TRULY MEXICAN

TRULY

MEXICAN

ROBERTO SANTIBAÑEZ

with JJ Goode and Shelley Wiseman

WILEY

John Wiley & Sons, Inc.

Published by John Wiley & Sons, Inc., Hoboken, New Jersey

Published simultaneously in Canada

For general information on our other products and services or for technical support, please contact our Customer Care Department within the United States at (800) 762-2974, outside the United States at (317) 572-3993 or fax (317) 572-4002.

Wiley also publishes its books in a variety of electronic formats. Some content that appears in print may not be available in electronic books. For more information about Wiley products, visit our Web site at www.wiley.com.

LIBRARY OF CONGRESS CATALOGING-IN-PUBLICATION DATA:

Santibañez, Roberto.
Truly Mexican / Roberto Santibañez with JJ Goode
Recipe Development by Shelley Wiseman
p. cm.
Includes index.
ISBN 978-0-470-49955-9 (cloth)
1. Cookery, Mexican. 2. Sauces. I. Goode, JJ II. Title.
TX716.M4S268 2011
641.5972—dc22
2010013151

Printed in China

10 9 8 7 6 5 4 3 2 1

CONTENTS

BASICS 1
ESSENTIAL INGREDIENTS AND TECHNIQUES

SALSAS 42
IGNITING THE FIRE OF FLAVOR

GUACAMOLES 100
THE CHUNKY AND THE SMOOTH

ADOBOS 120
SIMPLE PUREES WITH SOULFUL APPLICATIONS

MOLES & PIPIANES 148
MEXICO'S ICONIC SAUCES

MORE IDEAS FOR USING MEXICAN SAUCES 210

SIDES 244
FOR ROUNDING OUT YOUR MEAL

ACKNOWLEDGMENTS vi

INTRODUCTION vii

SOURCES 258

INDEX 259

ACKNOWLEDGMENTS

To my dear friends and co-authors, JJ Goode and Shelley Wiseman—without them I would have been lost in the forest!

To my editor, Pam Chirls, her assistant Rebecca Scherm, and my beloved friend and agent, Lisa Queen, for all their patience and hard work.

To Romulo Yanes, a photographer so talented that you might as well call him a magician. To Susan Victoria, whose props saved the day.

To my team at Fonda, especially Ruben Ortiz, Ana Andrade, and Maria Barrera, extraordinary cooks and three of the hardest working people I have ever met. Without their help at the restaurant, I never would have had time to cook for this book!

To Avocados from Mexico and Jacqueline Bohmer for her friendship and support.

To my mother, Mayan, and stepfather, Iker, and to my father, Guillermo, for a great education (culinary and otherwise), unconditional support, and all the love in the world. They instilled in me an eternal curiosity, which has pushed me toward the deepest, darkest places in search of knowledge.

To my beautiful sisters, Mayan and Ina, for inspiring me with their love and strength.

To great friends like Ricardo Muñoz, Sergio Remolina, Josefina Santacruz, Fany Gerson, Iliana de la Vega, Ana Elena Martinez, Phillip Hoffman, Cristina Castañeda, Gabriel Velasco, and Rafael Herera, who contributed to this book through recipes, knowledge, and inspiration.

To all the incredible women—mentors, friends, and incredible cooks—who taught me about the history and the pleasures of Mexican cooking. It's impossible to list them all but special mention goes to my mother, grandmother, and great aunts, and to Maria Dolores Torres Izabal, Guadalupe Pérez San Vicente, Cristina Barros, Lila Lomeli, Marilyn Tausend, Rachel Laudan, and last but certainly not least, Marta Lopez Matias, who has cooked for our family since I was born and contributed in a very special way to my development as a cook.

To Mark Miller, who has always been so supportive of and generous with me.

To Nick Malgieri for his friendship and always being my mentor!

To the Culinary Institute of America (the whole CIA team!) for their continuous support—and for believing in my crazy projects.

To Nicki Clendening, the best of the best—you are family!

To Jason, Shachar, and Chris from the Taco Truck for welcoming me into their fabulous partnership.

To Tom Gilliland, who gave a certain young and inexperienced Mexican the chance to cook at his wonderful restaurant in Austin, Texas. And to all the cooks at his restaurant, Fonda San Miguel, then and now.

To Molly Dinkins and Richard De Jong, who helped me get my visa!

To the late Josephina Howard, an inspirational cook and a voracious worker, who convinced me to come to the United States and taught me the value of looking at my home country's food from an outsider's perspective.

And finally, to one of the most special people in this world, whose amazing outlook on life and incredible sense of humor have put a smile on my face even in the toughest moments, whose sincerity, love, and incredibly sophisticated palate have helped build all that I am now. To Marco Diaz, my partner, my best friend and confidant, my business partner, and the best companion anyone could ever desire. Thank you, Marco.

INTRODUCTION

It's from a place of hope that I wrote this book. We've come a long way since the days when people in the United States thought the food of my home country was just beans and burritos. Today, Americans flock to Mexican restaurants to enjoy the food for the sophisticated, historically rich, and delicious cuisine it is. Now it's time to take the next step forward, to help home cooks over the wall of intimidation that stands between them and a fabulous *salsa verde* or *mole colorado*.

I understand the struggle of learning an unfamiliar cuisine. I was born and raised in Mexico City, and my family was always serious about food. When I was a boy, I remember listening as my mother composed her seemingly endless grocery lists over long phone calls with my grandmother and aunts. The following week would be a delicious blur of moles, tamales, pozoles, cakes, and long lunches that often stretched into dinners. Even as a kid, I would always peer over my grandmother's shoulder and into her cazuela. I only wanted to cook, cook, cook. So after college, I left my home in Mexico City, and enrolled at Le Cordon Bleu in Paris, the city's famous culinary school. At first, I was overwhelmed by the new techniques and ingredients—and a little dazed by all that butter and cream. Yet what made learning possible was the system that my teachers had inherited from men like Escoffier and Carême, the culinary revolutionaries of the past who refined and organized French sauce-making. They did it by breaking the cuisine down into meaningful categories, grouping sauces that were made using similar techniques. So instead of memorizing the recipes for 20 wildly different dishes, we learned to make one sauce that could be applied to 20 dishes. And with a couple of easy tweaks, that one sauce could be made into a dozen of others. This was tremendously empowering. And this sense of I-can-do-it enthusiasm, I decided, would be my gift to you.

To truly empower people, I knew I had to relegate a passion of mine—the history and culture of my home country—to the backseat. Fortunately, Mexican food already has some wonderful chroniclers—authors such as Rick Bayless, Susana Trilling, and Marilyn Tausend, have spent their careers showcasing the cuisine's vast regional variation. My objective is different. Instead of emphasizing this diversity, my goal is to show you how much the seemingly disparate food actually has in common.

That's why I chose to focus this book not on the street snacks or haute cuisine of Mexico, but on its condiments and sauces, to devote an entire chapter to the arsenal of exhilarating salsas, another to lush guacamoles, one to simple, soulful adobos, and another to the more elaborate (but decidedly doable) moles and pipianes. Because certain common techniques unite the recipes in each chapter, you'll find that once you can make, say, one adobo,

you're equipped to make dozens more. Plus, these recipes can be applied in so many different ways that learning to cook just a few can make your dinner table feel like a *fonda* or *taqueria*. A mole or adobo can turn a simple piece of fish or chicken into an impress-your-guests-feast, and just a tablespoon of salsa can ignite a simple grilled steak, plate of beans, and even a burger or sandwich. To help you turn these lovely sauces into full meals, I've also provided plenty of recipes for dishes that employ them and for staples like rice, beans, and tortillas that accompany them.

As you cook the recipes in this book, you'll find that you'll use the same simple techniques—roasting tomatoes and tomatillos or toasting dried chiles—again and again. And because I have devoted decades of my life to cooking, lecturing about, and teaching my native country's cuisine, I think I'm entitled to let you in on this secret without sounding dismissive of the masterful, creative, resourceful cooks of Mexico: Once you've roasted or toasted your ingredients, you're almost always just a whir of the blender and, sometimes, a simmer away from truly amazing Mexican food. That's why this book begins with the fundamentals, where I walk you through the Mexican way to prepare ingredients, the easy techniques that create the flavors we've all come to think of as Mexican. Once you learn the simple ways to prepare four or five ingredients—for instance, roasting tomatoes the Mexican way is as easy as popping them in a hot oven until their tops blacken—you can make just about any dish in the Mexican repertoire.

Although I'm sure this book will change the way you think about cooking Mexican food, I must admit that focusing on only the four categories was difficult for me. I wanted so badly to include a chapter on tamales. I wanted to write a treatise on the regional cuisines of Oaxaca and the food of the Yucatan. But I ultimately decided that this would distract from my mission and deserved space in another book. I had a similar struggle in deciding whether, and how, to whittle down the country's almost infinite repertoire of sauces. So as you're reading, remember: This book is by no means comprehensive, nor does it aim to be. Instead, I chose those sauces and dishes that contain accessible ingredients, illustrate important culinary concepts, and of course, taste amazing.

In the end, I had one simple goal in writing this book—to convert as many readers as I could from people who would love to cook Mexican food to people who cook Mexican food that they love.

BASICS

ESSENTIAL INGREDIENTS AND TECHNIQUES

A FEW YEARS BACK, I WAS TEACHING A COOKING CLASS, AND I HAD ROASTED A FEW TRAYS OF TOMATILLOS IN PREPARATION. AS I WAS HAULING THEM TO THE CLASSROOM, A STUDENT WALKED BY AND STOPPED ME. "UH OH, CHEF," HE SAID, NOTICING THAT THE TOMATILLOS' TOPS WERE BLACKENED. "LOOKS LIKE YOU BURNED THOSE." THAT I ACTUALLY HAD NOT BURNED THEM ILLUSTRATES AN IMPORTANT POINT: LEARNING TO COOK AN UNFAMILIAR CUISINE OFTEN MEANS UNLEARNING MANY OF THE PRINCIPLES YOU ONCE THOUGHT WERE UNIVERSAL.

Those used to cooking Italian food, which often involves sautéing garlic and onions in olive oil, might at first balk when they see a Mexican cook roast those same ingredients in a pan without oil until they're dark brown, blistered, and just cooked through. That's why my student had reacted with worry when he saw my tomatillos—he didn't yet know that they were *supposed* to blacken. And that's just one example of why this chapter is so important.

This chapter explores the ingredients, techniques, and equipment that make Mexican food taste recognizably Mexican—that make, for example, a cooked tomato salsa and an Italian tomato sauce taste so different despite their remarkably similar compositions. Of course, it doesn't cover every ingredient and technique—that would take an entire book as thick as a thousand tortillas—only unfamiliar ones that I use in multiple recipes or familiar ones that are so integral to my recipes that they deserve elaboration. It provides detailed descriptions of the techniques—for example, roasting tomatoes and tomatillos, toasting chiles and pumpkin seeds— that are particularly important to master. And it's here where I'll teach you how to make fresh corn tortillas. Each of my recipes will give you the direction you need to make amazing salsas, adobos, and moles, but you can refer to the particularly thorough instructions in this chapter the first few times you, say, roast tomatillos or garlic the Mexican way to ensure you do it perfectly. It's a bit like having me at the stove with you, helping you do everything just right. And I promise, cook through a few of my recipes, using this chapter as an occasional reference, and you will wind up with truly amazing Mexican food.

PREVIOUS PAGE, CLOCKWISE FROM TOP LEFT: Fresh arbol chiles (green and red), poblano chiles, serrano chiles, and jalapeño chiles (green and red)

FIVE COMMANDMENTS OF GREAT MEXICAN COOKING

1. **BUY THE BEST INGREDIENTS YOU CAN.** The better your tomatoes, chiles, and pork, the tastier the results.

2. TOAST CHILES AND ROAST TOMATOES, tomatillos, garlic, and onions the Mexican way—without oil, unless the recipe calls for it.

3. LOOK, TOUCH, AND SMELL. The heat of my oven and stovetop is probably a little bit different from that of yours. So our cooking times will also be a bit different. The best way to tell when ingredients are done toasting, roasting, or frying is to follow the visual cues and other descriptions I provide in this chapter and in my recipes. Times are just guidelines.

4. TEXTURE MATTERS. Salsa verde cocida is meant to be smooth, while salsa roja de molcajete still contains silky chunks of roasted tomato. Guacamoles that are meant to be chunky should not be mashed to mush. Adobos and some moles meant to have a velvety consistency should not be overly thick and gloppy. So pay attention to my descriptions of texture and the photographs that accompany my recipes.

5. SEASON TO TASTE. Before you serve anything from this book, take a taste. Ask yourself, does it need more sweetness, acidity, heat, or salt (which can boost those other flavors as well)? If so, gradually season the dish or sauce, always keeping in mind its purpose: Salsas meant to add spark by the teaspoonful should be intensely flavored, while saucy stews and moles you eat by the bowlful should be mellower but still packed with flavor.

A FEW NOTES ON MY RECIPES

SALT: Because a teaspoon of fine salt actually adds twice as much salt as a teaspoon of kosher salt, my recipes include amounts for both types, so the difference doesn't slip your mind.

SUBSTITUTIONS: In the cases that one ingredient may be substituted for another, I have listed my preferred choice first. For example, easier-to-find jalapeño chiles make a fine surrogate for the same number of serrano chiles. But when a recipe benefits from the slightly sharper, grassier flavor of serranos, I'll list the two chiles like so: "1 serrano or jalapeño chile."

SIZE: Whenever it makes sense to do so, I've listed ingredients by weight and added a number amount in parentheses. This allows you to be a flexible cook—for example, using one big, beautiful tomato instead of three smaller ones. For dried chiles, which can vary in size, weight is typically the best measure. But my chile charts (see pages 12 and 18) give you a choice by providing the average size of each chile.

ROASTING AND TOASTING: Each recipe takes you through the process of roasting and toasting ingredients, but for a refresher, you can always refer back to this chapter for a more detailed description of the process.

SERVING SUGGESTIONS: Many of my recipes for adobos, moles, and pipianes include a protein—chicken, fish, beef, or pork. And all my recipes include serving suggestions. Please keep in mind that these are simply suggestions. I encourage you to come up with your own ways of using Mexico's fabulous array of sauces—quail! goat! rabbit!—that fit with your budget, life, and taste.

INGREDIENTS

HERBS

AVOCADO LEAVES

The leaves of the native avocado criollo tree, available fresh in a few places close to the Mexican border and dried at just about any Mexican grocery store, provide a wonderful whiff of anise when you crush them between your fingers. They're used throughout the country—in Mexico City, Oaxaca, Morelos—for the subtle licorice flavor and aroma they contribute to beans, soups, and moles, just to name a few. If you're lucky enough to find fresh leaves, which should be bright green and glossy and look a bit like very large fresh bay leaves, store them in a resealable bag with some air remaining in it for a few weeks in the refrigerator. If you can only find dried leaves, look for those that are more or less whole. The whole leaves are about 5 inches long and 2½ inches wide; if they're broken, which they often are, use a few pieces to approximate the size of the whole leaves. Store them in a resealable bag in a cool, dark place for a few months, after which time they start to lose their perfume.

TOASTING AVOCADO LEAVES: To toast avocado leaves and bring out their aroma, heat a comal, griddle, or heavy skillet over medium-low heat. Toast the leaves, a few at a time, turning them over often, until they're fragrant and slightly browned, 1 to 2 minutes total.

CILANTRO

This herb, the leaves and stems of the coriander plant, has become inextricably associated with Mexican food, even though it's a relatively recent import to Mexico (it arrived with the Spanish). It probably caught on because of its similarity to pungent

native herbs like culantro, epazote, pepicha, oreja de león, and papalo. Scattered along with raw onions on tacos, added at the last minute to soups, and pounded into a paste for guacamole, cilantro is a familiar sight throughout Mexico and the United States.

Buy cilantro that's bright green with crisp stems. Avoid bunches with yellowing or browning leaves and limp stems. You may wash it as you wish, but I do it as soon as I bring the cilantro home. I typically keep the herb in a bunch, grabbing it by the stems and submerging it, leaves first, into plenty of cold water. I shake it around a bit, pull it out, and repeat this a few times. Then I dip the stems in cold water and do the same thing to them. Keeping the cilantro in a bunch, I'll stick it, stems first, into a large glass, like an edible bouquet, and let the excess water clinging to the leaves dry. Cilantro will stay fresh, bright green, and perky for a week or more if you then wrap it in a paper towel and put it in a resealable plastic bag with some air remaining inside. Store it in the lowest part of your refrigerator or in the vegetable drawer.

CHOPPING CILANTRO THE MEXICAN WAY: This method, rather than the obsessively minced, leaves-only French way, will give you the right texture and flavor for my dishes and will ensure your cilantro measurements match mine. Starting at the root end, cut off and discard the first two inches of the stems. Beginning at the stem end, chop the

LEFT: Chopped cilantro
RIGHT: Epazote

cilantro, making your way toward the leaves and leaving about ⅛ inch between each cut. Use your free hand to keep the leaves close together as you chop.

EPAZOTE

A little a day keeps the doctor away. The anti-parasite and anti-indigestion properties of this herb are probably why it made it into the everyday foods of Mexico. But cooks today add it to beans, soups (its flavor is essential to tortilla soup), salsas, and so much else just because it tastes great. It provides a strikingly pungent, herbaceous, woodsy flavor that newcomers to epazote don't soon forget. Whether I'm planning to sprinkle the chopped leaves raw over enchiladas or steep sprigs in salsa verde, I always insist on using the *fresh* herb. I'd rather not use epazote at all than cook with the dry version because the flavor is so different. Look for fresh epazote in Mexican markets or other markets in the American South, where it's occasionally called stinkweed or wormweed. What's not well known is that it grows wild just about everywhere—if you keep your eyes peeled, you'll see it growing on the streets of Brooklyn! Buy epazote with perky green leaves and crisp stems, and avoid epazote that has begun to brown or go limp. Store it the same way you would cilantro, but use it within three days.

HOJA SANTA

Also known as *hierba santa*, *acuyo*, and *momo*, the delicious "holy leaf" has some of the astringency of mint and a subtle anise flavor. Cooks steep it in soup and beans, wrap it around tamales before steaming, and blend it into sauces, like the mole amarillo from Oaxaca (see page 159). If you live in a city like New York, Los Angeles, or San Antonio (where hoja santa grows wild on the River Walk), you should be able to find the fresh leaf at Mexican grocery stores and markets. I don't like dry hoja santa nearly as much as the fresh herb because, like a lot of dried herbs, it takes on a tea-like flavor that just doesn't compare. If you find it fresh, give the leaves a quick rinse, let them dry, then layer them with paper towels (one leaf, one paper towel, then another leaf). Put the stack in a resealable bag with some air remaining inside, and put that in the refrigerator. The leaves will stay fresh for a couple of weeks.

MINT

Although both spearmint and peppermint are usually labeled simply "mint" in the grocery store, the former, with its more subtle, floral fragrance, provides the right flavor for Mexican dishes. Fortunately, it's easy to tell the difference: Spearmint has larger leaves, while the more aggressively flavored peppermint has small leaves and purple stems. If you can only find peppermint, don't worry: Start with a fourth of the amount my recipes call for and add more gradually, tasting to be sure it doesn't overpower the other flavors. And remember that unlike with cilantro, you only use the mint leaves and not the woody stems. Store it as you would cilantro, and it will keep for a week.

OREGANO

It's worth seeking out the dried herb labeled "Mexican oregano," which is more floral, subtle, and complex than regular oregano, for any dish in this book that calls for oregano. If you can't find it at your gourmet grocery store, at a local Mexican market, or from an online source, you may use regular dried oregano as long as you're cautious and start with a little less than the recipe calls for. In Oaxaca and other states in the southeast of Mexico, cooks use a special large-leafed oregano that you can't find in the United States. So in a couple of the moles in this book, I call for both regular oregano and marjoram, the combination of which provides a pretty close approximation of its flavor.

OPPOSITE, CLOCKWISE FROM TOP LEFT: Papalo, Mexican oregano, culantro, and pepicha

CHILES

The word may bring to mind spiciness, but there is so much more to these beloved fruits than their ability to bring a tingle to your tongue. In Mexico, there are dozens of types of chiles, eaten both fresh and dried, ripe and unripe, that span the spectrum from fiery and grassy to mild and raisiny sweet. And properly used—whether they're toasted, roasted, boiled, or raw—all of them bring an incredible depth of flavor to whatever they touch, from moles and adobos to salsas and beans. I've provided a rundown only of those I use for the recipes in this book, most of which you can find relatively easily. Most important, I tell you how to toast or roast each one—a simple but essential step toward coaxing out each chile's complex flavors and aromas.

As anyone who has mistakenly rubbed his or her eyes even hours after chopping chiles knows too well, you should be very careful whenever you handle them, especially incendiary ones like habaneros. The best way to spare yourself the pain is to wear disposable protective gloves. At the very least, wash your hands well with soap and water after contact. I go so far as to scrub my nails with a nailbrush!

FRESH CHILES

Fresh chiles have a way of imbedding themselves in your memory. And it's not just their spiciness, though a sliver of habanero can be so hot it will make the top of your head tingle. Roast the typically mild poblano, for instance, and it becomes faintly sweet with an unforgettably lovely tinge of bitterness.

But the ability of fresh chiles to set your mouth on fire is how they've earned their reputation. This heat is essential to the flavor of many Mexican dishes, so unless my recipe says otherwise, you should not discard the seeds and veins of small fresh chiles, because they are where most of this heat (and some great flavor and nutrients, too) lives. Larger chiles, such as poblanos, are not used for their heat, so they should be seeded.

Everyone knows that some types of chiles tend to be hotter than others, but there's also variation within each type. There's no way to tell at the store whether one jalapeño is hotter than the next, so I always buy a few more chiles than I think I'll need. That way, I can always add extra if I need to bump up the heat. In your kitchen, you can tell whether a chile is spicy without scalding your tongue: Just cut into it and carefully sniff the opening—the stronger the punch of spiciness, the hotter the chile. In general, look for fresh chiles with brightly colored, shiny, taut skins (a little wrinkling is ok) that are free of blemishes. Keep fresh chiles in the refrigerator in a plastic bag for up to a week.

Habanero chiles

FROZEN HEAT

Habaneros are not at everyone's neighborhood grocery store. And once you do find and buy a bunch of them, you'll probably use only one or two at a time, because they're so fiery. Instead of letting the leftover chiles languish in the refrigerator, put them in a resealable bag and pop them in the freezer. They'll keep there for a few months. When you're ready to use them, let them defrost for a few minutes at room temperature.

CHILE NAME	AVERAGE SIZE	AVERAGE WEIGHT	FLAVOR NOTES	HEAT LEVEL	HOW USED	ROASTING	SUBSTITUTIONS	OTHER NOTES
HABANERO	1 to 1½ inches in diameter	3 or 4 per ounce	Aromatic, tropical, almost fruity	Extremely spicy	Raw or roasted	8 to 12 minutes	Scotch bonnet chiles	They vary in color from pale green, red, yellow, and orange, to a mottled combination of these colors. (See photo on page 10.)
JALAPEÑO	3 inches x 1 inch	¾ to 1 ounce each	Sharp and pleasantly grassy	Moderately spicy to spicy	Raw, roasted, boiled, and sometimes stuffed	10 to 15 minutes	An equal number of serrano chiles	Red, ripe jalapeños are delicious but have a different flavor and should not be used in place of green, unripe jalapeños.
SERRANO	2½ to 3 inches x ½ inch	3 or 4 per ounce	Similar to jalapeños but even more intense	Spicy to very spicy	Raw, roasted, or boiled	10 minutes	An equal number of jalapeño chiles	A little harder to find than jalapeños, but worth the effort (See photo on page 13.)
POBLANO	5 to 6 inches x 2½ to 3 inches	4 ounces each	Subtly sweet with a slight grassy, bitter edge	Very mild	Roasted and sometimes stuffed	4 to 6 minutes on the stovetop or 6 to 8 minutes in the oven, plus about 15 minutes to steam	Chilacas if making rajas, and Anaheim or New Mexico hatch peppers if you're planning to stuff them	Poblanos with relatively flat sides are easier to roast and peel. (See photo on page 13.)
MANZANO	3 to 5 inches in diameter	¾ to 1 ounce each	Fruity like habaneros, fleshy like jalapeños	Extremely spicy	Like jalapeños and serranos	10 to 15 minutes	An equal number of habaneros	The only chile in Mexico with black seeds.

FRESH CHILES

Roasting transforms the aggressive, grassy flavor of fresh chiles into a lovely mild sweetness with subtle bitterness that's a beloved part of the Mexican flavor palate.

ROASTING LARGE FRESH CHILES, SUCH AS POBLANOS, ON THE STOVETOP: Set the chile on its side directly on the rack of a gas burner over medium-high heat (you can roast two chiles at the same time on one burner). Roast, turning over frequently with tongs, until the skin is blackened all over and the chile is soft but not mushy, 4 to 6 minutes. To complete the cooking and loosen the skin, put the charred chile in a bowl, cover the bowl with a plate, and set aside for 15 to 20 minutes.

ROASTING LARGE FRESH CHILES IN THE OVEN OR TOASTER OVEN: Set the oven to broil and preheat. Alternatively, you can preheat the oven to 500°F, or if the quantity of chiles is small enough, you can broil in a toaster oven. If you're using the oven broiler, position the rack 8 inches from the heat source. Roast the chile on a foil-lined baking pan, turning it over occasionally, until the skin is blistered and blackened all over and the chile is soft but not mushy, 6 to 8 minutes. To complete the cooking and loosen the skin, put the charred chile in a bowl, cover the bowl with a plate, and set it aside for 15 to 20 minutes.

LEFT, TOP: Roasted, peeled poblano
BOTTOM: Roasted poblano with charred skin still on
RIGHT: Serrano chiles roasting in a pan

A NOTE ON ROASTING

Since properly roasting and toasting is such an important part of making memorable Mexican food, I must give you a little extra advice to make sure you're successful at it.

First, remember, that when you're making Mexican dishes, you'll almost always be roasting and toasting vegetables and fruits without oil. This may seem odd at first, but I can assure you that your dinner will taste infinitely better as a result.

Also keep in mind that not all ovens and stoves are the same. What I consider medium-low heat might mean low to you, and therefore your chiles de árbol, for instance, might take a bit longer to toast than my instructions suggest. Here's the solution: Toast a test chile (or garlic clove or onion slice). If it's perfectly toasted in the time my instructions provide, then you and I agree on what constitutes a certain heat level. If it toasts in less time, your heat is higher than I'd suggest. If it takes more time to toast, then your heat is lower than I'd suggest. Next time you roast or toast, tweak your temperature so that your timing and mine match. But even more important than the time an ingredient takes to toast or roast is the finished product: Your primary goal should be to end up with chiles, onion, tomatillos, etc., with the coloring, blistering, and aroma that I describe in this chapter.

You'll also notice that the times and temperatures in this chapter don't always precisely match those in the recipes. There's a reason: This chapter is about fundamentals, about learning how to toast and roast and what the result should look and smell like. In the recipes, I've made simplicity my focus. For instance, if I have you roasting three items, in some cases I'd rather you roast them all at once than take three times as long to roast them separately. In the service of this convenience, I have tweaked the times and temperatures in my recipes accordingly.

Whether you roast on the stovetop or in the oven (I've provided instructions for both) is a matter of convenience, too. Whatever makes sense for you is what you should do. I've helped you out by suggesting one or the other in my recipes when I think it'll guide you toward the easiest process. I recommend roasting in the toaster oven, for instance, when you're dealing with small quantities of ingredients. And while you may not see many *abuelitas* in mountain villages using a toaster oven to roast tomatoes, let me assure you that the result is fantastic.

The oven broiler is far preferable to the separate broiler below your oven. That's because, ideally, whatever fruits and vegetables you're roasting should be eight inches from the heat source (in the toaster oven, this is not important because the heat isn't as intense) and in the separate broiler, you can't adjust the distance. If you don't have an in-oven broiler, roast in the oven at 500°F, or if you must, roast in the separate broiler, but be extra vigilant to prevent burning.

PEELING AND SEEDING ROASTED LARGE CHILES: Gently rub the outside of the chile with your fingers or a paper towel to remove the skin, which should slip right off. Don't hold the chile under running water while you do this or you'll sacrifice flavor. Make a slit lengthwise in the chile, then carefully scrape or scoop out the seeds (remove as much of the attached ribs as you can, but there's no reason to go nuts over them).

ROASTING SMALL FRESH CHILES, SUCH AS SERRANOS, ON THE STOVETOP: Put the chiles on a preheated comal, griddle, or heavy skillet set over medium-low heat. Cook (you should hear some popping and crackling as they cook), turning often so the entire surface has a chance to make contact with the pan, until the chiles are tender and their skins are blistered all over and blackened in spots, 10 to 15 minutes for jalapeños, about 10 minutes for serranos, and 8 to 12 minutes for habaneros.

ROASTING SMALL FRESH CHILES IN THE OVEN OR TOASTER OVEN: Set the oven to broil and preheat. Alternatively, you can preheat the oven to 500°F, or if the quantity of chiles is small enough, you can use a toaster oven. If you're using the oven broiler, position the rack 8 inches from the heat source. Roast on a foil-lined baking pan, turning the chiles over once or twice, until they're tender, blistered all over, and blackened in spots, about 15 minutes for jalapeños, about 10 minutes for serranos, and 8 to 12 minutes for habaneros.

PEELING ROASTED SMALL CHILES: There's no need to peel habaneros—actually, you can get away with leaving the skin on most small chiles—but I typically peel roasted serranos and jalapeños because I find it leads to a silkier final product. After the chiles are cool enough to handle, about 5 minutes, rub the outsides of the chiles with your fingers (put on protective gloves, to be extra careful) or a barely damp paper towel to remove the skin. If the skin doesn't come off easily, scrape it off with a small knife.

DRIED CHILES

If you've ever walked into a Mexican grocery store and wondered what the heck cooks do with the vast variety of dried chiles, get ready to find out. These chiles, which have typically been dried outside in fields or on patios, contribute a stunning flavor that's complex and concentrated, often reminiscent (not surprisingly) of dried fruit. To the inexperienced observer,

A NOTE ON SIZE

Dried chiles vary in size much more than fresh ones. You must keep this in mind as you follow my recipes: A salsa made with 10 small guajillos will taste very different and have a different texture than one made with 10 large guajillos. So for each type of dried chile I mention in this chapter, I've provided in my chile chart the dimensions (without the stems) of what I consider the standard-size chile. And that's the size I used when writing and testing the recipes. If the chiles you bought are smaller or larger, just estimate—use 2 small chiles to approximate 1 standard chile, and use a particularly large chile along with a small one to approximate 2 standard chiles. And to be really precise, go by the weights I have provided.

they all look basically the same, but once you get to know each one—and see how little effort it takes to incorporate them into dishes—a whole world of flavor will be revealed to you. Look for dried chiles that are the same deep color all over (rather than those with pale spots) and those that are pliable—if they're old or have been improperly stored, they'll feel brittle and crumble or snap in two when you try to bend them. You can resurrect brittle chiles by refrigerating them overnight in an airtight resealable bag with a square of just-damp paper towel. Store dried chiles in an airtight resealable bag, and keep them in a cool, dry place for up to six months.

TOASTING DRIED CHILES: Here's a revealing experiment: Take a few dried chiles, grind them to a powder, and give the powder a careful sniff. Then do the same with dried chiles of the same kind that have been toasted. The contrast is striking. The untoasted chiles smell pleasant but mild, while the toasted chiles will nearly knock you over—not with heat but with an intensely complex aroma. So if you haven't toasted chiles before, prepare to enter a delicious new world, where even familiar chiles seem new and exciting. It's as if they're urging you to cook with them.

The basic toasting process for all dried chiles is the same—a dry pan or comal, medium-low heat—but because chiles of different types are dramatically different—some thin-skinned and delicate, others thick-skinned and fleshy—they

OPPOSITE PAGE, CLOCKWISE FROM TOP LEFT: Cascabel chiles, toasted chipotle mecos (left) and untoasted chipotles mecos, pasilla de Oaxaca chiles, and chipotles moras

BELOW LEFT: Toasted chipotle moras RIGHT: Toasting guajillos on the comal

CHILE NAME	AVERAGE SIZE	AVERAGE WEIGHT	FLAVOR NOTES
ANCHO (dried ripe poblano)	4 to 5 inches × 2½ to 3 inches	2 per ounce	Mildly sweet, reminiscent of tamarind and raisin
DE ÁRBOL	3 inches × ⅓ inch	30 to 40 per ounce	Slightly acidic and nutty
CASCABEL	1 to 1½ inches in diameter	About 5 per ounce	A touch of lightly tart fruit, even a little tamarind-like
GUAJILLO	5 to 6 inches × 1 to 1½ inches	About 4 per ounce with stems, 5 or 6 per ounce without stems	A lovely earthy, woodsy flavor as well as some acidity
CHIPOTLE MECO (smoked, dried jalapeño)	3 to 3½ inches × about 1 inch	4 to 6 per ounce	Slightly more mellow than chipotles moras but still smoky and subtly sweet with a tobacco-toastiness
CHIPOTLE MORA (smoked, dried jalapeño)	2 to 2½ inches × ¾ to 1 inch	8 to 10 per ounce	Pronounced smokiness, with a touch of woodsy sweetness
PASILLA, PASILLA NEGRO, OR CHILE NEGRO (dried chiles chilaca)	7 to 8 inches × about 1½ inches	About 3 per ounce with stems, 4 per ounce without stems	Earthy flavor with subtle fruitiness and a note of licorice
PASILLA DE OAXACA, PASILLA OAXAQUEÑO, OR CHIPOTLE DE NAVIDAD	4 to 4½ inches × about 1½ inches	About 6 per ounce	Fabulously complex, with fruitiness and smokiness
MULATO (dried ripe poblano)	4 to 5 inches × 3 to 3½ inches	2 per ounce	The most intensely fruity of the dried chiles, it's fleshy, sweet, and prune-like.
PUYA (also occasionally spelled pulla)	3 to 4 inches × about ¾ inch	About 12 per ounce	Like smaller, hotter guajillos

HEAT LEVEL	DESEED / DEVEIN BEFORE TOASTING	TOASTING	OTHER NOTES
Mild	Yes	1½ minutes total, or until light-colored brown blisters appear and the chiles smell fragrant.	Be aware: Occasionally, you'll find anchos labeled as pasillas.
Very spicy	No	3 to 4 minutes total, or until they are dark brown and smell like toasted hazelnuts.	Don't confuse these with the fresh version. (See photo on page 91.)
Very spicy	See Other Notes	1 minute, or until they turn a slightly mottled lighter red.	These spherical chiles should be stemmed and broken into about three pieces before they're toasted, their seeds reserved in case the recipe calls for them. (See photo on page 16.)
Mild	Yes	1 minute total, or until they are fragrant and the outside has just barely changed color.	Because the chiles have particularly tough skins, I often strain sauces made with them, but this is optional. (See photo on page 17.)
Spicy	Depends on the recipe	3 to 5 minutes total, or until darker brown and even blackish blisters form and the chiles become slightly brittle; the chiles might puff up like balloons when they're nearly done.	Not to be confused with the more common chipotles moras, chipotles mecos are also smoked, dried jalapeños but they're made from a different type of jalapeño and smoked using a different process. (See photo on page 16.)
Very spicy	Depends on the recipe	3 to 5 minutes total, or until dark, blackish blisters appear on both sides and the chiles are brittle; the chiles might puff up like balloons when they're nearly done.	Don't mistake this smaller, wrinkly purplish-red chile for the slightly larger, tobacco-colored chipotle meco. (See photos on pages 16 and 17.)
Moderately spicy	Yes	1 minute total, or until the outsides have developed light colored blisters and the insides have turned a slightly lighter shade of brown; they will smell like raisins.	Be aware: occasionally, anchos are labeled as pasillas. (See photo on page 177.)
Spicy to very spicy	Depends on the recipe	3 minutes total, or until they develop some blisters and are fragrant; sometimes, they'll begin to puff up.	They can be hard to find in the United States but are worth seeking out; see Sources (page 258) for a mail-order source. (See photo on page 16.)
Mild	Yes	1½ minutes total, or until you see light-colored brown blisters and the chiles smell fragrant.	Mulatos and anchos are both dried poblano chiles, but mulatos are made from a variety that ripens purple instead of red. You may substitute anchos for mulatos, just note that anchos tend to be a little smaller, so you'll want to use more of them or rely on weight rather than number.
Moderately spicy to spicy	Depends on the recipe	1 to 1½ minutes total, or until the chiles are fragrant and the outsides have just barely changed color.	Puyas make a great substitute for the hard-to-find chile comapeño from Veracruz.

must be treated slightly differently. For example, some chiles take just a minute or so in the hot pan while others take several. Large dried chiles like guajillos and anchos should be seeded and deveined before they're toasted, because their many seeds can overwhelm the flavors of a sauce and affect its texture. Small chiles, like chiles de árbol and chipotles moras, on the other hand, typically should not be seeded, since their seeds provide just the right nuttiness and heat. The times I provide in my chile chart are helpful guidelines, but they're not gospel. Several variables—including the idiosyncrasies of your pan and stove and the dryness and thickness of your chiles—will affect toasting time. So use the times as a guide, keeping in mind that the visual and aroma cues I provide are what count.

Before you start, bear in mind that you must keep a close eye on the chiles, because they can quickly go from perfectly toasted to overly toasted. To that end, it helps to toast those chiles that cook quickly in batches of two or three. Overly toasted chiles taste bitter (though there are a few recipes in this book for which I actually recommend it!).

TOASTING DRIED CHILES

MAKING CHILE POWDERS

In my cupboard, you'll find a bunch of little jars filled with different chile powders—one with chiles de árbol, another with chipotles or cascabeles or piquines (a tiny dried chile just a little larger than a grain of Arborio rice). They're great for making quick salsas and adding bolts of flavor and spiciness to so many dishes. Making them is as simple as toasting the chiles as I've instructed and grinding them in a clean coffee or spice grinder (or even in a blender, if you must). For árbol chiles, I toast them a bit longer and more slowly than normal (about 8 minutes) over low heat, so the seeds get really toasty and nutty. Keep chile powder in a small airtight container away from light and heat, and not in the fridge, for up to three months. See recipe on opposite page.

Wipe each chile with a barely damp paper towel to remove any dust (after all, these guys are often dried outdoors), and snap or twist off the stem. Deseed and devein the chiles, depending on the type (see the chart on page 18).

Before toasting large chiles, remove the stems and cut each chile lengthwise with kitchen shears or a sharp knife. Open the chiles, lay them flat, and remove their seeds and as much of the veins as you can (there's no need to go nuts) with gloved hands, a towel, or a knife. Return each chile to its original shape (as if you had never cut into it) before toasting according to my instructions.

Preheat a comal, griddle, or heavy skillet over medium-low heat. Arrange the chiles in the skillet, a few at a time. Flip them often and press them down with a wooden spoon or tongs as you toast according to the instructions in the chart.

If any seeds escape the chiles as you're toasting and blacken in your pan, be sure to discard them.

Chile de árbol powder

CHILE POWDER
CHILE EN POLVO

MAKES ¼ CUP

1 ounce dried árbol (30 to 40), cascabel (about 5), or chipotle mora (8 to 10, purplish-red color) chiles, wiped clean and stemmed

HEAT a comal, griddle, or heavy skillet over low heat for árbol chiles and medium-low heat for cascabel and chipotle chiles.

FOR THE ÁRBOL CHILES, toast them, turning them over and pressing them down frequently with tongs, until they're browned all over with some blackened spots, about 8 minutes.

FOR THE CASCABEL CHILES, break each into about 3 pieces for easier toasting, then shake out and reserve the seeds. Toast the pieces, turning them over and pressing them down frequently with tongs, until they turn a lighter, slightly mottled red, about 1 minute. Remove the pieces. Toast the seeds in the skillet, shaking and tossing, until they're lightly browned and fragrant, 20 to 30 seconds.

FOR THE CHIPOTLE MORA CHILES, toast them, turning them over frequently, until dark, blackish blisters appear in spots (some will even puff up), 3 to 5 minutes.

GRIND or blend the chiles (and the toasted seeds, if you're using cascabel chiles) to a powder in a spice grinder or blender jar.

STORE in an airtight container in a cool, dark place (not in the refrigerator) for up to 3 months.

FRUITS AND VEGETABLES

AVOCADO

Whenever I mention avocados in this book, I'm talking about the dark, pebbly-skinned, Mexican Hass variety that you can buy just about everywhere all year-round nowadays. This fruit, with its creamy, buttery flesh and mellow fatty flavor, is very different from the other varieties of avocado you might see in markets in the United States—the larger, paler Fuerte, which has a pallid, watered-down flavor, and the Caribbean (or Florida) variety, which is less buttery and a bit fruity. Cooks in Veracruz and the Caribbean turn these into some tasty dishes, yet I always prefer the Hass—particularly those grown in Mexico. Because they're grown in the country's volcanic belt, a vast swatch of land in the High Plains from Colima to Veracruz to Oaxaca, their flavor is amplified by the mineral-rich soil, the cool nights in this mountainous area (which also makes them especially creamy), and a little cross-pollination with the native avocado trees. These native trees produce the avocado criollo, an itty-bitty fruit, only a bit bigger than a jalapeño with a beautiful background of anise. People in the High Plains of Mexico use a fresh tortilla to grab and crush the fruit. Then they take out the pit, sprinkle on some salt, and eat it—thin skin and all!

RIPENESS: Remember that the flesh of an avocado will get creamier and more delicious as it ripens, and unlike many fruits, the avocado ripens *after* it's off the tree. That means you can buy avocados that are still firm as long as you don't plan to use them for several days. If you're looking for avocados that will be ready to use within a day or two, you want to buy those that have begun to soften. Waiting until the fruit is properly ripe—neither too firm nor too soft—is the key to unlocking its creamy texture. Next time you have an avocado slowly ripening on the counter, let it get a bit softer than you typically do before cutting it open and tasting it. If you immediately think to yourself, "Ah, this is creamier and tastier than ever!" then you've been using avocados before they're perfectly ripe. Avoid those that feel mushy, that have any too-soft spots, and whose skin has separated from the flesh. These are too ripe.

STORAGE: Since I adore avocados, I almost always have them on hand in many stages of ripeness—some ready to use, and some a few days away. I encourage hard ones to soften by putting them in a closed paper bag and putting the bag on top of my refrigerator, near the back, where the residual heat accelerates the ripening. When my avocados are ripe, I stick them in the refrigerator, where they'll stay perfect for two or three days. (Just remove them from the refrigerator about an hour before you plan to use them.) If you only use one half of an avocado and want to store the other, save the half with the pit in the refrigerator wrapped tightly in plastic wrap. Make sure the wrap makes contact with the flesh to reduce browning. Use it within a day or so and scrape off any browned flesh with a knife.

Pitting avocados (see page 24)

SIZE: Finally, note that avocados vary in size. Large avocados weigh 8 to 9 ounces and small avocados weigh 5 to 6 ounces.

PITTING AND CUTTING AVOCADOS: I've seen plenty of creative ways to pit and cut avocados (some more successful than others), but this method is by far the best. Cut the avocado lengthwise all the way around the pit, twist the two halves to separate them, and remove the pit. To do this, place the flat part of the knife's blade against the exposed flesh, pierce the pit with the tip of your knife, turn your wrist so that the handle moves down and the tip moves up (to be safe, swaddle the hand holding the fruit in a kitchen towel). The pit will pop right out. (See photos on page 23.)

If you're going to blend the avocado, simply scoop out the flesh with a spoon. If you're making guacamole or some other dish that calls for irregular chunks, cut the flesh in a crosshatch pattern with a sharp knife, making sure not to cut through the skin, and then scoop out the flesh with a spoon. And finally, if you want neat slices of avocado, cut the avocado into quarters and carefully peel the skin off each piece with your fingers, as if you were peeling a hard-boiled egg, and then slice the fruit as you desire.

CHAYOTE

There are two kinds of chayote—the smooth-skinned, pale green kind that looks like a pear and the slightly larger, starchier one whose dark green skin is covered with spines. In Louisiana, many people eat the pale green kind and call it "mirliton." I've also seen it referred to as "vegetable pear." Both kinds have a delicious mild flavor and a

LEFT: Chayote
RIGHT: Easy-to-squeeze lime pieces (see opposite page)

hearty texture that falls somewhere in between potato and zucchini. In this book, I use them in *mole de olla*, for which they're peeled and cut, but cooks often boil them whole and then split them open as they would an avocado. As kids, my siblings and I would battle over who got to eat the small seed, which had become slightly soft and has this delicious nuttiness. Slices of the boiled chayote would end up floating in moles and stews or adorned with butter-sautéed onions and crema in a European-inspired treat.

GARLIC

There are still remote communities in Mexico, like those in the mountainous region called the Sierra Mixteca, where cooks don't use garlic. But this foreign import has become an important ingredient in the country's cuisine. In Spain, it's an upfront flavor in many dishes, but in Mexico it plays more of a supporting role—whether it's dry-roasted to highlight its mellow sweetness or used raw for a punch of flavor—to ingredients like chiles, tomatoes, and tomatillos.

ROASTING GARLIC ON THE STOVETOP: Put peeled cloves of garlic on a preheated comal, griddle, or heavy skillet set over medium-low heat. Roast, turning the cloves over every few minutes, until they are just tender and golden brown with some blackened spots (if you see a lot of black, turn your heat down slightly), 8 to 10 minutes. Each clove should be cooked through and soft enough that it gives when you squeeze it but far from the spreadably soft texture Italian cooks are after.

ROASTING GARLIC IN THE OVEN OR TOASTER OVEN: Set the oven or toaster oven to broil and preheat. Alternatively, you can preheat the oven to 500°F. If you're using the oven broiler, position the rack 8 inches from the heat source. Roast peeled garlic cloves on a foil-lined baking pan, turning them over occasionally until they're softened and golden brown with some deep brown spots, 15 to 20 minutes.

LIME

Although the lime (known in Mexico as *limón* or *limón verde*; *lima* is technically a different citrus) might be one of the first ingredients that comes to mind when you think about Mexican food, the fruit probably originated in Asia. No strangers to tartness—sour prickly pears and pineapple vinegars have been in our culinary arsenal for a very long time—Mexicans came to adore limes. Today we, especially those lime-fanatics from Mexico City, squeeze them over just about everything: tacos, soups, rice, tortillas, corn, melon, jicama, you name it! Fortunately, it's becoming more common to find the smoother skinned, light green limes common in Mexico in supermarkets

MAKING EASY-TO-SQUEEZE LIME PIECES

1. Holding the lime so that the stem end is facing up; cut off a piece by slicing through the lime lengthwise, not through the stem but slightly to the right of it. 2. Cut off another piece by making a similar off-center cut starting at either end of the flat side. 3. Do the same for the remaining rounded side of the lime. Now you have three easy-to-squeeze pieces.

in the United States, rather than the larger, bumpy dark green limes, which have a more bitter juice.

Have you ever cut into a lime only to find it barely has any juice? To be sure this doesn't happen, buy limes with smooth, glossy skin instead of those with dull, slightly bumpy skin. That's how you can be sure to select fruits that have especially thin skins and almost always contain more juice. Yet even these limes can vary in juice content—some will give you a generous two tablespoons, while others barely fill one—which is why my recipes call for a specific amount of juice, rather than the number of limes. Always buy a few more than you think you'll need, and if you don't end up using them within a day or two, store them in the vegetable drawer of the refrigerator for up to a week.

MANGO

It speaks to the place this fruit holds in the heart of Mexicans that silverware sets sold in my home country once included something called a mango fork. Mangoes are not indigenous to Mexico—they come from South Asia via the Spanish—but the fruits that grew in the country's volcanic soil developed an incredible flavor and aroma, particularly *mangos de manila*. This delicious variety, which may have arrived from the Philippines, has flesh that's almost as smooth as an avocado's, without those annoying fibers that get stuck in your teeth. But sadly, its thin, delicate skin makes it very difficult to export, though you will occasionally come across it in Mexican markets. The best mangoes common throughout the United States are ataulfo mangoes. They turn golden yellow when they're ripe and are much smaller than the ubiquitous Tommy Atkins variety, which Mexicans call mango *petacón* or "mango with a big butt" and can be frustratingly fibrous but are still tasty. If you plan to use mangoes right away, look for those with blemish-free skins (a little wrinkling is fine, but means the mango is on the edge of overly ripe) that are a bright yellow-orange color. Ripe mangoes should give slightly when you squeeze them and should smell sweet like some fantastic flower. You can also buy mangoes when they're firm and let them ripen at room temperature or encourage the process by putting them in a closed paper bag near the back of the refrigerator. Store unripe mangoes at room temperature, and ripe mangoes in the refrigerator for up to four days.

CUTTING MANGOES: Cut through the mango lengthwise on both sides of its pit. Cut the flesh in each half in a crosshatch pattern with a sharp knife, making sure not to cut through the skin. Scoop out the flesh with a spoon. Cut off any flesh remaining on the pit and use it as you wish.

ONIONS

My recipes call for two types of onion: red and white. Everybody knows red onions, but I find that people often confuse white onions (the kind most common in Mexican cooking) with any onions that aren't red, like Spanish onions. Look for signs at the supermarket for "white onions" or just look for onions whose skin, not just the flesh, is white. These onions have an especially delicate crisp texture and great sweetness without the sharp, ammonia-like flavor of Spanish onions.

ROASTING ONIONS ON THE STOVETOP: Cut the onions into ½-inch-thick round slices and put them (you may use only one or two rounds for any given recipe) on a preheated comal, griddle, or heavy skillet set over medium-low heat. Roast, carefully turning over each slice once, until both sides have developed black patches and the white flesh still visible is translucent, tender, but still firm, 15 to 20 minutes. If you start to see a lot of black before the onion is cooked through, don't worry, just turn your heat down (see page 28).

ROASTING ONIONS IN THE OVEN OR TOASTER OVEN: Set the oven to broil and preheat. Alternatively, you can preheat the oven to 500°F, or if the quantity of onion is small enough, you can use a toaster oven. If you're using the oven broiler, position the rack 8 inches from the heat source. Roast ½-inch-thick round slices on a foil-lined baking pan, carefully turning over each slice once, until both sides have developed black patches and the white flesh still visible is translucent, tender, but still firm, 15 to 20 minutes.

PINEAPPLE

Generally, this invigoratingly sweet-tart fruit is eaten as a snack, embellished perhaps by a little lime and chile. I highlight its tropical flavor in several of my salsas. I recommend buying whole pineapple and peeling it yourself. It is one of the few ingredients that I sometimes brush with a little oil before roasting; otherwise, the fruit's sticky sugars cause it to stick to the pan. Look for fragrant pineapples with yellow skin that yield slightly when you apply light pressure with your finger.

ROASTING PINEAPPLE: Cut whole, peeled pineapple into ½-inch-thick round slices. Set the oven to broil and preheat, or heat a lightly oiled grill pan over medium heat. If you're using the oven broiler, position the rack 8 inches from the heat source. Alternatively, you can preheat the oven to 500°F, or if the quantity of pineapple is small enough, you can use a toaster oven. Brush the slices with a little olive or vegetable oil and roast or grill them, turning over the slices once, until they're browned and slightly charred on both sides and tender, 5 to 6 minutes per side on the grill pan, and 8 minutes per side under the broiler. Cut out and discard the core from each slice.

TOMATOES

These fruits are indigenous to Mexico (the English word comes from the Nahuatl word *tomatl*) and one of the most common ingredients in its food. They add fresh jolts of flavor when raw and a beautiful balance of sweetness and acidity when cooked. They also provide silky body for sauces. In my recipes, I provide the weight as well as the number of tomatoes you'll need, so you can use the best tomatoes you can find, whether they're smaller plum tomatoes or bulky beefsteaks. The size, of course, will affect the cooking time, so expect particularly large tomatoes to take more time and smaller ones to take less, and rely on the visual cues I give you.

When you're planning to boil or roast tomatoes, look for those that are slightly soft and particularly heavy for their size. They're juicier and perfect for salsas and sauces made from cooked tomatoes. If you're planning to use tomatoes raw, as you would if you were making pico de gallo, look for bright-red tomatoes without blemishes, that are ripe but still a bit firm to the touch. Store firm tomatoes unwrapped at room temperature. Only when tomatoes are on the verge of overripe should you put them in the refrigerator.

NOTE: If you can't find great fresh tomatoes to cook, you can substitute high-quality canned tomatoes for boiled tomatoes and canned fire-roasted tomatoes for roasted

LEFT: Roasted onions
RIGHT: Roasted tomatoes

ones. Just drain and reserve their liquid before using them, so you can add it back little by little as you follow each recipe until you achieve the proper consistency. If you're using canned tomatoes, always taste your salsa or sauce first before you add salt because canned tomatoes can be salty.

CORING TOMATOES: To remove the tough little button on the stem end of the tomato, pierce the skin next to the button by about half an inch with a small, sharp knife and cut around it. Jiggle the knife to remove the button or scoop it out with a small spoon.

BOILING TOMATOES: Boiled tomatoes have a straightforward, clean tomato flavor and a silky, meaty texture.

Core each tomato and cut a small "X" through the skin on the bottom (opposite the stem end). Put the tomatoes in a pot with enough water to cover them. Bring the water to a simmer over medium-high heat. Lower the heat and simmer gently, turning the tomatoes carefully and occasionally, until they are tender but still intact, about 15 minutes. You know they're done when you can pierce their skins with a sharp paring knife without much resistance, as if you were sticking it into room-temperature butter. Drain them carefully, let them cool in a bowl, and remove the skins, which should slip right off.

ROASTING TOMATOES: Roasting tomatoes creates a more complex flavor than boiling, a lovely caramelized sweetness and pointed acidity. Since Mexicans don't use ovens as often as Americans do, the most common way to roast tomatoes is on a comal. But I prefer to roast them in the oven or toaster oven. When you roast them in a pan or comal, the skins stick to bottom, and I like to save myself the hassle of scrubbing afterward.

Set the oven to broil and preheat. Alternatively, you can preheat the oven to 500°F, or if the quantity of tomatoes is small enough, you can use a toaster oven. If you're using the oven broiler, position the rack 8 inches from the heat source. Core each tomato and cut a small "X" through the skin on the bottom (opposite the stem end). Roast the tomatoes, cored sides up, on a foil-lined baking pan until their tops have blackened and the tomatoes are cooked through to the core (there's no need to turn them over unless they're plum tomatoes, which lie on their sides), 20 to 30 minutes, depending on the size of the tomatoes. It's better to overcook them than undercook them. Remove the tomatoes, let them cool in a bowl to catch their juices, and remove the skins, which should slip right off. Don't leave any lovely liquid in the pan!

TOMATILLOS

By themselves, these unassuming relatives of the tomato (they're cousins, not brothers) taste a bit tart but otherwise unremarkable. But combine the raw fruit with just a few ingredients (perhaps some chiles and garlic) and you'll be shocked at how alive and distinctive they become—their meek acidity transforming into a brightness that awakens your palate. When the fruit is roasted or boiled, this brightness mellows into a gentle sweet-tartness, and the fruit's flesh becomes smooth and silky. Tomatillos, then, are not like the star solo trumpeter, but like the conductor of an orchestra: They provide this wonderful platform for flavor that lets other ingredients shine. And as usual, all you have to do to welcome tomatillos into your cooking is learn a few simple techniques.

The best way to choose tomatillos is to pull back the paper-like husk that encases the fruit and peek at the fruit itself. You want tomatillos that are as firm as grapes and free of bruises. (It's absolutely fine if the fruit is purplish.) The more taut the skins the better, but a little wrinkling is fine. Dark green tomatillos tend to be a little more tart than light green tomatillos. Don't worry too much about this, as you can always adjust the flavor of your sauce or salsa by adding lime juice or vinegar to bump up the tartness or a little sugar to add sweetness. Tomatillos are tough little things—you can store them, husked and washed or not, loose in the vegetable drawer for several weeks—as long as they're dry and kept away from moisture.

RINSING TOMATILLOS: Beneath their husks, on the skin of the fruit, you'll feel a slightly sticky substance. It's natural but slightly bitter tasting and should be rinsed off. Here's how you do it: Put the husked tomatillos in a bowl filled with water. Rub them with your fingers, changing the water once or twice, if necessary, until they feel less sticky.

LEFT: Boiled tomatillos
RIGHT: Roasted tomatillos

BOILING TOMATILLOS: Put the tomatillos in a pot with just enough water to cover them. Bring the water to a simmer over medium-high heat. Lower the heat and simmer gently, carefully turning those that float near the surface so they cook evenly, until the tomatillos have turned a khaki-green color and are soft but still intact, about 15 minutes. To make sure that they're done, cut into one: It should be cooked to the core. If they're not soft at the core, leave them in the cooking water for about 15 minutes to finish cooking. Drain them carefully (you don't want them to burst open). Unlike with tomatoes, you don't need to remove their skins.

ROASTING TOMATILLOS: Roasting tomatillos transforms the mildly tart fruit into something complex and intensely flavorful. As the sugars caramelize, the fruit gives up a dark amber syrup and the flesh takes on a silky texture that reminds me of cooked plums. The process is easy, and nearly identical to that of roasting tomatoes.

ROASTING ON THE STOVETOP: Put husked, rinsed tomatillos on a preheated comal, griddle, or heavy skillet (do not use cast iron) set over medium-low heat. (If you put them stem side down, they'll stay put, rather than rolling around the pan.) Roast the tomatillos until the undersides have blackened and the lower halves have turned a khaki-green color, 10 to 15 minutes. Carefully turn them over and roast until the other sides have blackened and the tomatillos are cooked through to the core, 10 to 15 minutes more. Remember, it's better to overcook them than undercook them, and you don't need to remove their skins. Let them cool in a bowl to catch their juices.

ROASTING IN THE OVEN OR TOASTER OVEN: Set the oven to broil and preheat. Alternatively, you can preheat the oven to 500°F, or if the quantity of tomatillos is small enough, you can use a toaster oven. If you're using the oven broiler, position the rack 8 inches from the heat source. Roast the tomatillos, stem side down, on a foil-lined baking pan, turning them over once halfway through, until their tops and bottoms have blackened and the tomatillos have collapsed like deflated balloons and turned a khaki-green color, 20 to 30 minutes. Check them occasionally, remove any that have finished roasting, and scoop out some of the syrup that has developed on the bottom of the pan, so it doesn't burn. If the tops and bottoms are blackened but the tomatillos don't seem soft all the way through, put them in a bowl and cover it, or leave them in a turned-off oven or toaster oven for 5 minutes, so they can continue to cook gently. Let them cool in a bowl to catch their juices.

XOCONOSTLE

There are several types of prickly pear adored in Mexico, but the one included in a couple of recipes in this book is the *xoconostle*. Unlike the other kinds, which have sweet flesh flecked with tiny edible seeds, xoconostles are tart, only slightly less sour than limes, with a flavor that's as much vegetable as fruit, with several medium-size seeds. Cooks all over Mexico, and particularly in the High Plains in the center of the country, use the fruit to make bracing salsas and drop it into bubbling stocks or *moles de olla*, letting its acidic tang seep into the liquid. To find them in the United States, you'll probably have to head to a market that caters to Mexicans. Choosing xoconostle (also known as sour prickly pear or *tuna agria*) is not like choosing peaches or mangoes. Because they grow under the harsh sun in desert and semi-desert areas, sour prickly pears are homely little fruits. On the same plant, you can find fruits in shades of pale magenta, green, and yellow, all with rugged skins. Neither pristine appearance nor ripeness is all that important—as long as the fruit is heavy for its size, without wet spots or mushiness. Be careful when you pick them up as their little spines can prick you. Store them on your counter and use them within a few days, or in your vegetable drawer, where they'll stay for up to two weeks.

NUTS AND SEEDS

PEANUTS

So many Mexicans grow up snacking on peanuts spiked with chile and lime (or the soy sauce–laced ones called *cacahuates japoneses*) or gobbling their grandmothers' *encacahuatados*, a peanut-focused category of pipianes. Native to the Americas, this nut (technically, it's a legume) performs best in recipes when it's roasted or fried in its raw state. Look for shelled, raw, skinless peanuts in your local natural foods store. If you must, you can substitute roasted unsalted peanuts for raw ones—in that case, you do not have to fry them as you would if they were raw. Store them in an airtight container in a cool, dark place for up to one month and in the freezer for up to six months.

PUMPKIN SEEDS

Cooks in Mexico adore this healthful seed, turning it into moles, pipianes, and even sweets like brittle, cookies, and marzipan-like confections. When my recipes call for pumpkin seeds, I always mean hulled raw pumpkin seeds, which are small and pastel green. You'll find them at your local natural foods store. Store them in an airtight plastic bag in the freezer for up to six months. You can use them straight from the freezer.

TOASTING PUMKPIN SEEDS: Some recipes call for toasted pumpkin seeds. Heat a small, heavy skillet (preferably one with raised sides) over medium heat. Toast the pumpkin seeds, stirring them constantly, until most of them have puffed up slightly and they're only slightly browned, 5 to 8 minutes. (See photo on page 188.)

SESAME SEEDS

There's a saying in Mexico that you use when you keep bumping into somebody: *"Eres ajonjoli de todos los moles."* To paraphrase: You are like the sesame seed; you're in all moles. Indeed, Mexicans use these seeds for so many sauces that you'll surely bump into them often, whether sprinkled on moles or made into a sauce with ancho chiles. It's important to note that my recipes call for unhulled sesame seeds, which are a bit darker and larger than the pearly white ones you see on your hamburger bun. If you use the hulled seeds, your sauce will be more likely to break. Look for unhulled sesame seeds in natural foods stores and Mexican markets. Store them in an airtight container in a cool, dark place for up to two months and in the refrigerator for up to six months.

TOASTING SESAME SEEDS: Some recipes call for toasted sesame seeds. Heat a small, heavy skillet with raised sides (this will make it easier to stir the tiny seeds) over medium heat. Toast the sesame seeds, stirring and tossing them constantly so they don't burn and so they all make some contact with the pan, until they're fragrant and a shade or two darker, about 4 minutes. Listen closely, and you'll hear some of them pop and see a little steam rising from the pan when they're just about done.

LEFT: Untoasted, unhulled (top) and hulled sesame seeds
RIGHT: Regular cinnamon (left) amd Mexican cinnamon (right) (see page 35)

PANTRY

LARD

On the streets of Mexico, when you order a *gordita* or *sope* from a vendor, he might drizzle a little *manteca*, or melted lard, on top. Beans refried in lard are indescribably delicious. For many cooks, making tamales or fresh flour tortillas without lard is unthinkable. But, you might ask, isn't rendered pork fat terrible for you? Well, what if I told you that this widely misunderstood ingredient has more good fat and less bad fat than butter? The real thing is hard to find in the United States. Many products labeled "lard" have been hydrogenated, which undoes its relative healthfulness; or the lard available is snowy white raw lard rather than the freshly rendered, light tan fat you see in Mexico and many Latin markets. That said, I've used vegetable shortening and white raw lard when nothing else was available. And in my tamale recipe (see page 227), I provide a way to substitute easy-to-find vegetable oil for lard. But for the truly committed, there's nothing quite like making lard yourself and filling your kitchen with that soft, porky aroma. It'll keep for a few weeks in your refrigerator.

LARD MANTECA

MAKES 1½ CUPS   **ACTIVE TIME: 10 MINUTES**   **START TO FINISH: 30 MINUTES**

1 pound pork fat, either from fatback, belly, or trimmed from the shoulder, cut into approximately ½-inch cubes

¼ teaspoon kosher salt, or ⅛ tsp fine salt

PUT the fat in a medium saucepan with the salt, and add ½ cup of water. Bring the water to a boil over high heat. Reduce the heat to medium, and cook at a vigorous simmer until the water has evaporated (you'll notice the furious bubbling will subside) and the small pieces of fat that remain are golden (you might also see a bit of smoke when it's ready), about 20 minutes. Scoop out the crunchy pieces (snack on them— they're *chicharrones!*), strain the golden liquid into a heat-proof bowl, and you're ready to use it as a flavor-packed cooking fat, or let it solidify in the fridge before you use it to make tamales or pastries.

MASA

The word means dough, but it speaks to corn's venerated status in Mexico that masa immediately signifies a specific kind. Made into so many delicious items—tortillas, tamales, gorditas, and little dumplings that float in moles, just to name a few—masa is made from a starchy corn that's dried and cooked in hot water mixed with slaked lime or ashes. This ingenious process, known as nixtamalization, transforms the chemical structure of the corn, turning the unremarkable, undigestible dried corn into something nutritious and tremendously delicious. The result of this miracle of culinary science is the swollen kernels known as nixtamal, which gets ground into masa. In Mexico, many cooks still do this themselves, making nixtamal into a paste on a *metate*, a sort of flat stone mortar, or at least make the nixtamal and take it to a local mill to be ground. If they plan to make tamales, they'll ask for a slightly coarser grind than they would for tortillas. But more often, Mexicans buy their masa from a *tortilleria* (tortilla shop), and nowadays, it's often not freshly ground but rather made from powdered dried masa rehydrated with water. Fresh masa is wonderful if you can find it—depending on where you live, this can be pretty easy or really difficult—but since it doesn't travel well, you can't have it mailed to you. Fortunately, masa flour (fresh masa that has been dried and powdered) makes a solid substitute and is easy to find. The most common brands are Maseca and Minsa.

MEXICAN CHOCOLATE

Centuries ago, the Maya, Aztec, and other peoples in the Americas drank chocolate in slightly bitter beverages. The stuff Mexicans use today is spiked with cinnamon and, unlike the smooth, creamy chocolate Americans and Europeans are used to, contains crunchy grains of sugar. Besides incorporating it into all sorts of desserts, cooks add small amounts to some adobos and moles for the lovely background flavor it provides. If you can find or order an artisanal product, like the Seasons of My Heart brand, buy it right away. Mexican chocolate is also available in most large supermarkets (look for the Ibarra or Abuelita brands), any Mexican market, and by mail order, but if you must, substitute the same amount of semisweet chocolate and add a pinch of cinnamon.

MEXICAN CINNAMON

This fragrant, mellow cinnamon—flaky curls of bark labeled "canela" in Latin grocery stores and known elsewhere as Ceylon, Sri Lankan, or "true" cinnamon—adds an irreplaceable flavor to sweets, adobos, moles, and braising sauces. It is not interchangeable with the aggressively spicy cinnamon (which is actually cassia) found most often in American supermarkets, either ground into a powder or in tough sticks. Canela is pretty easy to find, but if you must, you can substitute ⅛ teaspoon ground regular cinnamon for every ½-inch stick of canela. And note that in contrast to the delicate canela, sticks of common cinnamon can be too tough to grind. So if you do use them, steep the sticks in the sauce and remove them before serving.

OIL FOR COOKING

Most Mexican cooks use vegetable oil. I prefer safflower oil, which they used for many years before moving on to the more affordable oil, but vegetable and mild olive oil both work well. They're certainly better than corn oil, which is gaining ground in Mexico, but I find corn oil adds an unpleasant flavor to whatever you're cooking.

SALT

You can use any kind of salt you want, but it's important to note that one teaspoon of fine salt is half the volume of the same weight of coarser kosher salt. For example, one teaspoon of fine salt is equivalent to two teaspoons of kosher salt. My recipes take this into account, offering you amounts for both types, so the important difference doesn't slip your mind. When you're pounding ingredients with salt in a molcajete or mortar, it will be much easier to create a paste if you use kosher salt. In general, you should add salt gradually, and remember that everyone has a different tolerance for salt levels in food. But also keep in mind that the addition of salt can magically boost flavor without making a sauce or dish taste "saltier."

TORTILLAS

Nearly every meal in Mexico features tortillas. Served warm, the delicate disks are used like bread to sop up sauces or turned into Tacos (pages 212–214), Enchiladas (pages 216–224), and so many other delicious dishes. Even day-old tortillas are put to use: They're fried to make crunchy Tortilla Chips or Tostadas (page 229), which are sometimes soaked in sauce to make spicy, sloppy Chilaquiles (page 231).

A friend once asked me where I buy my tortillas, and I told him that I don't typically buy them—rather, I make them myself. "But," he said incredulously, "that must be so hard and take so much time!" So I dragged him into my kitchen and showed him how easy and fun it is to make your own tortillas and how far superior they are to anything you can buy at the supermarket. It takes a little practice to perfect, but even your first attempts will produce tasty tortillas.

Store-bought tortillas can last for two weeks in the refrigerator. Wrap any homemade tortillas you don't use in a kitchen towel, put them in an airtight plastic bag, and store the bag in the fridge. Eat them within a day or two, heating them through on a comal or skillet first, if you're using them for tacos or as an accompaniment for salsas, adobos, moles, and pipianes. Use them within two days for enchiladas and

DID YOU KNOW?

As any Mexican will tell you, tortillas have a top and a bottom. You might dismiss this as crazy talk, until you look closely at a homemade one. On one side, you'll notice a thin layer that has separated from the rest, which happened when the tortilla puffed up during cooking. This is the top of the tortilla. This thin layer acts as a barrier, protecting the tortilla from becoming soggy too quickly. So if you're a stickler (or if I'm coming over for dinner), you'll make sure this side is facing the sky, whether you're serving tacos or a stack of warm tortillas with dinner.

three days, when they're a bit stale, to make tortilla chips, tostadas, and chilaquiles.

BUYING AND HEATING STORE-BOUGHT TORTILLAS: If you're pressed for time or, for some other reason, don't make tortillas yourself, you should buy the best you can find. Sometimes that means seeking out a local tortilla factory (you'd be surprised at how many there are in the United States) or asking a local restaurant if they'll sell you some of their freshly made tortillas. But you might have to settle for those you can find at your local supermarket. While commercially made flour and corn tortillas don't compare to the homemade sort, they can actually be quite delicious as long as you give them enough time in the pan. I've noticed that most people cook them for about 15 seconds per side, which will leave you with gummy, gritty tortillas that will break when you fold them. Instead, heat a comal, griddle, or heavy skillet over medium-high heat. When it's hot, add a tortilla. After 30 seconds, you should see steam escaping from underneath the disk. If you don't, turn the heat up a bit before you heat the next tortilla. After another 15 seconds, flip the tortilla. Soon, you should see some pockets of air forming. Cook it for another 45 seconds, flip it once more (you'll see a few golden brown spots), and cook it for a final 15 seconds. Flour tortillas take about the same amount of time to cook as corn tortillas, but they deserve slightly lower heat, more frequent flipping, and, occasionally, a little less time because they're more susceptible to burning. Eat the tortillas right away or keep them warm in a tortilla basket.

MAKING CORN TORTILLAS: Mexicans also eat flour tortillas, especially in the North, but corn tortillas are the most common kind in Mexico. I went back and forth, trying to decide whether to provide instructions that were brief but less helpful or long and more helpful. I finally settled on the latter because if I'm urging you to make tortillas, I'd better take the time to make sure you can do them right. If the text looks daunting, that's only because it's packed with details. Look more closely and you'll see that making tortillas is as easy as making a two-ingredient dough, pressing balls of it into disks, and cooking those disks in a pan. Sure, your first few will take a little more time to make as you read and reread the instructions, but before you know it, you won't have to refer to the instructions at all.

If you can get fresh masa, you can skip the step of making the dough. My recipe differs in two important ways from the classic you'll see in many other cookbooks. I add salt to the masa flour to bump up the flavor, and I make particularly moist masa dough, because I find that it's the secret to the perfect texture.

TRICK: HEATING TWO TORTILLAS AT A TIME

This easy technique helps to keep the tortillas from drying out and lets you warm up two at once.

Put two tortillas in a hot pan, one (tortilla 1) directly on top of the other (tortilla 2). After about 45 seconds, turn over the stack so that tortilla 2 is on top and tortilla 1 is on the bottom. Turn over tortilla 2 only, so that it's still on top of tortilla 1. After about 45 seconds, turn over the stack, then turn over tortilla 1 only, so that it's still on top of tortilla 2. After another 45 seconds, turn over the stack and cook for a final 45 seconds.

CORN TORTILLAS TORTILLAS DE MAÍZ

MAKES ABOUT SIXTEEN 5- TO 6-INCH TORTILLAS

2 cups corn tortilla flour (also called masa harina)

¼ teaspoon fine salt, or ½ teaspoon kosher salt

1¾ cups barely hot water (see note), plus more as needed

WHAT YOU'LL NEED: A good tortilla press (see page 41); a shallow pan (preferably a flat one like a comal or griddle); a kitchen towel; a tortilla basket, large bowl, or a plastic bag; and two circles of plastic about 7 inches in diameter.

MAKE THE PLASTIC CIRCLES: Find a grocery bag made of thin plastic (one that's translucent works perfectly), and lay it flat on a cutting board. Put an upside-down plate or bowl, whose diameter is about 7 inches, on top of the bag, then trace the edge of the plate or bowl with the tip of a sharp knife. You can use these two circles again and again as long as you wipe them clean after each tortilla-making session.

MAKE THE DOUGH: Combine the masa harina and salt in a large bowl. Add the water and mix with your hands, incorporating all the bits of dough stuck to the bowl. Knead it for a minute with your palm so you can be sure that there are no spots of dry flour. You should have a smooth dough that feels like slightly sticky Play-Doh and leaves a light film on your hands. Cover the bowl with plastic wrap and let it sit for 5 minutes. Meanwhile, put a comal, griddle, or heavy skillet over medium-high heat until it just begins to smoke.

MAKE THE DISKS: Open your tortilla press and put one of the plastic circles in the center of the press's bottom plate. Roll a small piece of masa dough (2 tablespoons should do it) with your palms into a 1¼-inch ball, about the size of a Ping Pong ball, and put it in the center of the plastic circle. Put the other plastic circle centered on top of the ball and press down lightly with your palm, then close the tortilla press, pushing down on the handle with some force, jiggling the handle a little once the press is closed. At this point, you can tell whether your dough is perfectly wet. If the edges of your first disk crack and look ragged, then gradually add a little more water to your dough. If they get stuck to the plastic circle, the dough is too wet and you should gradually add a little more masa.

OPEN the press and rotate your tortilla 180°, making sure it's still centered. Close the press again and jiggle the handle. If the

tortilla has an even thickness, you're ready to cook it. If not, give it another turn and press. As you get a feel for the idiosyncrasies of your press, you'll figure out how hard to press down on the handle and whether, or how often, you'll need to rotate your tortilla. Your tortilla should be 5 to 6 inches in diameter. If for some reason it tears, don't worry—roll the disk back into a ball and try again.

COOK THE TORTILLAS: Open the press and take out the plastic-encased tortilla. Holding it in one hand, carefully peel off the plastic from one side. Switch hands and remove the plastic from the other side. Drape the tortilla on your open hand so that about two-thirds of it hangs over the pinky side. Position your hand so that it's parallel to the pan and your palm is facing up. Turn your wrist as you gently lay the tortilla flatly on the surface. Resist the temptation to flop the tortilla onto the pan. Cook the tortilla for 20 seconds (be as precise as possible): You should see a little steam and the edges just barely begin to lift from the pan's surface. If you don't see any steam at this point, try turning up the heat slightly before you cook your next tortilla. Lift an edge of the tortilla using a spatula, or if you're brave, your fingers, and carefully flip the tortilla. Cook it for 45 seconds. Flip it again, and cook for another 45 seconds. If you've done everything right, the tortillas should puff up a bit. Also, both sides should have developed a few brown spots. (If they haven't, the heat is a bit too low. If the spots look black, the heat is a bit too high. Adjust the heat before you cook your next tortilla.) Flip the tortilla once more and cook it for 30 seconds.

WRAP THEM UP: Put the cooked tortilla in a kitchen towel–lined basket or bowl and cover it. As you cook each tortilla, layer it on top of the others in the towel and cover it again, which keeps them moist and warm and also completes the cooking process.

NOTE: I've found that the ideal range of temperature is 105° to 115°F. Eventually you won't need a thermometer—once you get the feel for it, a dip of your finger will tell you whether the water is just right.

NOTE: The tortillas stay warm for up to 30 minutes. To reheat homemade tortillas held longer, cook each tortilla on a hot comal for 30 seconds on each side, and return it to the towel-lined basket.

ESSENTIAL EQUIPMENT

BLENDER

Thank heaven for this modern kitchen tool. Every time I make moles, adobos, or one of my smooth salsas, I wince at how laborious cooking was before the invention of the blender. In fact, in many parts of Mexico, you can still see women grinding pastes the old-fashioned way, in molcajetes or metates, their arms straining as they crush ingredients against the rough volcanic stone. Of course, there are still things it can't do quite as well as the molcajete or metate, such as turning chiles, salt, and vegetables into pastes for some guacamoles and chunky salsas, yet I'm going to go out on a limb and call it the most useful piece of equipment in my kitchen after my comal. The good news is you don't need some fancy 20-speed blender. In fact, I prefer a machine that has only two options: blend and pulse. The important thing is that it's strong and sturdy.

CAZUELA

There's something romantic about this deep, heavy earthenware pot that Mexicans use to make saucy stews. Not only does its width make it great for sautéing and its depth make it fabulous for frying sauces (it contains any splattering), but I'd also swear that the material from which cazuelas are made imparts a lovely flavor to moles, pipianes, adobos, and guisados. But really, a heavy-bottomed Dutch oven (like the ones made by Le Creuset) or even a deep stainless-steel pot works just as well.

COMAL

In nearly every Mexican kitchen, you'll find the round, flat pan made of clay, cast iron, or steel, known as a comal. It's this, not the oven, that Mexican cooks use to dry roast garlic, onions, tomatoes, tomatillos, you name it! In modern kitchens in Mexico and America, though, many of these tasks can be done (and in some cases are even better done) in an oven or toaster oven. Still, I use my comal so often. Because it doesn't have raised edges, you can wield tongs, spatulas, even fingers

CAST IRON

You can use almost any shallow pan for dry roasting, but I don't recommend using a cast-iron skillet. I have more than once had to throw out mine because the oil-less cooking had left some gunk on the surface that I just couldn't get off. Dry roasting, boiling, or otherwise cooking tomatoes, tomatillos, and other highly acidic ingredients in cast iron is another no-no because the acidity in those fruits can corrode the cast iron and ruin your skillet, and react with the cast iron to create unwanted flavors.

without limitations, flipping tortillas and pressing down on chiles to make sure every bit makes contact with the hot comal. You certainly don't need a comal to make great Mexican food, but they're inexpensive and very helpful. I love my heavy, cast-iron comal. I use it for everything except tomatoes and tomatillos, which would corrode the well-seasoned surface. For those, I use a lighter (but not flimsy), almost equally lovely steel comal or the oven.

FREEZER AND REFRIGERATOR

As you read my recipes, you'll notice that many of the sauces in this book keep well in the freezer and refrigerator. Once you've cooked through the book a bit, you'll find yourself making, say, *salsa verde cocida* or pork in adobo, and freezing the result—giving you a sort of magic Mexican pantry that you can dip into on a weeknight and pull out a fabulous dinner in minutes. Just make sure that you let food reach room temperature before storing it in the refrigerator or freezer or else it won't cool quickly enough and will raise the temperature of the food around it.

MOLCAJETE

First things first: You can make every recipe in this book even if you don't own this wide, shallow mortar. But the vessel is incredibly useful for grinding chiles, garlic, and roasted vegetables of all kinds into just the right paste for salsas and guacamoles, not to mention show-stoppingly beautiful. If you're lucky enough to find a relatively smooth, grit-free, charcoal-colored molcajete made entirely of high-quality volcanic rock, buy it immediately. It'll be expensive (expect to spend around $60), but worth it. If you can only find the light-colored, white-speckled ones sold throughout the United States, you're better off buying a nice marble mortar and pestle, which you can find in almost any good cookware store. If you do buy the molcajete I prefer, do this before you use it: Grind a few small batches of raw white rice, a couple of tablespoons at a time, to a powder in it. The first few times, you'll notice that the ground rice looks gray, not white. Keep grinding small batches until the powder is white, which means you've dislodged and removed any loose bits of rock.

TORTILLA PRESS

If you're ready to impress your friends by making your own delicately doughy tortillas—it's much easier than you think (see Corn Tortillas, page 39)—you need to buy a tortilla press, which will turn a little ball of masa dough into a disk ready for your comal or skillet. Light, cheap ones never do the job as well as heavy wooden, cast-iron, or cast-aluminum ones. A good press will cost anywhere from $25 to $60, and it'll be worth every penny. One of my favorite readily available presses is the one from Imusa USA with the word *Victoria* printed on its top.

SALSAS

IGNITING THE FIRE OF FLAVOR

IMAGINE BITING THROUGH A SOFT, HOMEMADE CORN TORTILLA AND INTO CHARRED PIECES OF STEAK OR SALTY, JUICY CHUNKS OF PORK. THE THOUGHT OF THOSE FLAVORS AND TEXTURES IS ALREADY MAKING YOU HUNGRY, BUT THIS IS JUST THE KINDLING. SALSA IS THE SPARK THAT IGNITES THE FIRE OF FLAVOR.

From the silky smooth to the thick and chunky, the salsas in this chapter are used to deliver an exhilarating bolt of flavor and a welcome dose of lip-tingling heat that takes even the most delicious dishes to new heights. Of course, the concept of a mouth-awakening condiment is not uniquely Mexican—the British use vinegars, Germans use mustards, Vietnamese use the chile-spiked dipping sauce called *nuoc cham*, and Americans use ketchup—but Mexico's repertoire is probably the most diverse and exciting. No one can say for sure why this is, but I bet the reason has something to do with the creative spirit of Mexicans and the country's incredible diversity of cultures, climates, and ingredients.

Salsas feature such a wide variety of tastes and textures that, to the uninitiated, they can seem irreconcilably different. Pico de gallo brings a fresh and crunchy combination of chopped tomatoes, jalapeños, and onions with the tart tug of lime. Salsa negra is nearly black and thick, the consistency of brownie dough, with the intense smoky sweetness of scorched chipotles. Salsa with roasted habaneros, pineapple, and tomatoes tastes complexly sweet and fiery and has a smooth, soupy texture interspersed with soft chunks of fruit.

Yet besides being united by their common purpose, salsas are also united by techniques that are more similar than you might expect. Ingredients, either raw or cooked, are chopped up or pureed in the blender jar (or if you're ambitious, pounded in the molcajete). Occasionally the result is fried in a little oil. That's it. And since you already know how easy it is to roast, boil, and toast ingredients (see the Basics chapter), making salsa is a snap. To make your life really easy, I've broken the universe of salsas into two categories—raw and cooked—and grouped them by ingredient. That way, you'll know precisely where to look in this book when you find a bunch of gorgeous tomatoes at the farmers market or come across tomatillos at a bodega.

Generally, when you taste a salsa, keep in mind its purpose, besides a few salsas meant for cooking (see pages 92–99). It's not meant to be eaten by the spoonful (though sometimes, I bet you'll be tempted!). When you make a salsa and taste it, it might seem so spicy or tangy that you think to yourself, "Wow, did I go overboard?" Before you answer, remember, you want something that packs a big punch, because just a small spoonful is meant to electrify an entire taco, sandwich, or bowl of soup.

Besides the intensity of flavor, each salsa has its own perfect world, where all its components are in just the right balance. But finding that balance is not as simple as following a recipe—even the most carefully written one. That's because particular ingredients can vary in flavor. One jalapeño is fiery, while another is more mild. Dark green tomatillos are more tart than light green ones. So it happens that you'll fastidiously follow a recipe that you've made many times before and find it doesn't turn out precisely as spicy or tart or sweet as you remember. But fear not! My recipes help guide you toward the right flavor and also give you the tools to tweak the flavors if necessary.

3 KEYS TO GREAT SALSA

1. SALT IS AN ESSENTIAL, if often overlooked, component to successful salsas, heightening their spicy, tart, tangy, and even sweet flavors. Use it liberally, but add it gradually.

2. YOU CAN MAKE MANY SALSAS IN ADVANCE, up to several hours earlier for some and a few days earlier for others. But when you do, remember that more often than not, the heat of the chiles dwindles as time passes. So if you're planning to wait before serving a salsa, compensate by adding extra chile.

3. CONDIMENT SALSAS ALWAYS TASTE BEST AT ROOM TEMPERATURE, so keep this in mind when you're thinking of serving leftover salsa stored in the refrigerator or making a salsa from cooked ingredients. Let the chilled salsa come up to room temperature and give the hot salsa time to cool down.

RAW SALSAS There is no salsa police. There are no unbending rules that dictate which salsas must go with what dishes. But there are some time-honored combinations and principles that will help guide you. One of those is that raw salsas are used to provide contrast. Generally, they go great with fattier dishes, like braised short ribs, because their sharp, fresh acidity cuts into richness, giving you a little relief so you can dive into that next bite. Raw salsas also provide textural contrast. Chopped salsas, like pico de gallo, with the gentle crunch of onion or cucumber or pineapple make a lovely pairing with the buttery flesh of fish or a quesadilla with oozy melted cheese.

RAW TOMATO SALSAS

This indigenous fruit is the star of these salsas, so buy the best ones you can find. In fact, if you can't find great tomatoes, these salsas won't taste nearly as good as they should, so either try my Cucumber Salsa (page 59) or focus on another exciting category of salsas. And whenever you're using tomatoes raw, use those that are ripe but still pretty firm. Softer tomatoes, which are juicier, work better for cooked tomato salsas.

PICO DE GALLO FRESH TOMATO SALSA

The Spanish name for this salsa means "rooster's beak," and originally referred to a salad of jicama, peanuts, oranges, and onions. But today, whether you're in Minneapolis or Mexico City, if you ask for pico de gallo, you'll get the familiar cilantro-flecked combination of chopped tomato, onion, and fresh chiles. This tart, crisp condiment (also known as salsa Mexicana) has become so common on Mexican tables that it seems like no coincidence that its colors match those of the national flag. Besides finding firm ripe tomatoes and seeding them, the key to this salsa is adding plenty of lime juice and salt, and not skimping on the chiles. Because without a burst of acidity and heat, you're just eating chopped tomatoes.

MAKES 2 CUPS   ACTIVE TIME: **15 MINUTES**   START TO FINISH: **15 MINUTES**

¾ pound tomatoes (about 2 medium), seeded and finely diced (1½ cups)

⅓ cup chopped cilantro

¼ cup finely chopped white onion

1 small fresh jalapeño or serrano chile, finely chopped, including seeds, or more to taste

1 tablespoon freshly squeezed lime juice, or more to taste

½ teaspoon fine salt, or 1 teaspoon kosher salt

MIX all the ingredients together in a bowl. Season to taste with additional chile, lime juice, and salt.

Serve it with Adobo-Marinated Fish (page 130), Adobo-Marinated Shrimp (page 132), Grilled Adobo-Marinated Skirt Steak (page 135), Adobo-Marinated Chicken (page 133), Tacos (pages 212–214), Quesadillas (page 225), Carnitas (page 240), Beans with Pork (page 232), or Tortilla Chips (page 229).

This salsa keeps in the refrigerator for up to one day. Before you serve it, stir it well and drain any excess liquid that has accumulated in the bowl.

FRESH TOMATO SALSA WITH PARSLEY, MINT, AND OLIVE OIL

SALSA LIBANESA

This salsa is a delicious melding of cultures—pico de gallo meets vinaigrette—and my tribute to Mexico City's significant Lebanese population. Olive oil gives it a silky texture, vinegar provides a lovely tang, and fresh parsley and mint team up with Mexican dried oregano to give a nod to the Middle East. My late aunt was married to a Lebanese man, and I can imagine her serving this to him beside a plate of lentils, but I love to spoon the salsa over grilled steak, lamb chops, or *molletes,* those lovely open-face sandwiches of beans and melted cheese.

MAKES 1½ CUPS   ACTIVE TIME: **20 MINUTES**   START TO FINISH: **1 HOUR AND 20 MINUTES (PLUS MAKING ÁRBOL CHILE POWDER)**

½ pound tomato (about 1 medium-large), seeded and finely diced (1 cup)

⅓ cup finely diced red onion

¼ cup olive oil

2 tablespoons freshly squeezed lime juice

2 tablespoons sherry vinegar, or more to taste

2 tablespoons chopped fresh flat-leaf parsley (leaves only)

1 tablespoon chopped fresh mint (leaves only)

1 tablespoon sugar

1 teaspoon Árbol Chile Powder (see page 21) or cayenne pepper (see note), or more to taste

½ teaspoon fine salt, or 1 teaspoon kosher salt

¼ teaspoon dried oregano, preferably Mexican, crumbled

MIX the ingredients together in a bowl. Let the mixture sit for 1 hour at room temperature before you serve it. Season to taste with additional vinegar, chile powder, and salt.

Serve it with Grilled Adobo-Marinated Skirt Steak (page 135), Adobo-Marinated Chicken (page 133), Tacos (pages 212–214), Quesadillas (page 225), Tortilla Chips (page 229), rice, beans, or any other side you like (pages 246–256).

This salsa keeps in the refrigerator for up to one day. Before you serve it, stir it well and drain any excess liquid that has accumulated in the bowl.

NOTE: Purchased cayenne pepper is a fine substitute for árbol chile powder in this recipe, so long as it's added gradually and to taste. But in recipes where árbol chile powder plays a major role, don't make this substitution.

FRESH YELLOW TOMATO SALSA
PICO DE GALLO AMARILLO

I didn't often see yellow tomatoes in the markets of Mexico, but when I came to the United States, they seemed to be everywhere. So I decided to have some fun with them, and dreamed up this colorful salsa. It has a few more ingredients than the typical pico, but the addition of scallions, habaneros, and orange juice takes it to another level of deliciousness. Of course, you can substitute any kind of tomato for the yellow beauties, just as long as it's ripe and delicious.

MAKES 2½ CUPS   ACTIVE TIME: **20 MINUTES**   START TO FINISH: **20 MINUTES**

1 pound yellow tomatoes (about 3 medium), seeded and finely diced (2 cups)

⅓ cup finely chopped red onion

1 large scallion (white and green parts), finely sliced

¼ cup finely diced red bell pepper

1 tablespoon minced fresh jalapeño or serrano chile, including seeds, or more to taste

3 tablespoons freshly squeezed orange juice

1½ tablespoons freshly squeezed lime juice, or more to taste

½ teaspoon minced fresh habanero chile, including seeds, or more to taste

¾ teaspoon fine salt, or 1½ teaspoons kosher salt

MIX all the ingredients together in a bowl. Season to taste with additional chiles, lime juice, and salt.

Serve it with Adobo-Marinated Fish (page 130), Adobo-Marinated Shrimp (page 132), Grilled Adobo-Marinated Skirt Steak (page 135), Adobo-Marinated Chicken (page 133), Tacos (pages 212–214), Quesadillas (page 225), Tortilla Chips (page 229), rice, beans, or any other side you like (pages 246–256).

This salsa keeps in the refrigerator for up to one day. Before you serve it, stir it well and drain any excess liquid that has accumulated in the bowl.

RAW TOMATILLO SALSAS Tomatillos are getting easier and easier to find in the United States, whether at the farmers market in summertime or the supermarket all year-round. If you've never used them before, you'll be shocked at how little you have to do to harness their bright, tart flavor. Remember when you're selecting tomatillos to look beneath the husks for taut skins that are free of blemishes. And keep in mind that the fruit's acidity varies (dark green tomatillos are a bit more tart than lighter, paler ones), and you can always tweak the acidity of salsas made with raw tomatillos with lime juice.

FRESH TOMATILLO SALSA
SALSA VERDE CRUDA

Let me be dramatic for a second: I live for this salsa! Few things make me happier than going to my favorite taquerias in Mexico City, ordering tacos with carnitas, barbacoa, or other tasty braised meats, and spooning on salsa verde cruda. Really, though, I'll add it to almost anything that benefits from a bolt of tartness and spiciness. It always amazes me that a salsa that takes so little effort can deliver such tremendous flavor. You just toss tomatillos, such unassuming little fruits, along with a few other easy-to-find ingredients in the blender, puree, and you're done. Each time you make it, it'll get even better as you get a sense of the balance of flavors—tweaking the level of tomatillos' acidity with a little lime juice and adding just the right amount of salt to make it all sing.

MAKES 1½ CUPS   ACTIVE TIME: 15 MINUTES   START TO FINISH: 15 MINUTES

½ pound tomatillos (5 or 6), husked, rinsed, and coarsely chopped

½ cup chopped cilantro

2 fresh serrano or jalapeño chiles, coarsely chopped, including seeds, or more to taste

2 tablespoons chopped white onion

1 large garlic clove, peeled

¾ teaspoon fine salt, or 1½ teaspoons kosher salt

PUT the tomatillos in the blender jar first, then add the remaining ingredients. Blend until the salsa is very smooth (the tomatillo seeds will still be visible), at least a minute. Season to taste with additional chile and salt, and blend again.

Serve it with Adobo-Marinated Fish (page 130), Grilled Adobo-Marinated Skirt Steak (page 135), Adobo-Marinated Chicken (page 133), Tacos (pages 212–214), Quesadillas (page 225), Beans with Pork (page 232), Carnitas (page 240), Mexican-Style Noodles (page 235), rice, beans, or any other side you like (pages 246–256).

This salsa tastes best no more than a few hours after you make it.

BLENDING STUBBORN TOMATILLOS

It takes a minute or so for the blades of the blender jar to catch raw chopped tomatillos. Once they do, all the ingredients will be pulled toward them. Be patient, and do not add any water. If the tomatillos don't liquidize after a minute or so, stop the blender, prod them with a wooden spoon, and try to blend again.

FRESH TOMATILLO SALSA WITH AVOCADO SALSA VERDE CRUDA CON AGUACATE

It's a cinch to turn simple fresh tomatillo salsa into the kind of tart, creamy, slightly soupy condiment that you find in Mexico City's incredible taquerias. You just blend in an avocado and add a little more salt and chile. The addition of water gives it just the right texture. Even though it acts like salsa, strictly speaking it's a guacamole— yet as long as you promise to spoon some on my taco, I don't care what you call it!

MAKES 2½ CUPS **ACTIVE TIME: 20 MINUTES** **START TO FINISH: 20 MINUTES**

1 recipe Fresh Tomatillo Salsa (opposite page)

1 large or 2 small ripe Mexican Hass avocados, halved and pitted

2 fresh serrano or jalapeño chiles, coarsely chopped, including seeds, or more to taste

½ cup water

¼ teaspoon fine salt, or ½ teaspoon kosher salt

PUT the fresh tomatillo salsa in the blender jar, scoop the avocado flesh into the jar, and add the remaining ingredients. Blend until smooth. Season to taste with additional chile and salt, and blend again.

Serve it with Adobo-Marinated Fish (page 130), Adobo-Marinated Shrimp (page 132), Grilled Adobo-Marinated Skirt Steak (page 135), Adobo-Marinated Chicken (page 133), Tacos (pages 212–214), Quesadillas (page 225), Beans with Pork (page 232), Tortilla Chips (page 229), Carnitas (page 240), rice, beans, or any other side you like (pages 246–256).

This salsa tastes best no more than a few hours after you make it.

FRESH TOMATILLO AND MANZANO CHILE SALSA

SALSA FRESCA DE TOMATILLO CON CHILE MANZANO

From the foot of the volcano Nevado de Toluca and the mind of Señora Delia Gasca, my partner's mother, this fresh salsa makes brilliant use of the quirky chile manzano, which is shaped like an apple (hence the name), has beautiful black seeds, and delivers blistering heat that mercifully doesn't obscure the chile's unique flavor. Because chiles manzanos can be tough to find, you can use habanero instead. The flavor won't be the same, but the variation will still offer a similarly delicious change of pace from raw tomatillo salsa made with serranos or jalapeños.

MAKES 1 CUP   ACTIVE TIME: **15 MINUTES**   START TO FINISH: **15 MINUTES**

½ pound tomatillos (5 or 6), husked, rinsed, and coarsely chopped

1 pencil-thin scallion (white and green parts), coarsely chopped

1 large garlic clove, peeled, or more to taste

½ fresh manzano chile or habanero chile, including seeds, or more to taste

2 whole allspice berries

2 whole black peppercorns

½ teaspoon fine salt, or 1 teaspoon kosher salt

PUT the tomatillos in the blender jar first, then add the remaining ingredients. Blend until smooth, at least a minute. Season to taste with additional garlic, chile, and salt, and blend again.

Serve it with Adobo-Marinated Fish (page 130), Grilled Adobo-Marinated Skirt Steak (page 135), Adobo-Marinated Chicken (page 133), Tacos (pages 214–214), Quesadillas (page 225), Beans with Pork (page 232), Carnitas (page 240), rice, beans, or any other side you like (pages 246–256).

This salsa tastes best the day it's made.

Tomatillos

RAW SALSAS WITH OTHER FRUITS AND VEGETABLES

These recipes take fruits, which are already so tasty, and turn them into something even more delicious with a little help from chiles and fresh juices. No cooking necessary.

SPICY FRESH PINEAPPLE SALSA
SALSA DE PIÑA PICANTE

It's funny, a lot of the taste experience I aim to create when I make a salsa—a lovely texture, a balance of flavors—is embodied in the pineapple, a fruit so good I often don't embellish it with anything at all. With a starting point that tasty, it's a snap to make a salsa that wins you wide smiles at the table.

MAKES 1½ CUPS   **ACTIVE TIME: 30 MINUTES**   **START TO FINISH: 30 MINUTES**

1 cup diced fresh pineapple

⅓ cup finely chopped fresh jalapeño chiles, including seeds, or more to taste

¼ cup chopped cilantro

¼ cup finely chopped red onion

3 tablespoons freshly squeezed lime juice, or more to taste

2 tablespoons freshly squeezed orange juice

1½ teaspoons sugar, or more to taste

½ teaspoon fine salt, or 1 teaspoon kosher salt

MIX all the ingredients together in a bowl. Season to taste with additional chile, lime juice, sugar, and salt.

Serve it with Adobo-Marinated Fish (page 130), Adobo-Marinated Shrimp (page 132), Grilled Adobo-Marinated Skirt Steak (page 135), Adobo-Marinated Chicken (page 133), Tacos (pages 212–214), Quesadillas (page 225), Tortilla Chips (page 229), or Carnitas (page 240).

This salsa keeps in the refrigerator for up to one day. Before you serve it, drain any excess liquid that has accumulated in the bowl.

FRESH MANGO AND PINEAPPLE SALSA SALSA DE PIÑA Y MANGO

Two fruits adored in Mexico come together in this colorful, summery salsa. As with most fruit-based salsas, you're looking for a bold sweetness reined in by a little acidity and plenty of heat from chiles (remember, the salsa will tone down as it rests). The better the fruit tastes, the better this salsa will taste, so buy fresh pineapple and preferably either the perfumed, silky-textured ataulfo mangoes or mangoes de manila, though any ripe, fresh mango will be delicious.

MAKES 4½ CUPS   ACTIVE TIME: **40 MINUTES**   START TO FINISH: **40 MINUTES**

2 cups diced fresh pineapple (from ½ pineapple)

1 large firm-ripe mango, peeled, pitted, and diced (1½ to 2 cups)

1 red bell pepper, finely diced (¾ cup)

½ cup chopped cilantro

¼ cup finely chopped red onion

2 tablespoons freshly squeezed lime juice, or more to taste

1 teaspoon fine salt, or 2 teaspoons kosher salt

1 fresh habanero chile, finely chopped, including seeds

MIX all the ingredients except the habanero together in a large bowl. Add ½ teaspoon of the chopped habanero, and then add more to taste, remembering that the more heat the better here. Season to taste with additional lime juice and salt.

Serve it with Adobo-Marinated Fish (page 130), Adobo-Marinated Shrimp (page 132), Grilled Adobo-Marinated Skirt Steak (page 135), Adobo-Marinated Chicken (page 133), Tacos (pages 212–214), Quesadillas (page 225), Tortilla Chips (page 229), or Carnitas (page 240).

This salsa keeps in the refrigerator for up to one day. Before you serve it, drain any excess liquid that has accumulated in the bowl.

FRESH PEACH SALSA

SALSA FRESCA DE DURAZNO

When the weather gets warm in the town of Coatepec Harinas, my partner's mother uses the peaches from her ranch for this summery salsa. It can turn the most basic plate of grilled fish or pork into a thrilling meal, especially if you get the balance between sweetness and tartness right, dialing up the former with a little sugar or the latter with a little lime juice. If you can't find epazote, try adding a pinch of fresh oregano. And finally, if you're in the mood, do as Delia Gasca does and mix in a tablespoon of silver tequila just before you serve the salsa.

MAKES 2¼ CUPS   ACTIVE TIME: **30 MINUTES**   START TO FINISH: **30 MINUTES**

1 pound firm-ripe peaches (4 small or 2 large)

3 tablespoons finely chopped red onion

3 tablespoons freshly squeezed lime juice, or more to taste

2½ teaspoons sugar, or more to taste

1½ teaspoons minced fresh epazote (about 5 leaves)

1½ teaspoons minced fresh habanero chile, including seeds, or more to taste

½ teaspoon fine salt, or 1 teaspoon kosher salt

FILL a 2- to 3-quart pot halfway with water and bring the water to a boil over high heat. Cut a small "X" through the skin on the bottom (opposite the stem end) of each peach and add the peaches to the boiling water for 15 seconds to loosen their skins. Transfer the peaches to a bowl of icy cold water so they cool quickly, then peel and pit them, and dice the flesh.

STIR the peaches and the remaining ingredients together in a bowl. Season to taste with additional lime juice, sugar, chile, and salt

Serve it with Adobo-Marinated Fish (page 130), Adobo-Marinated Chicken (page 133), Carnitas (page 240), or Tortilla Chips (page 229).

This salsa is best eaten the day it's made.

Ingredients for
Fresh Peach Salsa

PAPAYA SALSA SALSA DE PAPAYA

I came up with this modern creation while I was in Merida, the capital of the Yucatán, where you see a ton of papaya, habanero, and the heat-free chile dulce (probably the great-grandfather of the bell pepper). So I combined all these elements—substituting bell pepper for the hard-to-find chile dulce—in a salsa that takes full advantage of papaya's musky sweetness. It's the perfect accent for grilled tuna or beef, raw oysters on the half shell, or a simple salad of avocado and shrimp. To get the right texture and flavor, use firm-ripe papayas—if the fruit's soft, eat it for breakfast instead—and make sure the salsa gets a spicy kick.

MAKES 2½ CUPS   **ACTIVE TIME: 25 MINUTES**   **START TO FINISH: 25 MINUTES**

1 pound firm-ripe papaya, peeled, seeded, and finely diced (2 cups)

¼ cup finely diced red bell pepper

¼ cup finely diced red onion

1 pencil-thin scallion (white and green parts), finely sliced (2 tablespoons)

1 tablespoon freshly squeezed lime juice, or more to taste

1 tablespoon freshly squeezed lemon juice

1 teaspoon minced fresh habanero chile, including seeds, or more to taste

¼ teaspoon fine salt, or ½ teaspoon kosher salt

MIX all the ingredients together in a bowl. Season to taste with additional lime juice, chile, and salt.

Serve it with Grilled Adobo-Marinated Skirt Steak (page 135) or Tortilla Chips (page 229).

This salsa keeps in the refrigerator for up to one day. Before you serve it, drain any excess liquid that has accumulated in the bowl.

CUCUMBER SALSA PICO DE PEPINO

Sometimes you want the crisp freshness of pico de gallo, but you just can't find worthy tomatoes. So I came up with this marvelous substitute that's so tasty I make it even during the height of tomato season.

MAKES 2 CUPS   ACTIVE TIME: **25 MINUTES**   START TO FINISH: 1½ **HOURS**

1 (10- to 12-ounce) cucumber, peeled, seeded, and diced (2 cups)

⅔ cup chopped cilantro

½ cup finely diced seeded fresh red pepper, such as Italian frying pepper, Hungarian pepper, or bell pepper

⅓ cup finely diced red onion

⅓ cup freshly squeezed orange juice

2½ tablespoons freshly squeezed lime juice, or more to taste

1 tablespoon mild olive oil

1½ teaspoons minced fresh habanero chile, including seeds

¾ teaspoon fine salt, or 1½ teaspoons kosher salt

½ teaspoon dried oregano, preferably Mexican, crumbled

Sugar, if necessary

MIX all the ingredients together and let the salsa sit for 1 hour. Season to taste with additional lime juice and salt, and add sugar if the orange juice isn't very sweet.

Serve it with Adobo-Marinated Fish (page 130), Adobo-Marinated Shrimp (page 132), Grilled Adobo-Marinated Skirt Steak (page 135), Adobo-Marinated Chicken (page 133), Tacos (pages 212–214), Quesadillas (page 225), Tortilla Chips (page 229), rice, beans, or any other side you like (pages 246–256).

This salsa keeps in the refrigerator for up to one day. Before you serve it, drain any excess liquid that has accumulated in the bowl.

COOKED SALSAS
The salsas in this section have at least one ingredient that's been toasted, roasted, boiled, or sautéed. Sometimes, all the ingredients—maybe habaneros, tomatoes, onions, and garlic—are cooked before they're mixed together. Occasionally, the entire salsa is cooked in oil. These salsas tend to feature silky, soupy textures and smooth flavors: By that I mean that through cooking, the ingredients have lost their jagged edges—that piercing acidity and prickly spiciness. Cooked salsas can be plenty tart and incredibly fiery, but these components are more unified among the rest of the flavors, which creates a more balanced flavor compared to the fresh and crazy raw salsas.

Cooked salsas also play a slightly different role from raw salsas. While you typically serve raw salsas to offer contrast, you often serve cooked salsas to urge the already existing flavors in a dish forward. For instance, in Mexico City, cooks often serve barbacoa with salsa borracha, which is made with toasted pasilla chiles and the funky fermented drink called *pulque,* because the dark, earthy flavors of the salsa match up with the dark, gamy flavors of the long-cooked lamb or goat.

ROASTED TOMATO SALSAS
Roasting tomatoes the Mexican way (without oil) intensifies their sweetness and acidity, leaving you with their unadulterated essence and a silky, meaty texture. Although you can roast them in a comal or skillet, I find that tomatoes turn out best (and cause the least mess) roasted on a foil-lined pan under the broiler in your oven or toaster oven.

SIMPLE ROASTED TOMATO SALSA
SALSA ROJA DE MOLCAJETE

Some of my friends get the impression that I spend all day every day cooking lavish meals. But like everyone else, I'm often so busy I can hardly find time to go through my mail. When I'm pressed for time but still want a Mexican meal, I'll pick up a roast chicken at the market or scramble some eggs, warm up some tortillas and maybe some leftover beans, and make salsa de molcajete. As soon as I get home from work, I'll stick the tomatoes and chiles in the toaster oven, and by the time I'm finished paying that last bill, they're ready to be turned into this dead-simple condiment, one of the most common in Mexico.

This salsa is best when the garlic, roasted chiles, and salt are pounded to a paste by hand in a molcajete, mortar, or even with a knife on a cutting board. But you can use a blender, if you follow these instructions: Put the garlic, roasted chiles, salt, and about one-third of the roasted tomatoes in the blender and puree until fairly smooth. Then add the remaining tomatoes and pulse a few times in order to keep the texture chunky.

MAKES **1 CUP**   ACTIVE TIME: **15 MINUTES**   START TO FINISH: **45 MINUTES**

1 pound tomatoes (about 3 medium)

2 fresh serrano or jalapeño chiles, stemmed, or more to taste

1 small garlic clove, peeled

½ teaspoon kosher salt, or ¼ teaspoon fine salt

SET the oven or toaster oven to broil and preheat. Alternatively, you can preheat the oven to 500°F. If you're using the oven broiler, position the rack 8 inches from the heat source. Core the tomatoes and cut a small "X" through the skin on the opposite ends. Cook the tomatoes, cored sides up, and the chiles on a foil-lined baking pan (it's not necessary to turn the tomatoes, but you should turn the chiles as they roast) until the chiles are tender, blistered all over, and blackened in spots, about 15 minutes. Remove them and continue to cook the tomatoes until their tops have blackened and the tomatoes are cooked to the core, 20 to 30 minutes total. Let them cool slightly.

SLIP the skins from the tomatoes, and remove the skins from the chiles (you might have to use a paring knife).

PUT the peeled chiles, garlic, and salt (the coarseness of kosher salt helps you make the paste) in a molcajete or other large mortar, and pound them to a paste. You can also mince and mash the ingredients together on a cutting board with a large knife, and then transfer the paste to a bowl.

ADD the tomatoes to the chile mixture and pound to a coarse puree. Season to taste with additional salt.

Serve it with Adobo-Marinated Chicken (page 133), Tacos (pages 212–214), Quesadillas (page 225), rice, beans, or any other side you like (pages 246–256).

This salsa keeps in the refrigerator for up to two days.

SIMPLE ROASTED TOMATO SALSA WITH ONION AND CILANTRO

SALSA ROJA CON CEBOLLA Y CILANTRO

A bit of crunchy onion, some cilantro, and a good squirt of lime juice turn the three-ingredient salsa de molcajete into an even livelier sauce that's great on quesadillas and tacos. If you're not afraid of tweaking tradition in the name of flavor, try this salsa with a drizzle of olive oil!

MAKES 1½ CUPS   ACTIVE TIME: **25 MINUTES**   START TO FINISH: **45 MINUTES**

1 recipe Simple Roasted Tomato Salsa (page 60)

¼ cup chopped cilantro

¼ cup finely chopped white onion

1 tablespoon freshly squeezed lime juice, or more to taste

Fine salt or kosher salt to taste

MIX together the salsa, cilantro, onion, and lime juice in a bowl. Season the mixture to taste with additional lime juice and salt.

Serve it with Adobo-Marinated Chicken (page 133), Tacos (pages 212–214), Quesadillas (page 225), Tortilla Chips (page 229), rice, beans, or any other side you like (page 246–256).

This salsa keeps in the refrigerator for up to one day.

ROASTED CHERRY TOMATO SALSA
SALSA DE TOMATITOS

Sometimes I find that the best tomatoes in the market are the itty-bitty ones piled in little containers. So instead of roasting the big boys, I'll let the sweet-tart flavor of the little guys concentrate in the oven and then toss them in a garlic-chile paste. Since I'm obsessive about skins, I make the effort to peel each tomato, so I can fully enjoy its silky texture, but feel free to skip that step.

MAKES 2 CUPS   ACTIVE TIME: **30 MINUTES**   START TO FINISH: **40 MINUTES**

1 pint (10 ounces) red cherry or grape tomatoes

1 pint (10 ounces) yellow cherry or pear tomatoes

2 fresh jalapeño or serrano chiles, stemmed, or more to taste

2 garlic cloves, peeled

1 teaspoon kosher salt, or ½ teaspoon fine salt

1 tablespoon freshly squeezed lime juice, or more to taste

SET the oven to broil and preheat. Alternatively, you can preheat the oven to 500°F. If you're using the oven broiler, position the rack 8 inches from the heat source. Put the tomatoes and jalapeños on a large foil-lined baking pan and roast, turning the jalapeños over once, until softened and blackened in spots, 10 to 15 minutes. Remove the tomatoes and chiles from the oven and let them cool slightly. Slip the skins from the tomatoes, and remove the skins from the chiles (you might have to use a paring knife).

POUND the garlic with the chiles and salt (the coarseness of kosher salt will help you make the paste) to a paste in a molcajete or other mortar. You can also mince and mash the ingredients together on a cutting board with a large knife, and then transfer the paste to a bowl.

ADD the peeled tomatoes to the molcajete or bowl with the paste and stir. Season to taste with lime juice and additional salt.

Serve it with Adobo-Marinated Chicken (page 133), Tacos (pages 212–214), Quesadillas (page 225), Tortilla Chips (page 229), rice, beans, or any other side you like (page 246–256).

This salsa keeps in the refrigerator for up to two days.

ROASTED TOMATO AND PINEAPPLE SALSA SALSA DE JITOMATE CON PIÑA

Unlike most of the salsas in this book, this modern one—that is, a creation at which my grandmother would have smiled and rolled her eyes—takes some time to make. But not only does it pay off in a big way, it's also a pleasure to prepare: peeking into the oven as the pineapple and tomatoes begin to brown, basking in the amazing aroma that fills your kitchen as a poblano blackens on the stovetop. Before you know it, you're ready to toss everything together in a big bowl and taste how the sweetness of the pineapple plays off the slight bitterness of the roasted poblano, how the punch of garlic and the spicy tingle of chiles de árbol make music in your mouth.

MAKES 4 CUPS   **ACTIVE TIME: 1¼ HOURS**   **START TO FINISH: 1¾ HOURS**

1 pound tomatoes (about 3 medium)

4 (½-inch-thick) round slices peeled fresh pineapple

½ tablespoon mild olive oil or vegetable oil

1 medium red onion, peeled whole and cut into ½-inch-thick round slices

5 garlic cloves, peeled

3 dried árbol chiles, wiped clean and stemmed

1 small (approximately 3-ounce) poblano chile

¼ teaspoon whole allspice berries

2 tablespoons chopped jalapeño chiles, including seeds

½ cup chopped cilantro

½ cup freshly squeezed orange juice

3 tablespoons freshly squeezed lime juice

2 tablespoons distilled white vinegar, or more to taste

2 tablespoons water

1½ teaspoons sugar, or more to taste

1½ teaspoons fine salt, or 1 tablespoon kosher salt

SET the oven to broil and preheat. Alternatively, you can preheat the oven to 500°F. If you're using the oven broiler, position the rack 8 inches from the heat source. Have ready a large bowl to hold the ingredients that you'll remove from the oven as they finish roasting.

CORE the tomatoes and cut a small "X" through the skin on the opposite ends. Brush both sides of the pineapple slices with the oil and arrange them on a foil-lined baking pan with the tomatoes, cored sides up. Cook, turning the pineapple slices once, until they're tender and well browned on both sides, 15 to 20 minutes, and the tomatoes' tops have blackened and the tomatoes are cooked to the core, 20 to 30 minutes total. Let the cooked ingredients cool to room temperature.

MEANWHILE, heat a comal, griddle, or heavy skillet over medium-low heat. Working in batches, if necessary, roast the onion slices, garlic, and árbol chiles, turning the garlic and chiles occasionally and carefully turning the onion rounds once, until the chiles are deep brown, 3 to 4 minutes; the garlic is just tender and golden brown with some blackened spots, 8 to 10 minutes; and the onion rounds are softened and charred on both sides, 15 to 25 minutes.

WHILE you cook the chiles, garlic, and onions, turn another burner to high and roast the poblano chile on the rack of the burner (or directly on the heating element of an electric stove), turning frequently with tongs, until it is blistered and charred all over, 4 to 6 minutes. Put the roasted poblano in a bowl and cover with a plate to steam, 15 to 20 minutes.

CORE the pineapple slices and chop them finely. Slip the skins from the tomatoes and chop the tomatoes coarsely. Finely chop the onions, and mince the garlic.

FINELY grind the toasted árbol chiles and the allspice in a clean coffee or spice grinder or the blender jar.

RUB off the skin from the poblano chile with a paper towel. Then cut the chile open lengthwise, cut out the seed pod, veins, and stem, and lay the chile flat. Wipe the chile clean of seeds with another paper towel and cut into ¼-inch dice.

MIX the roasted and ground ingredients in a large bowl. Stir in the jalapeño, cilantro, orange juice, lime juice, vinegar, water, sugar, and salt. Season to taste with additional vinegar, sugar, and salt.

Serve it with Adobo-Marinated Fish (page 130), Adobo-Marinated Shrimp (page 132), Grilled Adobo-Marinated Skirt Steak (page 135), Adobo-Marinated Chicken (page 133), Carnitas (page 240), Tacos (page 212–214), Quesadillas (page 225), or Tortilla Chips (page 229).

This salsa keeps in the refrigerator for up to one day.

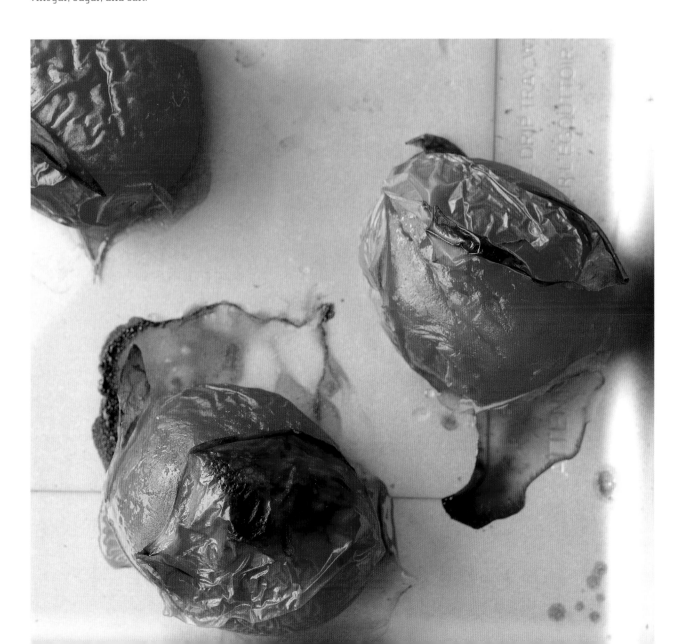

TOMATO AND MANGO COCKTAIL SALSA SALSA COCTEL DE JITOMATE Y MANGO

American cocktail sauce gets its zip from horseradish, but this Mexican version is all about a silky tomato base revved up by the heat of habaneros, the tang of lime juice, and tequila-marinated mango. Serve it as a dip for simply cooked shrimp, hot or cold, or for rounds of jicama and cucumber.

MAKES 2½ TO 3 CUPS   **ACTIVE TIME: 30 MINUTES**   **START TO FINISH: 1¼ HOURS**

1 (10-ounce) firm-ripe mango, peeled, pitted, and finely diced

3 tablespoons tequila, preferably reposado

1 teaspoon sugar, or more to taste

1 pound tomatoes (about 3 medium)

½ cup finely diced red onion

1 generous tablespoon freshly squeezed lime juice

1½ teaspoons minced fresh habanero chile, including seeds, or more to taste

1⅛ teaspoons fine salt, or 2¼ teaspoons coarse salt

2 tablespoons chopped cilantro

TOSS together the mango, tequila, and sugar in a bowl and let the mixture stand for 1 hour.

SET the oven or toaster oven to broil and preheat. Alternatively, you can preheat the oven to 500°F. If you're using the oven broiler, position the rack 8 inches from the heat source. Core the tomatoes and cut a small "X" through the skin on the opposite ends. Put the tomatoes, cored sides up, on a foil-lined baking pan, and roast until their tops have blackened and the tomatoes are cooked to the core, 20 to 30 minutes. Let them cool to room temperature.

SLIP the skins from the tomatoes. Coarsely chop the tomatoes or mush them with your fingers in a wide bowl. Stir the onion, lime juice, habanero, and salt together with the tomatoes. Stir in the mango mixture and cilantro just before serving. Season to taste with additional salt.

Serve it as a dip for simply cooked shrimp, hot or cold, or for rounds of jicama and cucumber.

This salsa keeps in the refrigerator for up to one day.

ROASTED TOMATILLO SALSAS When you roast tomatillos, the crisp, tart fruits transform into something silky and syrupy with a complex acidity. The gradual progression of recipes here—from simple to complex—shows you how once you get comfortable with just a few techniques, you can make a surprisingly wide variety of salsas. Soon you will even learn to create your own salsas, substituting roasted garlic for raw here and chiles de árbol for chiles chipotles there, depending on what you like and what you have on hand. Keep in mind that the fruit's acidity varies (dark green tomatillos are a bit more tart than lighter, paler ones) and you can always tweak the flavor of salsas made with roasted tomatillos with apple cider vinegar or even a little squirt of lime juice.

ROASTED TOMATILLO SALSA WITH TOASTED CHILE POWDER

SALSA DE TOMATILLO CON CHILE SECO EN POLVO

In my cupboard, next to the sugar, Mexican oregano, and other staples, you'll find an assortment of chile powders (see page 21), in unassuming little jars, that pack a huge punch of flavor. Freshly toasted chiles ground up will become serious weapons in your culinary arsenal and make the chile powders sold in supermarkets taste like cake flour by comparison. When I roast tomatillos, out comes one of these powders and, with a little garlic and salt, I have a wildly good salsa. I love using powder made from toasted chiles de árbol, which adds dramatic heat and a lovely nuttiness, but I've given you the option of using smoky chipotles moras or fiery, lightly acidic chiles cascabeles.

MAKES ½ CUP   ACTIVE TIME: **10 MINUTES**   START TO FINISH: **40 MINUTES**

½ pound tomatillos (5 or 6), husked and rinsed

1 garlic clove, peeled

2 teaspoons Árbol Chile Powder or Chipotle Mora Powder, or 4 teaspoons Chile Cascabel powder (page 21), or more to taste

¾ teaspoon kosher salt, or a rounded ¼ teaspoon fine salt

SET the oven or toaster oven to broil and preheat (alternatively, you can preheat the oven to 500°F), or heat a comal, griddle, or heavy skillet over medium-low heat. If you're using the oven broiler, position the rack 8 inches from the heat source.

PUT the tomatillos on a foil-lined baking pan or comal and roast, turning them over once halfway through, until their tops and bottoms have blackened and the tomatillos are a khaki-green color and cooked to the core, 20 to 30 minutes. Let them cool to room temperature.

PUT the garlic, chile powder, and salt (the coarseness of kosher salt helps you make the paste) in a molcajete or other mortar and pound to a paste. You can also mince and mash the ingredients together on a cutting board with a large knife, and then transfer the paste to a bowl. Add the roasted tomatillos to the chile mixture and pound to a coarse puree. Season to taste with additional chile powder and salt.

Serve it with Grilled Adobo-Marinated Skirt Steak (page 135), Adobo-Marinated Chicken (page 133), Tacos (pages 212–214), Quesadillas (page 225), Tortilla Chips (page 229), rice, beans, or any other side you like (pages 246–256).

This salsa keeps in the refrigerator for up to five days.

Roasted Tomatillo Salsa with Toasted Chile Powder (page 67) with two tomatillos left to be pounded.

ROASTED TOMATILLO SALSA WITH CHILES CASCABEL

SALSA DE TOMATILLO ASADO CON CHILES CASCABEL

I adore the taste of chiles cascabeles, the little spherical chiles that, when they're dried, you can hold by the stem, shake, and listen to their seeds rattle around. They contribute an acidity, similar to that of tart dried fruit, to the salsa that you won't soon forget. After you've made this a few times, try swapping six cloves of roasted garlic for the one raw clove for a delicious variation.

MAKES ABOUT 1 CUP   **ACTIVE TIME: 15 MINUTES**   **START TO FINISH: 35 MINUTES**

½ pound tomatillos (5 or 6), husked and rinsed

4 cascabel chiles, wiped clean and stemmed

½ cup water

1 garlic clove, peeled

½ teaspoon apple cider vinegar, or more to taste

Rounded ¼ teaspoon fine salt, or
¾ teaspoon kosher salt

———————————————

SET the oven or toaster oven to broil and preheat. Alternatively, you can preheat the oven to 500°F. If you're using the oven broiler, position the rack 8 inches from the heat source.

PUT the tomatillos on a foil-lined baking pan and roast, turning them over once halfway through, until their tops and bottoms have blackened and the tomatillos are a khaki-green color and cooked to the core, 20 to 30 minutes. Let them cool slightly.

MEANWHILE, break each cascabel chile into about 3 pieces for easier toasting, and shake out and reserve the seeds. Heat a small heavy skillet over medium-low heat, and toast the chile pieces, turning them over and pressing them down frequently with tongs until they turn a lighter, slightly mottled red color, about 1 minute. Remove the chile pieces. Put the chile seeds in the skillet and toast, shaking and tossing, until lightly browned and fragrant, 20 to 30 seconds.

PUT the roasted tomatillos, chiles, and seeds in the blender jar with the water, garlic, vinegar, and salt and blend until smooth (some tomatillo seeds will still be visible). Season to taste with additional salt and vinegar.

Serve it with Grilled Adobo-Marinated Skirt Steak (page 135), Adobo-Marinated Chicken (page 133), Tacos (pages 212–214), Quesadillas (page 225), Tortilla Chips (page 229), rice, beans, or any other side you like (pages 246–256).

This salsa keeps in the refrigerator for up to five days.

ROASTED TOMATILLO SALSA WITH CHIPOTLE AND ROASTED GARLIC

SALSA DE TOMATILLO ASADO CON CHIPOTLE

That simple blueprint—tomatillos, chiles, garlic—that you follow to make the previous salsa will lead you to another super salsa. The difference? You roast the garlic. That seemingly minor change takes barely any extra effort—after all, you're already roasting and toasting the other ingredients—but adds so much complexity and a haunting sweetness that plays off those tangy tomatillos. As for chiles, I love using smoky chipotles, but chiles de árbol add nuttiness and serious heat, while pasillas de Oaxaca, if you can get your hands on them, one-up chipotles with smokiness and a touch of fruitiness. The choice is yours.

MAKES 1¼ CUPS   **ACTIVE TIME: 25 MINUTES**   **START TO FINISH: 40 MINUTES**

½ pound tomatillos (5 or 6), husked and rinsed

3 chipotle mora chiles (purplish-red color), wiped clean and stemmed

6 garlic cloves, peeled

½ cup water

Rounded ¼ teaspoon fine salt, or ½ teaspoon kosher salt

SET the oven or toaster oven to broil (alternatively, you can preheat the oven to 500°F) and preheat. If you're using the oven broiler, position the rack 8 inches from the heat source.

PUT the tomatillos on a foil-lined baking pan and roast in the oven, turning them over once halfway through, until their tops and bottoms have blackened and the tomatillos are a khaki-green color and cooked to the core, 20 to 30 minutes. Let them cool to room temperature.

MEANWHILE, heat a comal, griddle, or heavy skillet over medium-low heat and toast the chiles and roast the garlic on the comal, turning them over frequently until the chiles have puffed up and are blistered in spots, 3 to 5 minutes, and the garlic is tender and golden brown with some blackened spots, 8 to 10 minutes.

PUT the roasted tomatillos, chiles, and garlic in the blender jar with the water and salt and blend until smooth (the tomatillo seeds will still be visible). Season to taste with additional salt.

Serve it with Grilled Adobo-Marinated Skirt Steak (page 135), Adobo-Marinated Chicken (page 133), Tacos (pages 212–214), Tortilla Chips (page 229), rice, beans, or any other side you like (pages 246–256).

This salsa keeps in the refrigerator for up to five days.

TRY MAKING THIS SALSA WITH OTHER CHILES:

Substitute 6 dried árbol chiles or 2 pasillas de Oaxaca for the chipotle mora chiles. See Basics (pages 18–19) for specific toasting instructions for these chiles.

ROASTED TOMATILLO SALSA WITH CHIPOTLE AND ÁRBOL CHILES

SALSA DE TOMATILLO ASADO CON CHIPOTLE MORA Y CHILE DE ÁRBOL

Now we're cooking. Building on the basic blueprint, this salsa adds yet more layers of complexity, using two types of chiles, roasted garlic, and even a few spices. It's the salsa to show off with when connoisseurs of Mexican cuisine come over, but it's easy enough for a weeknight dinner.

MAKES 1¼ CUPS   **ACTIVE TIME: 25 MINUTES**   **START TO FINISH: 40 MINUTES**

½ pound tomatillos (5 or 6), husked and rinsed

8 dried árbol chiles, wiped clean and stemmed

2 chipotle mora chiles (purplish-red color), wiped clean and stemmed

1 garlic head (about 12 cloves), cloves separated and peeled

10 whole allspice berries

1 large whole clove

½ teaspoon fine salt, or 1 teaspoon kosher salt

———————————————

SET the oven or toaster oven to broil (alternatively, you can preheat the oven to 500°F) and preheat. If you're using the oven broiler, position the rack 8 inches from the heat source.

PUT the tomatillos on a foil-lined baking pan and roast, turning them over once halfway through, until their tops and bottoms have blackened and the tomatillos are a khaki-green color and cooked to the core, 20 to 30 minutes. Let them cool to room temperature.

Meanwhile, heat a comal, griddle, or heavy skillet over medium-low heat and toast the chiles and roast the garlic on the comal, pressing down on the árbol chiles until they are brown all over and blackened in spots and chipotle mora chiles have puffed up and are blistered in spots, 3 to 5 minutes. Continue roasting the garlic, turning it over frequently, until it is tender and golden brown with some blackened spots, 8 to 10 minutes.

PUT the roasted tomatillos, chiles, and garlic in the blender jar with the allspice, clove, and salt and blend until smooth (the tomatillo seeds will still be visible). Season to taste with additional salt.

Serve it with Grilled Adobo-Marinated Skirt Steak (page 135), Adobo-Marinated Chicken (page 133), Tacos (pages 212–214), Tortilla Chips (page 229), rice, beans, or any other side you like (pages 246–256).

This salsa keeps in the refrigerator for up to five days.

ROASTED TOMATILLO SALSA WITH JALAPEÑO AND CHIPOTLE

SALSA DE TOMATILLO ASADO CON JALAPEÑO Y CHIPOTLE

One of the more elaborate salsas you'll find, it's not nearly as complicated as it seems at first. As usual, the main ingredients roast, getting all charred and intense, and then you mix them all together. The combination of tomatillos and tomatoes provides a fantastic interplay of sweet and tart, and the two types of chiles, one fresh and one dried, give you a mouthful of both sharp heat and smoky spice.

MAKES **ABOUT 1½ CUPS**   ACTIVE TIME: **50 MINUTES**   START TO FINISH: **50 MINUTES**

½ pound tomatoes (about 2 medium)

½ pound tomatillos (5 or 6), husked and rinsed

1 large fresh jalapeño chile, stemmed

2 (½-inch-thick) round slices white onion

1 garlic head (about 12 cloves),
cloves separated and peeled

¼ cup water

2 tablespoons canned chipotles in
adobo, including sauce

1½ teaspoons white distilled vinegar, or more to taste

¾ teaspoon fine salt, or 1½ teaspoons kosher salt

⅛ teaspoon cumin seeds

2 tablespoons chopped cilantro

SET the oven to broil and preheat. Alternatively, you can preheat the oven to 500°F. If you're using the oven broiler, position the rack 8 inches from the heat source. Have ready a large bowl to hold the ingredients that you'll remove from the oven as they finish roasting.

CORE the tomatoes and cut a small "X" through the skin on the opposite ends. Arrange the tomatoes, cored sides up, tomatillos, and jalapeño on a foil-lined shallow baking pan and roast, turning the jalapeño once or twice, until it's tender, blistered all over, and blackened in spots, 10 to 15 minutes; turning the tomatillos over once halfway through, until their tops and bottoms have blackened and the tomatillos are khaki green and cooked to the core, 20 to 30 minutes; and without turning the tomatoes, until they are blackened and cooked to the core, 20 to 30 minutes. Let the cooked ingredients cool to room temperature.

MEANWHILE, heat a comal, griddle, or heavy skillet over medium-low heat, and roast the onions and garlic, turning the garlic over frequently, until it's just tender and golden brown with some blackened spots, 8 to 10 minutes, and carefully turning the onion rounds once, until they're softened and charred on both sides, 15 to 25 minutes.

REMOVE the skin from the jalapeño (you might have to use a paring knife) and discard. Add the chile to the blender jar with the roasted garlic, water, chipotles in adobo, vinegar, salt, and cumin, and blend until smooth. Add the tomatillos and pulse several times until you have a coarse puree, then transfer to a large bowl.

SLIP the skins from the tomatoes. Coarsely chop the tomatoes and finely chop the onions and stir them into the salsa along with the cilantro. Season to taste with additional vinegar and salt, and add a little more water if the salsa is too thick.

Serve it with Grilled Adobo-Marinated Skirt Steak (page 135), Adobo-Marinated Chicken (page 133), Tacos (pages 212–214), Tortilla Chips (page 229), rice, beans, or any other side you like (pages 246–256).

This salsa keeps in the refrigerator for up to five days.

SPICY COOKED TOMATILLO TABLE SALSA SALSA VERDE PICANTE

My delicious Cooked Green Salsa (page 99) is perfect for enchiladas and huevos rancheros, but it becomes a taco-worthy condiment once you rev up the spice level with a few roasted jalapeños or serranos and add a little chopped onion for crunch. It's one of the salsas on offer at just about every taqueria, and you'll understand why when you try it on tacos filled with cactus, carnitas, or grilled beef.

If you use a molcajete for this recipe and it isn't big enough to hold all the sauce, add some of the cooked green salsa to the chile paste, stir well, and transfer the mixture to a large bowl. Then add the remaining green salsa and stir well.

MAKES 1½ CUPS   **ACTIVE TIME: 10 MINUTES**   **START TO FINISH: 25 MINUTES (PLUS MAKING COOKED GREEN SALSA)**

2 fresh jalapeño or serrano chiles, stemmed

¼ teaspoon kosher salt, or ⅛ teaspoon fine salt

1 cup Cooked Green Salsa (page 99)

¼ cup chopped cilantro

¼ cup finely chopped white onion

Lime juice, if necessary

───────────────

HEAT a comal, griddle, or heavy skillet over medium-low heat, and roast the chiles, turning often, until tender, blistered all over, and blackened in spots, 10 to 15 minutes. Remove the skins from the chiles (you might have to use a paring knife).

POUND the chiles with the salt (the coarseness of kosher salt helps you make the paste) in a molcajete or other mortar (or mince and mash to a paste with a knife on a cutting board and transfer to a bowl). Add some of the cooked green salsa and mash together with a pestle, then stir in the remaining green salsa as well as the cilantro and onion. Season to taste with additional salt and lime juice, if necessary. You can serve it right away, but I like it best after it sits for an hour, so the flavors have time to blend.

Serve it with Grilled Adobo-Marinated Skirt Steak (page 135), Adobo-Marinated Chicken (page 133), Tacos (pages 212–214), Quesadillas (page 225), Tortilla Chips (page 229), rice, beans, or any other side you like (pages 246–256).

This salsa keeps in the refrigerator for up to one day.

COOKED SALSAS MADE WITHOUT TOMATOES OR TOMATILLOS When roasted chiles, fruits, or vegetables star in salsa, you get truly thrilling flavors—many of them like nothing you've tasted before. These are the salsas that you rarely spot in the United States, and that will make a splash at dinner whether your guests are new to Mexican food or visiting from Oaxaca.

FRIED SERRANO CHILE SALSA
SALSA DE CHILE FRITO

This recipe from a family friend in Oaxaca demonstrates the strong Spanish influence on a lot of Mexican food. The grassy flavor and heat from the serrano chiles is very Mexican, but the chiles are fried (a technique the Spanish brought to the New World) and the mayonnaise-like emulsion you end up with is similar to what the Spanish call alioli (and the French call aïoli). Originally pounded painstakingly in a mortar and pestle, this smooth, almost creamy chile sauce is turned out wonderfully by the blender.

MAKES ¾ CUP ACTIVE TIME: 10 MINUTES START TO FINISH: 20 MINUTES

¼ cup mild olive oil

5 fresh serrano chiles, stemmed

½ cup coarsely chopped white onion

¼ cup water

1 garlic clove, peeled

¼ teaspoon fine salt, or ½ teaspoon kosher salt

HEAT the oil in a small saucepan over medium heat, then add the chiles and fry them, turning them with tongs until they're blistered all over, about 2 minutes. Using tongs, transfer the chiles to the blender jar.

ADD the onion to the oil in the same saucepan and cook, stirring, until it's slightly softened and golden on the edges, about 3 minutes. Transfer the onion to the blender jar with a slotted spoon and let the oil cool for at least 10 minutes.

ADD the cooled oil to the blender jar along with the water, garlic, and salt and blend until the sauce is very smooth. Season to taste with additional salt.

Serve it with Corn Tortillas (page 39), Adobo-Marinated Fish (page 130), Adobo-Marinated Shrimp (page 132), Grilled Adobo-Marinated Skirt Steak (page 135), Adobo-Marinated Chicken (page 133), Tacos (pages 212–214), rice, beans, or any other side you like (pages 246–256).

This salsa keeps in the refrigerator for up to two days.

JALISCO-STYLE GUAJILLO SALSA

SALSA DE GUAJILLO ESTILO JALISCO

In Jalisco, a state in north-central Mexico, cooks rub goat or lamb with a guajillo chile mixture and cook the meat slowly until it's meltingly tender. It's called *birria*—no one makes it quite like my friend Alejandro Garcia—and it's a local riff on the more ubiquitous slow-cooked dish called Barbacao (page 146). It's typically served with this stunning salsa, an earthy, tangy blend of dried guajillo and chiles de árbol, that tastes great on just about any preparation of lamb or beef, like grilled chops or skirt steak. Anyone unfamiliar with this salsa should make it right away (because it's so delicious!) and should pay particular attention to getting the flavor hierarchy right: The strongest flavors should come from the earthy, barely sweet guajillos and the nutty, spicy chiles de árbol. Next you'll taste a smack of garlic, and finally the spices—cumin and even a whisper of ginger. And yes, you read the recipe right: You don't have to toast the chiles!

MAKES 1¾ TO 2 CUPS   **ACTIVE TIME: 15 MINUTES**   **START TO FINISH: 30 MINUTES**

1½ ounces guajillo chiles (about 6), wiped clean, stemmed, slit open, seeded, and deveined

½ ounce dried árbol chiles (15 to 20), wiped clean and stemmed

2 large garlic cloves, peeled

1 (1 × ½-inch) piece fresh ginger, peeled and sliced

¾ cup water for blending, or more if necessary

1 teaspoon apple cider vinegar, or more to taste

½ teaspoon fine salt, or 1 teaspoon kosher salt

¼ teaspoon ground cumin

PUT the chiles in a medium pot with enough water to cover them and bring the water to a simmer. Cook until they are soft and a brighter red color, about 15 minutes. Add the garlic and ginger to the chiles and simmer for 1 minute.

DRAIN the chiles, garlic, and ginger and add them to the blender jar along with the ¾ cup of fresh water, vinegar, salt, and cumin. Blend until smooth, gradually adding water (no more than ¼ cup) if necessary to puree, at least 2 minutes. Strain the salsa through a medium-mesh sieve for a silky smooth sauce. Season to taste with additional vinegar and salt.

Serve it with Grilled Adobo-Marinated Skirt Steak (page 135), Adobo-Marinated Chicken (page 133), Adobo Braised Lamb (page 146), Tacos (pages 212–214), Tortilla Chips (page 229), rice, beans, or any other side you like (pages 246–256).

This salsa keeps in the refrigerator for up to five days or in the freezer for up to one month.

The blender turns a few ingredients into the fantastic, smooth Jalisco-style Guajillo Salsa.

GINGER: THE SECRET WEAPON

If you take a look at the ingredient list for the Jalisco-Style Guajillo Salsa (page 77), you might be surprised to see an ingredient more commonly associated with Asian cuisine: ginger. I have seen a lot of ginger in my many trips to the markets of Mexico. When you ask what it's used for, people like to be coy and tell you that they use it for tea or for medicinal purposes. But the truth is that cooks often add it to their food. When the Spanish arrived in Mexico in the sixteenth century, they had just ended eight centuries of Arabic domination, so the Spanish food that originally pervaded Mexico was closer to the Moorish-influenced cuisine than the more Mediterranean cuisine of modern Spain. That means in the 1700s, the food of the upper classes in Mexico was full of seasonings like ginger, mace, cumin, cinnamon, and cloves. When indigenous peoples got a taste of this food, they must have been horrified, but gradually, the spices made their way into everyday food. Today, so many dishes—from salsas to adobos to moles—include these spices, not as major flavors, but as a quarter teaspoon here and a half teaspoon there. The result is a delicious background flavor that was once foreign but now is thoroughly Mexican.

ROASTED PINEAPPLE SALSA
SALSA DE PIÑA ASADA CON HABANERO

Pineapple's bright sweet-tart flavor becomes sweeter and more complex as the sugars caramelize on the grill or under the broiler. Like most fruit salsas, a high heat level—thank you, habaneros—keeps all that beautiful sweetness in check. This salsa brings to mind *tacos al pastor*—the amazing taqueria specialty of pork roasting on a vertical spit with a piece of pineapple on top, dripping its juices onto the charred meat—so I often serve it with roast pork or Carnitas (page 240), but it also goes great with grilled fish or shrimp. I thank my dear friend, the wonderful chef-instructor at the Culinary Institute of America, Sergio Remolina for inspiring this recipe. Cheers, Sergio!

MAKES 2½ CUPS   **ACTIVE TIME: 35 MINUTES**   **START TO FINISH: 35 MINUTES**

4 (½-inch-thick) round slices fresh pineapple (½ pineapple)

¼ cup mild olive oil or vegetable oil

1 medium red onion, finely chopped (1 cup)

½ cup chopped cilantro

¼ cup freshly squeezed lime juice, or more to taste

2 fresh habanero chiles, minced, including seeds

½ teaspoon fine salt, or 1 teaspoon kosher salt

———————————————

SET the oven to broil (alternatively, you can preheat the oven to 500°F) and preheat, or heat a lightly oiled grill pan over medium heat. If you're using the oven broiler, position the rack 8 inches from the heat source.

BRUSH the pineapple slices with some of the oil and roast or grill them until they're browned on both sides and tender, 5 to 6 minutes a side on the grill pan, or 8 minutes a side under the broiler. Let them cool to room temperature.

DICE the pineapple (about ⅛ inch), discarding the core, and mix it in a bowl with the remaining ingredients. Season to taste with additional lime juice and salt.

Serve it with Adobo-Marinated Fish (page 130), Adobo-Marinated Shrimp (page 132), Grilled Adobo-Marinated Skirt Steak (page 135), Adobo-Marinated Chicken (page 133), Tacos (pages 212–214), Tortilla Chips (page 229), rice, beans, or any other side you like (pages 246–256).

This salsa keeps in the refrigerator for up to one day.

HABANERO-ORANGE SALSA
SALSA DE HABANERO CON NARANJA

This creation of mine was inspired by *xnipec,* the classic type of salsa found in the Yucatán. In the Mayan language, the name means "dog's nose," because those who eat these fiery, habanero-based condiments find themselves with a runny one, wet like that of man's best friend. Heat is the key, so resist the temptation to discard the chile seeds. Keep in mind that since you want to let the salsa sit for about an hour before serving to allow the flavors to develop, the heat level will have mellowed a bit by the time you eat the salsa. In the finished salsa, the roasted ingredients should be floating freely in lime and orange juice, a combination that approximates the sour orange common in the Yucatán.

MAKES 1½ CUPS   ACTIVE TIME: 15 MINUTES   START TO FINISH: 1½ HOURS

1 small red onion, cut into ½-inch-thick round slices

8 pencil-thin scallions, trimmed to 6 or 7 inches

1 fresh habanero chile, stemmed

1 cup freshly squeezed orange juice

2 tablespoons freshly squeezed lime juice, or more to taste

3 tablespoons chopped cilantro

½ teaspoon fine salt, or 1 teaspoon kosher salt

HEAT a comal, griddle, or heavy skillet over medium-low heat. Roast the onion slices, scallions, and habanero chile on the comal, turning the onion slices over once and turning the scallions and habanero occasionally, until the habanero is browned in spots and soft, 8 to 12 minutes; the scallions are tender and browned with some black patches but the greens are still moist, 10 to 12 minutes; and the onions are tender and charred on both sides, 15 to 25 minutes.

WHEN the roasted vegetables and chiles are cool enough to handle, mince them and add them to a bowl with the orange and lime juices, cilantro, and salt.

LET the salsa stand for an hour so the flavors can develop. Season to taste with additional lime juice and salt.

Serve it with Adobo-Marinated Fish (page 130), Adobo-Marinated Shrimp (page 132), Adobo-Marinated Chicken (page 133), Tacos (pages 212–214), rice, beans, or any other side you like (pages 246–256).

This salsa will keep in the refrigerator for one day.

DRUNKEN SALSA SALSA BORRACHA

Whenever I'm ogling a steaming heap of barbacoa, anxiously anticipating my first bite of the impossibly tender slow-cooked goat or lamb, I'm equally excited to try the salsa borracha that often comes alongside. Traditionally, this slightly funky and intensely delicious pasilla-based salsa, common throughout Mexico's central high plains, is made with *pulque,* the fermented sap of the maguey plant. To mimic its light sweetness and fermented flavor, I substitute beer and a little sugar. Of course, there's no need to wait to make this salsa until you have barbacoa around—it goes great with duck, beef, and just about any preparation of lamb.

MAKES 1¼ CUPS   **ACTIVE TIME: 35 MINUTES**   **START TO FINISH: 1 HOUR**

1⅔ ounces pasilla chiles (5), wiped clean, stemmed, slit open, seeded, and deveined

¼ cup water for blending, or more if necessary

½ cup dark Mexican beer

2 garlic cloves, peeled

2 teaspoons apple cider vinegar, or more to taste

1 teaspoon fine salt, or 2 teaspoons kosher salt

½ teaspoon sugar

⅛ teaspoon ground cumin

¼ cup chopped cilantro

¼ cup finely chopped white onion

HEAT a comal, griddle, or heavy skillet over medium-low heat, and toast the chiles, 2 or 3 at a time, turning them over and pressing them with tongs frequently, until they're slightly blistered and the insides are tobacco colored, 1 to 1½ minutes total per batch.

PLACE the chiles in a bowl and add enough cold water to cover them. Soak the chiles until they're softened, about 30 minutes. Drain and discard the soaking water.

PUT the ¼ cup of fresh water in the blender jar with the chiles and the rest of the ingredients, except for the cilantro and onion, and puree until the salsa is fairly smooth but still has some texture.

POUR the salsa into a serving bowl and season to taste with additional salt and vinegar. Stir the cilantro and onion into the salsa.

Serve it with Carnitas (page 240), Grilled Adobo-Marinated Skirt Steak (page 135), Adobo-Braised Lamb (page 146), Tacos (pages 212–214), Tortilla Chips (page 229), rice, beans, or any other side you like (pages 246–256).

This salsa keeps in the refrigerator for up to three days.

BURNT CHIPOTLE CHILE SALSA

SALSA DE CHILE CHIPOTLE QUEMADO Y MIEL DE MAGUEY

When I explained how to toast chiles in the Basics chapter, I told you to be careful *not* to burn them. But for this unforgettable sweet and tangy salsa, from the highlands of Veracruz (and the kitchen of my friend Sergio Remolina), I want you to toast chipotles mecos to the brink of burnt, until they're brittle and blistered with black patches (see page 16). Blended with sautéed onion, agave syrup, and apple cider vinegar, they create a thick salsa like no other—just four main ingredients that add up to a wildly complex flavor where tartness tugs at sweetness, and where gentle bitterness, warm spiciness, and bold smokiness keep every bite exciting. The stunning dark color demonstrates why it's also called salsa negra.

MAKES 1 CUP   **ACTIVE TIME: 30 MINUTES**   **START TO FINISH: 1¼ HOURS**

3 tablespoons mild olive oil or vegetable oil

1 medium white onion, finely chopped (1¼ cups)

1¼ ounces chipotle meco chiles (5, tobacco-color), wiped clean and stemmed

¾ cup water

¼ cup agave syrup, or more to taste

¼ cup apple cider vinegar, or more to taste

1 garlic clove, peeled

1 teaspoon fine salt, or 2 teaspoons kosher salt

HEAT 2 tablespoons of the oil in a medium skillet over medium heat and cook the onion, stirring occasionally, until golden and lightly caramelized, 10 to 15 minutes.

MEANWHILE, heat a comal, griddle, or heavy skillet over medium-low heat, and toast the chiles, turning them over frequently, until puffed, deep brown (with some black blisters) all over and brittle again (they become softer at first), 8 to 10 minutes. Remove them from the heat and let them cool slightly.

CRUMBLE the chiles into the blender jar, then add the onion, water, agave syrup, vinegar, garlic, and salt and blend until smooth, at least 2 minutes.

HEAT the remaining tablespoon of oil in the skillet over medium heat until it shimmers, then carefully add the sauce (you can swish a little water around in the blender jar to get the remaining sauce out). Simmer, stirring occasionally, until the sauce thickens slightly and its color changes from brownish to purplish, 10 to 15 minutes (use a splatter screen so the sauce doesn't make a mess of the stove). Turn the heat to low, and cook for another 25 minutes or until it's so thick that when you tip the skillet it barely moves. Let the salsa cool to room temperature before you serve it, and season to taste with additional salt, agave syrup, and vinegar.

Serve it with Grilled Adobo-Marinated Skirt Steak (page 135), Tacos (pages 212–214), Tortilla Chips (page 229), rice, beans, or any other side you like (pages 246–256).

This salsa keeps in the refrigerator for up to five days or in the freezer for up to one month.

The thick texture and dark color of Burnt Chipotle Salsa

CHIPOTLE AND ROASTED GARLIC SALSA

SALSA DE CHIPOTLE CON AJO ASADO

Sometimes I think Mexican cooks are magicians. Because here's yet another salsa with just three main ingredients that tastes so complex you'd think that it involves a whole cupboard's worth of stuff. Brick red with a silky, creamy (but cream-free) texture, it wallops you with smoky, garlicky, tongue-scalding spice. I add it to almost anything from turkey sandwiches to soups to beans.

MAKES ½ CUP   **ACTIVE TIME: 25 MINUTES**   **START TO FINISH: 25 MINUTES**

⅓ ounce chipotle mora chiles (3, purplish-red color), wiped clean and stemmed

6 garlic cloves, peeled

½ cup water

1 teaspoon apple cider vinegar, or more to taste

½ teaspoon fine salt, or 1 teaspoon kosher salt

HEAT a comal, griddle, or heavy skillet over medium-low heat, and toast the chiles and garlic, turning them over frequently, until the chiles have puffed up and are blistered in spots, 3 to 5 minutes, and the garlic is just tender and golden brown with some blackened spots, 8 to 10 minutes. Put the chiles and garlic in the blender jar with the remaining ingredients and puree until smooth, at least 2 minutes. Season to taste with additional vinegar and salt.

Serve it with Grilled Adobo-Marinated Skirt Steak (page 135), Adobo-Marinated Chicken (page 133), Tacos (pages 212–214), Tortilla Chips (page 229), rice, beans, or any other side you like (pages 246–256).

This salsa keeps in the refrigerator for up to five days or in the freezer for up to one month.

BEET SALSA WITH HABANERO
SALSA DE BETABEL CON HABANERO

Although I created this fun, modern salsa for a friend looking to give gravlax a Mexican twist, I found that this chunky beet relish—sweet, spicy, and tart all at once—makes an amazing addition to grilled beef or any salad containing goat cheese or feta. In fact, add a little cheese and it can become a salad itself!

MAKES 3 CUPS   **ACTIVE TIME: 30 MINUTES**   **START TO FINISH: 2¾ HOURS**

3 medium beets, rinsed and stems removed

2 pencil-thin scallions (white and green parts), thinly sliced

⅓ cup freshly squeezed orange juice

¼ cup chopped cilantro

¼ cup finely diced yellow bell pepper

¼ cup freshly squeezed lime juice, or more to taste

2 tablespoons olive oil

1 fresh habanero chile, minced, including seeds

½ teaspoon fine salt, or 1 teaspoon kosher salt

PREHEAT the oven to 450°F and tightly wrap the beets in foil.

BAKE the beets until they are tender, about 1¼ hours. Let them stand wrapped in foil for 15 minutes to help loosen the skins, then open the foil and peel the beets when they're cool enough to handle. Finely dice the beets; you will have 1½ to 2 cups.

MIX the beets in a bowl with the remaining ingredients and let the salsa stand at room temperature for 20 minutes before you serve it. Season to taste with additional lime juice and salt.

Serve it with Tortilla Chips (page 229) or Grilled Adobo-Marinated Skirt Steak (page 135).

This salsa keeps in the refrigerator for up to one day.

PEANUT AND ÁRBOL CHILE SALSA

SALSA DE CACAHUATE Y CHILE DE ÁRBOL

Many of my American friends are surprised and a bit put off to hear that Mexicans use peanuts in salsas, but it's actually quite common—after all, we even make peanut drinks! I think what comes to mind, and what might sound unpleasant, is peanut butter on a taco, so let me assure you that this salsa is nothing like Jif. Instead, blended peanuts are the creamy canvas for this pourable sauce and its flavor comes from the nutty, prickly heat of chiles de árbol and sautéed onions and garlic. One taste and you'll find yourself spooning it over roast chicken and grilled steak, serving it as a dip for shrimp, and yes, even adding it to your tacos.

MAKES 1 CUP   ACTIVE TIME: **15 MINUTES**   START TO FINISH: **15 MINUTES**

2 tablespoons mild olive oil

½ cup finely chopped white onion

¼ cup roasted unsalted peanuts

6 dried árbol chiles, wiped clean and stemmed

8 whole black peppercorns

6 whole allspice berries

4 garlic cloves, peeled and finely chopped

⅛ teaspoon dried thyme leaves

½ cup water

1 teaspoon apple cider vinegar

½ teaspoon fine salt, or 1 teaspoon kosher salt

HEAT the oil in a small (7- to 8-inch) heavy skillet over medium-low heat, then add the onion, peanuts, árbol chiles, peppercorns, allspice, garlic, and thyme and fry, stirring constantly, until the onion is translucent, about 2 minutes.

POUR all the ingredients from the skillet into the blender jar, then add the water, vinegar, and salt, and blend until very smooth, adding more water 1 tablespoon at a time, if necessary, to obtain a silky puree. You will need to blend for at least 2 minutes. Be careful when you're blending hot ingredients: Cover the top with a kitchen towel, and hold the top firmly in place with your hand. Let the salsa cool to room temperature before you serve it. Season to taste with additional salt.

Serve it with Grilled Adobo-Marinated Skirt Steak (page 135), Adobo-Marinated Chicken (page 133), Tacos (page 212–214), Tortilla Chips (page 229), rice, beans, or any other side you like (pages 246–256).

This salsa keeps in the refrigerator for up to five days or in the freezer for up to one month.

The peanuts, chiles, onions, and spices after frying and before blending

D.F.-STYLE ROASTED SERRANO SALSA

SALSA DE SERRANO CON CEBOLLA ESTILO D.F.

You might not associate Maggi and Worcestershire sauce with Mexican cooking, but these intense liquids have become staples of the Mexican pantry. Taqueria-goers often add a few drops of yeasty Maggi to their tacos (on top of salsa!), and my grandmother used to make a sauce for sautéed fish by deglazing the pan with Worcestershire, lime juice, and butter. Despite the obvious affection for these ingredients, particularly in Mexico City (aka D.F.), traditionalists still bang their heads over salsas like this one. I wonder if they still would after they taste it on tacos or simple quesadillas.

MAKES ½ CUP   **ACTIVE TIME: 15 MINUTES**   **START TO FINISH: 1½ HOURS**

2 (½-inch-thick) round slices white onion

3 fresh serrano chiles, stemmed

4 garlic cloves, peeled

3 tablespoons freshly squeezed
lime juice, or more to taste

3 tablespoons water

1 teaspoon mild olive oil

¾ teaspoon fine salt, or 1½ teaspoons kosher salt

½ teaspoon Worcestershire sauce

¼ teaspoon Maggi seasoning sauce

SET the oven or toaster oven to broil and preheat. Alternatively, you can preheat the oven to 500°F. If you're using the oven broiler, position the rack 8 inches from the heat source. Have ready a bowl to hold the ingredients that you'll remove from the oven as they finish roasting.

PUT the onion slices, chiles, and garlic on a foil-lined baking pan and roast, turning the chiles and garlic over once or twice and turning over the onion slices once, until the chiles are blistered all over and blackened in spots, about 10 minutes; the garlic is just tender and golden brown with some blackened spots, 15 to 20 minutes; and the onion slices are softened and charred on both sides, 15 to 20 minutes.

WHEN the chiles are cool enough to handle, remove the skins (you might have to use a paring knife). Chop the onion slices, chiles, and garlic very finely, and put them in a bowl with the remaining ingredients and mix well. Let the salsa stand for 1 hour at room temperature before you serve it. Season to taste with additional lime juice and salt.

Serve it with Grilled Adobo-Marinated Skirt Steak (page 135), Tacos (pages 212–214), Quesadillas (page 225), Tortilla Chips (page 229), rice, beans, or any other side you like (pages 246–256).

This salsa keeps in the refrigerator for up to two days.

GREEN CHILE PASTE PASTA DE CHILE VERDE

This intense paste of chile and garlic makes a great condiment by itself—it'll liven up beans, soups, warm tortillas, even a sandwich—but it's also something I stick in the freezer and take out whenever I want to make a no-hassle salsa roja. All you have to do is roast tomatoes (you can even use canned, as long as they're very high-quality) and mix a cup of them with up to three tablespoons of this paste—depending on how spicy you like your salsa. If you throw in a couple tablespoons of chopped cilantro and white onion and a little lime juice, even better.

MAKES 1 CUP   **ACTIVE TIME: 30 MINUTES**   **START TO FINISH: 30 MINUTES**

10 ounces small fresh green chiles, such as serranos (30 to 40) or jalapeños (about 10), stemmed

1 garlic head (about 12 cloves), cloves separated and peeled

¼ cup water, or more if necessary

1½ tablespoons mild olive oil

1 teaspoons fine salt, or 2 teaspoons kosher salt

SET the oven to broil and preheat. Alternatively, you can preheat the oven to 500°F. If you're using the oven broiler, position the rack 8 inches from the heat source.

PUT the chiles and garlic cloves on a foil-lined baking pan, and roast, turning once, until the chiles are tender, blistered all over, and blackened in spots, 10 to 15 minutes, and the garlic is tender and golden brown with some blackened spots, 15 to 20 minutes.

PUT the chiles and garlic in the blender jar along with the water, oil, and salt. Blend until smooth, adding more water by the tablespoonful if necessary. Season to taste with additional salt.

Serve it with Corn Tortillas (page 39), Adobo-Marinated Fish (page 130), Adobo-Marinated Shrimp (page 132), rice, beans, or any other side you like (pages 246–256).

The paste keeps in the refrigerator for up to five days or in the freezer for up to one month. For easy access, freeze the paste in an ice cube tray then store the cubes in the freezer in a plastic bag.

SWEET STRAWBERRY SALSA WITH ÁRBOL CHILES

SALSA DULCE DE FRESA CON CHILES DE ÁRBOL

Here's something you don't see every day: a salsa you eat for dessert. Sure, purists may cringe, but I bet they'd be singing a different tune if they drizzled some over vanilla ice cream or fresh berries—the tomatillos provide a lovely tang, and the chiles contribute just enough *oomph*.

MAKES 1½ CUPS   **ACTIVE TIME: 20 MINUTES**   **START TO FINISH: 40 MINUTES**

2 dried árbol chiles, wiped clean and stemmed

2 tomatillos, husked and rinsed

1 pound strawberries, rinsed, hulled, and quartered (3½ cups)

½ cup sugar

10 whole black peppercorns

2 whole cloves

2 small Turkish bay leaves or 1 small California bay leaf

¼ teaspoon fine salt, or ½ teaspoon kosher salt

HEAT a heavy skillet over medium-low heat and roast the tomatillos and toast the chiles, turning the chiles over and pressing down on them frequently with tongs, until they are browned all over and with some blackened spots, 3 to 4 minutes. Remove the chiles and continue to roast the tomatillos, turning them over only once, until their tops and bottoms have blackened and the tomatillos are a khaki-green color and cooked to the core, 20 to 30 minutes total.

ADD the strawberries to the tomatillos in the hot skillet and cook, stirring over medium heat, until they start to give off liquid. Add the toasted chiles, sugar, peppercorns, cloves, bay leaves, and salt and cook until the strawberries are soft, about 5 minutes.

TRANSFER the mixture to the blender jar and blend until the spices break down and the salsa is very smooth, about 1 minute, then strain the mixture through a fine-mesh sieve, pressing on and then discarding the solids.

This salsa keeps in the refrigerator for up to three days.

Chiles de árbol fresh, dried and toasted, dried

SALSAS FOR COOKING
This subset of cooked salsas has a different purpose. Instead of condiments, think of these as super flavorful cooking liquids. They're less spicy and intense than condiment salsas, because you want to be able to slurp them with a spoon when you use them to make enchiladas, eggs, and fabulous meat stews.

SIMPLE COOKED TOMATO SALSA
RECAUDO DE JITOMATE

If you ask a Mexican who doesn't typically cook, "Well, what can you make?" he'll probably describe this sauce. That's how simple it is. Rather than toasting and roasting ingredients, this recipe employs a technique you see often in Mexico and one that you'll surely be familiar with. You add the chopped ingredients to some oil and cook away. It's a great thing to keep in the refrigerator—a few tablespoons will add Mexican flavor to eggs or vegetables like sautéed mushrooms or zucchini.

MAKES **4 CUPS**   ACTIVE TIME: **35 MINUTES**   START TO FINISH: **1 HOUR**

¼ cup mild olive oil

2 cups finely chopped white onion

1½ tablespoons minced garlic

1 fresh jalapeño or serrano chile, minced, including seeds

2 pounds tomatoes (about 6 medium), cored and finely chopped

3 bay leaves (optional)

1 teaspoon fine salt, or 2 teaspoons kosher salt

1 to 2 teaspoons sugar, if necessary

HEAT the oil in a 2- to 3-quart heavy saucepan over medium heat. Add the onion, garlic, and chile, and cook, stirring, until the onions are translucent, about 5 minutes. Add the tomatoes, bay leaves (if using), and salt, and simmer, stirring occasionally, until the sauce is slightly thickened, about 20 minutes. Remove and discard the bay leaves. Season to taste with sugar, but only if the sauce is too acidic, and additional salt.

This salsa keeps in the refrigerator for up to five days or in the freezer for up to one month.

CHUNKY TOMATILLO SAUCE
ENTOMATADO

Like Simple Cooked Tomato Salsa (page 92), this sauce is as easy as chop, sauté, and simmer—a slightly different method than the dry roasting you see in most other recipes in this book. The chunky, sweet-tart result is just the thing for cooking chicken or pork and reminds me of my dinners at home as a boy in Mexico City.

MAKES 4 CUPS   ACTIVE TIME: **30 MINUTES**   START TO FINISH: **1 HOUR**

3 tablespoons mild olive oil or vegetable oil

1 large white onion, sliced

½ teaspoon fine salt, or 1 teaspoon kosher salt

4 large garlic cloves, finely chopped

¼ cup chopped canned chipotles in adobo, including sauce

¼ cup grated piloncillo, or brown sugar

2 pounds tomatillos (20 to 24), husked, rinsed, and cut into eighths

1 (5-inch) piece canela (Mexican cinnamon)

1 large sprig epazote, optional

1 tablespoon white distilled vinegar, or more to taste

HEAT the oil in a 4- to 5-quart wide heavy pot over medium heat until it shimmers. Add the onion slices and the salt, and cook, stirring, until the onions are translucent, about 5 minutes. Add the garlic, chipotles in adobo, and piloncillo and cook, stirring, about 1 minute. Add the tomatillos, cinnamon, epazote, and vinegar. Stir and bring the mixture to a simmer. Cook, covered, over medium-low heat until the tomatillos have broken down but the sauce is still chunky and the liquid is slightly syrupy, about 30 minutes. Season to taste with additional salt and vinegar. Discard the epazote and cinnamon.

Serve as part of Chicken in Chunky Tomatillo Sauce (page 238).

This salsa keeps in the refrigerator for up to five days or in the freezer for up to one month.

NOTE: Piloncillo is a type of Mexican raw sugar that has a lovely molasses-like flavor and comes in a pestle-shape block. It is available at Mexican grocery stores or by mail order (see Sources, page 258).

TOMATO AND HABANERO SALSA
CHILTOMATE

This tomato sauce might seem Italian if it weren't for those habaneros, which make it taste so very Mexican. Many tomato sauces in my home country use chiles, but the addition of the fiery, fruity habanero is the Yucatan touch. Chiltomate makes great enchiladas, sauteed shrimp, chicken and vegetable stew, or huevos *motuleños,* a local riff on rancheros: bean-topped corn tortillas crowned with fried eggs, peas, ham, and chiltomate. Many Yucatan cooks wouldn't dare blend the habanero into the sauce (instead, they'd steep it, then remove it), but I do because the result is amazing.

MAKES **ABOUT 2 CUPS**   ACTIVE TIME: **20 MINUTES**   START TO FINISH: **1 HOUR**

1½ pounds tomatoes (about 4 medium-large)

1 fresh habanero chile, stemmed

1 small garlic clove, peeled

½ teaspoon fine salt, or 1 teaspoon kosher salt

2 tablespoons mild olive oil

½ cup finely chopped white onion

SET the oven to broil and preheat. Alternatively, you can preheat the oven to 500°F. If you're using the oven broiler, position the rack 8 inches from the heat source. Have ready a large bowl to hold the ingredients that you'll remove from the oven as they finish roasting.

CORE the tomatoes and cut a small "X" through the skin on the opposite ends. Put the tomatoes, cored sides up, and the habanero on a foil-lined baking pan, and roast, turning over the habanero once or twice but not turning the tomatoes, until the chile is browned in spots and soft, 8 to 12 minutes, and the tomatoes' tops have blackened and the tomatoes are cooked to the core, 20 to 30 minutes.

SLIP the skins from the tomatoes, then puree the tomatoes, habanero, garlic, and salt in the blender jar until smooth. Be careful when you're blending hot ingredients: Cover the top with a kitchen towel, and hold the top firmly in place with your hand.

HEAT the oil in a medium saucepan over medium-low heat, then cook the onion over medium-low heat until it's translucent, about 5 minutes. Add the blended tomato sauce and simmer, uncovered, stirring occasionally, for 10 minutes, gradually adding a little water (no more than 4 tablespoons), if necessary, to maintain the same consistency. Season to taste with additional salt.

Turn it into Enchiladas (pages 216–224) or Chilaquiles (page 231).

This salsa keeps in the refrigerator for up to five days or in the freezer for up to one month.

Chicken Stewed with Tomato Sauce and Vegetables (page 237)

RANCHERA SAUCE SALSA RANCHERA

This light tomato sauce, so common throughout Mexico, has a touch of heat and sweetness. It's so versatile: Like the previous recipe, you can use it as a braising liquid (see Chicken in Tomato Sauce, page 237), pour some on a plate of eggs, and use it to make Chilaquiles (page 231).

MAKES **2 CUPS**   ACTIVE TIME: **15 MINUTES**   START TO FINISH: **1 HOUR**

1½ pounds tomatoes (about 4 medium-large)

1 fresh serrano or jalapeño chile, coarsely chopped, including seeds

1 large garlic clove, peeled

2 tablespoons mild olive oil or vegetable oil

⅔ cup chopped white onion

½ teaspoon sugar

Rounded ¼ teaspoon fine salt, or ¾ teaspoon kosher salt

1 (1-inch) piece canela (Mexican cinnamon), or ¼ teaspoon ground cinnamon

---

SET the oven or toaster oven to broil and preheat. Alternatively, you can preheat the oven to 500°F. If you're using the oven broiler, position the rack 8 inches from the heat source.

CORE the tomatoes and cut a small "X" through the skin on the opposite ends. Roast the tomatoes, cored sides up, on a foil-lined baking pan until their tops have blackened and the tomatoes are cooked to the core, 20 to 30 minutes.

SLIP the skins from the tomatoes. Put the tomatoes, chile, and garlic in the blender jar, and blend until smooth. Be careful when you're blending hot ingredients: Cover the top with a kitchen towel, and hold the top firmly in place with your hand.

HEAT the oil in a medium heavy saucepan over medium heat until it shimmers. Add the onion and cook, stirring, until the onion is translucent, about 5 minutes. Add the tomato mixture, and bring it to a boil. As the tomato mixture is cooking, swish a little liquid around in the blender jar and add it to the pan. Reduce the heat, stir in the sugar, salt, and cinnamon, and simmer the sauce, stirring occasionally, until it has thickened slightly, about 20 minutes.

Turn it into Chicken in Tomato Sauce (page 237), Enchiladas (pages 216–224), or Chilaquiles (page 231).

This salsa keeps in the refrigerator for up to five days or in the freezer for up to one month.

ROASTED TOMATO SALSA WITH CHIPOTLE AND HABANERO CHILES

SALSA DE JITOMATE ASADO CON CHIPOTLE Y HABANERO

In Mexico, chile-spiked tomato sauces are as common as ketchup is in the United States. In Mexico City, where I'm from, we make them with roasted serranos or jalapeños. In the Yucatán, they'll almost always use habaneros. And throughout the country, you'll find *albóndigas* (meatballs) covered in a smoky chipotle-laced version. This recipe is a hybrid that brings together two chiles that get along magically. It's just the thing for Adobo-Marinated Skirt Steak (page 135), Enchiladas (pages 216–224), eggs, meatballs, and just about any dish that you associate with European tomato sauces.

MAKES 5 CUPS   **ACTIVE TIME: 30 MINUTES**   **START TO FINISH: 1¼ HOURS**

3 pounds tomatoes (about 10 medium)

2 chipotle mora chiles (purplish-red color), wiped clean and stemmed

½ fresh habanero chile, stemmed, including seeds

3 small garlic cloves, peeled

1 teaspoon fine salt, or 2 teaspoons kosher salt

½ teaspoon sugar

¼ cup mild olive oil or vegetable oil

1 medium white onion, thinly sliced

1 (½-inch) piece canela (Mexican cinnamon), or ⅛ teaspoon ground cinnamon

1 cup water

SET the oven to broil and preheat. Alternatively, you can preheat the oven to 500°F. If you're using the oven broiler, position the rack 8 inches from the heat source. Have ready a large bowl to hold the ingredients that you'll remove from the oven as they finish roasting.

CORE the tomatoes and cut a small "X" through the skin on the opposite ends. Put the tomatoes, cored sides up, and the chipotle and habanero chiles on a foil-lined baking pan, and roast, turning the chiles over once, until the chipotles have puffed up and are blistered in spots, 3 to 5 minutes, and the habanero is browned in spots and softened, 8 to 12 minutes. Remove the chiles from the pan and continue cooking the tomatoes, without turning, until their tops have blackened and the tomatoes are cooked to the core, 20 to 30 minutes total.

SLIP the skins from the tomatoes, then put the tomatoes in the blender jar with the chiles, garlic, salt, and sugar and blend until smooth. Be careful when you're blending hot ingredients: Cover the top with a kitchen towel, and hold the top firmly in place with your hand. Work in batches to avoid blending with a full jar.

HEAT the oil in a medium heavy saucepan over medium heat and cook the onion and the cinnamon, stirring, until the onion is softened and translucent, about 5 minutes.

STRAIN the blended tomato mixture through a medium-mesh sieve into the saucepan with the onions. Add the cup of water and simmer, stirring occasionally, until the sauce has thickened slightly, about 30 minutes. Season to taste with additional salt or sugar.

Turn it into Chicken in Tomato Sauce (page 237), Enchiladas (pages 216–224), or Chilaquiles (page 231).

This salsa keeps in the refrigerator for up to five days or in the freezer for up to one month.

COOKED GREEN SALSA
SALSA VERDE COCIDA

This versatile cooking salsa has a mouth-puckering tang and spicy zip that makes it a great foil for rich meats like pork. It also turns eggs into fabulous huevos rancheros and is a great partner for tortillas—either Chilaquiles (page 231) or Enchiladas (pages 216–224). Any leftover sauce can be turned into Spicy Cooked Tomatillo Table Salsa (page 74).

MAKES 4 CUPS   ACTIVE TIME: **20 MINUTES**   START TO FINISH: **1 HOUR**

2 pounds tomatillos (20 to 24), husked and rinsed

2 fresh jalapeño chiles, stemmed

3 small garlic cloves, peeled

1 teaspoon fine salt, or 2 teaspoons kosher salt

1 teaspoon ground cumin

½ cup chopped cilantro

1 tablespoon mild olive oil or vegetable oil

PUT the tomatillos and jalapeños in a 4- to 5-quart heavy pot with enough water to cover and bring the water to a simmer. Lower the heat and simmer gently, turning the tomatillos and chiles occasionally, until the tomatillos have turned a khaki-green color and are tender, but still intact, about 15 minutes. If necessary, let the tomatillos stand in the pan off the heat for up to 15 minutes more to finish cooking the insides.

GENTLY drain the tomatillos and chiles in a colander, being careful to keep the tomatillos intact. Put the tomatillos, jalapeños, garlic, salt, and cumin in the blender jar and pulse just until the tomatillos are coarsely chopped. Add the cilantro and blend until the sauce is smooth and flecked with cilantro (the tomatillo seeds should still be visible). Be careful when you're blending hot ingredients: Cover the top with a kitchen towel, and hold the top firmly in place with your hand. Work in batches to avoid blending with a full jar.

WIPE the pot clean and heat the oil in the pot over medium heat until it shimmers. Carefully pour the salsa into the oil (it may splatter), and bring it to a simmer. As it's simmering, swish a little water around in the jar and add it to the pot. Simmer gently until slightly thickened, about 10 minutes. Transfer the salsa to a heatproof 4-cup measure, and add water (if necessary) until the salsa measures 4 cups but is still thick enough to coat the back of a spoon. Season to taste with additional salt.

Turn it into Enchiladas (pages 216–224) or Chilaquiles (page 231) or use it with Pork Braised in Tomatillo Sauce (page 239).

This salsa keeps in the refrigerator for up to three days or in the freezer for up to one month.

SALSA VERDE CON EPAZOTE

The recipe above makes a fabulous sauce for Chilaquiles (page 231), but for an equally delicious and more typical partner, omit the cilantro and cumin, and add an 8-inch sprig of epazote (or a small bunch of younger, more delicate epazote) when you begin to simmer the sauce. Discard the epazote before serving.

Pork Braised in Cooked Green Salsa (page 239)

GUACAMOLES

THE CHUNKY AND THE SMOOTH

GUACAMOLE IS THE CULMINATION OF THE MEXICAN LOVE AFFAIR WITH THE AVOCADO, A FRUIT SO COMMON IN MY HOME COUNTRY THAT ONE MIGHT LITERALLY FALL AT YOUR FEET FROM A TREE IN MICHOACÁN OR EVEN MEXICO CITY. THE FRUIT'S UBIQUITY SURELY ACCOUNTS FOR THE POPULARITY OF GUACAMOLE. THE AVOCADO'S RICH, BUTTERY FLESH, WHICH IS SO TASTY SPRINKLED WITH JUST A LITTLE SALT, BECOMES SOMETHING UNFORGETTABLE WHEN IT'S MIXED WITH CHILES, ONIONS, HERBS LIKE CILANTRO AND EPAZOTE, OR EVEN, IN THE REGION OF GUANAJUATO, THE CRUNCHY PIG SKINS CALLED CHICHARRONES.

The word *guacamole* is a combination of the Spanish word *aguacate* (or *ahuacatl* in Nahuatl, the language spoken by the Aztecs), which means avocado, and the word *mole*, which essentially means "a mixture." So really, any time an avocado is smashed and mixed with other ingredients, you can call it a guacamole. Yet as anyone who has been disappointed by an utterly bland avocado mush knows, there's an art to turning the collection of basic ingredients into a dish worthy of the designation. And once you try it my way, I promise it will spoil you for almost any other guacamole.

In America, guacamole has established its place at the table as a snack or appetizer, served in a big bowl with lots of chips. That's a delicious way to eat it, though one you rarely see on my family's table. Instead, we add it to soups, scoop it on white rice, serve it alongside grilled meats, and spoon spicy versions on tacos. One of my favorite ways to eat it couldn't be easier: inside a warm, soft corn tortilla.

Once you follow a few of my recipes, you'll begin to understand the simple techniques that make truly great guacamoles and the balance of flavors I want you to achieve. Of course, I will tell you how each version is served in my scrupulously traditional home country, but once you understand the basics, you can serve guacamoles however you like—on a burger, a sandwich, or even, and you'll have to trust me on this, a hot dog!

Guacamoles fall into two major categories: chunky and smooth. Chunky ones tend to be more rustic and reflective of guacamole's roots than smooth ones. But that's not to say I haven't included a few modern interpretations as well. Almost every version I provide a recipe for is a variation on a winning theme: the chile and onion are almost always present, but they partner with everything from lime and cilantro to apple and blue cheese!

Of course, no matter what you add to guacamoles, the star is the flavor and texture of the avocado. So to make truly great guacamoles, try to find Mexican Hass avocados, which I consider the best in the world, and use them only when they are perfectly ripe. For more on this (and on selecting, cutting, and storing avocados) refer to the Basics chapter (pages 22–24), but since this deserves repeating:

Remember, many people use avocados before they're ripe enough. So next time you make guacamole, use an avocado that's a bit softer than you're used to. You might just have an avocado revelation.

Smooth guacamoles tend to be more modern than their chunky counterparts. But they're just as exciting, and easy to make: Rather than mashing your ingredients in a molcajete or bowl, you toss them in the blender to make a silky, creamy, and pourable dip for vegetables and chips or a condiment for anything from tacos to turkey sandwiches.

Whatever kind you decide on, it'll taste best if you make the guacamole right before you plan to serve it because with time, the ingredients that make guacamoles exciting—the tart lime, the heat of chiles, and the punch of herbs—quickly lose their intensity. Also, when avocado flesh is exposed to the air for too long, it turns brown. This is the result of a process called oxidization, and while it affects the fruit's flavor only a little, the unappealing color is something to be avoided. (Smooth guacamoles for which avocado is blended with acidic ingredients won't oxidize nearly as quickly.) If you expect to be pressed for time come guacamole day, you can prep all the ingredients, except for the avocado, in advance (even as far ahead as the night before, if you refrigerate them in airtight containers). If you must make guacamole in advance, store it in the refrigerator with a piece of plastic wrap pressed against the surface to prevent discoloration. Be sure to take it out an hour before you plan to use it, so it comes to room temperature, and give it a stir. Never, ever microwave guacamole.

KEEP IT CHUNKY!

Remember, guacamoles meant to be chunky should not be mashed to mush. For a good model, look at the avocado in the photo on page 112.

CLASSIC GUACAMOLE
GUACAMOLE TÍPICO

The secret to this guacamole, the reason that it's so alive with heat and flavor, is in its method. Instead of simply chopping onion, cilantro, and chile, and tossing them with avocado, I start by mashing those three ingredients along with a generous sprinkle of salt into an intensely flavored, bright green paste. Only then do I scoop out pieces of perfectly ripe avocado and toss it all together. The result is a bit like salad properly dressed in vinaigrette: Every creamy piece of avocado gets coated with the paste, so every bite starts with a pop of heat, salt, and herbs, and ends with the mellow, buttery flesh of the fruit. Sometimes, like the good lime-loving Mexico City guy that I am, I'll add a spritz of lime juice right before I serve it. But imagine, this is guacamole so flavor-packed that the citrus squirt, a staple in most American versions, is optional.

MAKES ABOUT 1¾ CUPS   **ACTIVE TIME: 15 MINUTES**   **START TO FINISH: 15 MINUTES**

2 tablespoons finely chopped white onion

1 tablespoon minced fresh serrano or jalapeño chile, including seeds, or more to taste

½ teaspoon kosher salt, or ¼ teaspoon fine salt

¼ cup chopped cilantro, divided

1 large or 2 small ripe Mexican Hass avocados, halved and pitted

A squeeze of lime, if desired

MASH the onion, chile, salt (the coarseness of kosher salt helps you make the paste), and half of the cilantro to a paste in a molcajete or other mortar. You can also mince and mash the ingredients together on a cutting board with a large knife or a fork, and then transfer the paste to a bowl.

SCORE the flesh in the avocado halves in a crosshatch pattern (not through the skin) with a knife and then scoop it with a spoon into the mortar or bowl. Toss well, then add the rest of the cilantro and mash coarsely with a pestle or a fork. Season to taste with lime juice (if you'd like) and additional chile and salt.

Serve it with Corn Tortillas (page 39), Adobo-Marinated Fish (page 130), Grilled Adobo-Marinated Skirt Steak (page 135), Adobo-Marinated Chicken (page 133), Tacos (pages 212–214), Quesadillas (page 225), Tortilla Chips (page 229), rice, beans, or any other side you like (pages 246–256). Or turn it into Tangy Guacamole Enchiladas with Guajillo-Tomatillo Beef (page 223).

It's best to eat guacamole right away, but you can store it in the refrigerator for up to an hour with a piece of plastic wrap pressed against the surface to prevent discoloration. Let it come to room temperature before you serve it.

CLASSIC GUACAMOLE WITH TOMATO OR TOMATILLO

For an easy twist on the classic guacamole, stir in ¼ cup finely diced, seeded tomato or ¼ cup finely chopped raw tomatillo just before you serve it.

The chile paste that makes this guacamole so great

PINEAPPLE AND CUCUMBER GUACAMOLE GUACAMOLE CON PIÑA Y PEPINO

This is yet another wonderful recipe from my partner's mother, Delia, who lives in avocado country and is so enamored with the fruits she grows that she turns them into beverages and desserts, not to mention plenty of guacamoles. This is one of her finest inventions and gives you so much in each bite—the soft crunch of cucumber, the sweet-tart flavor of pineapple, and the creamy pleasure of this chapter's featured fruit. Plenty of heat and lime give it life and make it a great companion for anything grilled—salmon, shrimp, steak, whatever! Because it's more like a pineapple-avocado salad than a guacamole with a little pineapple, I often treat it as an appetizer salad and serve it to my guests in bowls with spoons.

MAKES 5 CUPS   **ACTIVE TIME: 30 MINUTES**   **START TO FINISH: 30 MINUTES**

1 (10- to 12-ounce) cucumber, peeled, seeded, and diced (½ inch)

½ cup finely diced red onion

2 fresh serrano or jalapeño chiles, minced, including seeds, or more to taste

2 tablespoons freshly squeezed lime juice, or more to taste

¾ teaspoon fine salt, or 1½ teaspoons kosher salt

2 large or 4 small ripe Mexican Hass avocados, halved and pitted

½ pineapple, peeled, cored, and diced (½ inch)

½ cup chopped cilantro, divided

STIR together the cucumber, onion, chiles, lime juice, and salt in a large bowl. Score the flesh in the avocado halves in a cross-hatch pattern (not through the skin) with a knife and then scoop it with a spoon into the bowl and gently stir together (do not mash). Stir in half the cilantro and the pineapple last so the fresh acidity is distinct from the avocado. Season to taste with additional chile, lime juice, and salt. Transfer the guacamole to a wide dish and sprinkle the remaining cilantro on top.

Serve it with Corn Tortillas (page 39), Adobo-Marinated Fish (page 130), Grilled Adobo-Marinated Skirt Steak (page 135), Adobo-Marinated Chicken (page 133), Tacos (pages 212–214), Quesadillas (page 225), Tortilla Chips (page 229), rice, beans, or any other side you like (page 246–256).

Because of the acid in the pineapple, this salsa will not discolor as quickly as other guacamoles. Store it in the refrigerator for up to 2 hours with a piece of plastic wrap pressed against the surface. Let it come to room temperature before you serve it.

This special guacamole is kept chunkier than most.

FRUIT GUACAMOLE GUACAMOLE CON FRUTAS

This festive guacamole, my riff on a traditional recipe from Guanajuato introduced to me by my friend Maria Dolores Torres Izabal, is packed with unexpected fruits that provide a thrilling foil to all that creamy avocado—the juicy, sweet-tart bursts from grapes; the toasty, aromatic flakes of coconut; and luscious chunks of peach. It's hearty enough to be an appetizer all by itself, served in martini glasses or empty coconut shells.

MAKES **ABOUT 3 CUPS**   ACTIVE TIME: **25 MINUTES**   START TO FINISH: **25 MINUTES**

¼ cup flaked coconut, preferably unsweetened, divided

1 large or 2 small ripe Mexican Hass avocados, halved and pitted

1 tablespoon finely chopped white onion

2 teaspoons minced fresh serrano or jalapeño chile, including seeds, or more to taste

½ teaspoon fine salt, or 1 teaspoon kosher salt

1 cup finely diced peeled fresh peaches (1 to 2), mango, or pineapple, divided

12 purple grapes, halved, divided

12 green grapes, halved, divided

Pomegranate seeds (optional)

PREHEAT the oven to 350°F, then spread the coconut flakes on a baking pan and toast in the oven until golden, stirring occasionally, 5 to 8 minutes.

SCORE the flesh in the avocado halves in a crosshatch pattern (not through the skin) with a knife and then scoop it with a spoon into a bowl along with the onion, chile, salt, and the most of the peaches, grapes, and toasted coconut, mixing with a fork to combine and mashing the avocado slightly. Season to taste with additional chile and salt.

SPRINKLE the rest of the peaches, grapes, and toasted coconut on top, and garnish with the pomegranate seeds (if you like).

Serve it with Tortilla Chips (page 229), Corn Tortillas (page 39), or Grilled Adobo-Marinated Skirt Steak (page 135).

It's best to eat guacamole right away, but you can store it in the refrigerator with a piece of plastic wrap pressed against the surface to prevent discoloration for up to an hour. Let it come to room temperature before you serve it.

APPLE-TEQUILA GUACAMOLE
GUACAMOLE CON MANZANA Y TEQUILA

The combination seems unusual at first blush, but it turns out that crunchy pecans (toasted and then tossed in a little butter) and crisp pieces of apple create a textural marvel when paired with creamy avocado. And the tequila, which soaks into the apples and charges their flavor, somehow doesn't make the whole dish taste boozy. Instead, it makes the chiles and cilantro taste even more potent and delicious. Make sure to mix the ingredients together at the last minute, so they all retain their own identities.

MAKES 2 CUPS   ACTIVE TIME: **35 MINUTES**   START TO FINISH: **1¼ HOURS**

FOR THE APPLE

1 large crisp, sweet apple, such as Gala or McIntosh, peeled, cored, and finely diced

1 tablespoon silver (blanco) tequila

1 tablespoon freshly squeezed lime juice

FOR THE PECANS

¼ cup pecan halves, sliced crosswise or coarsely chopped

1 teaspoon butter

⅛ teaspoon fine salt, or ¼ teaspoon kosher salt

FOR THE GUACAMOLE

1 fresh serrano or jalapeño chile, stemmed

2 tablespoons finely chopped white onion

1 teaspoon coarse salt, or ½ teaspoon fine salt

3 tablespoons chopped cilantro, divided

1 large or 2 small ripe Mexican Hass avocados, halved and pitted

TOSS the apple with the tequila and lime juice in a bowl and let the mixture stand for 30 minutes to 1 hour.

PREHEAT the oven or toaster oven to 350°F. Spread the pecans on a small baking pan and bake until golden and fragrant, 7 to 8 minutes. Add the butter to the pan and toss to melt the butter and coat the pecans. Sprinkle with salt, tossing to coat.

HEAT a comal, griddle, or heavy skillet over medium-low heat and roast the chile, turning it over with tongs once or twice, until tender, blistered all over, and blackened in spots, 10 to 15 minutes. Remove the skin from the chile (you might have to use a paring knife).

MASH the chile, onion, salt (the coarseness of kosher salt will help you make the paste), and 2 tablespoons of the cilantro to a paste in a molcajete or other mortar. You can also mince and mash the ingredients together on a cutting board with a large knife or a fork, and then transfer the paste to a bowl.

SCORE the flesh in the avocado halves in a crosshatch pattern (not through the skin) with a knife and then scoop it with a spoon into the mortar or bowl. Toss well, mashing the avocado coarsely with a pestle or fork.

STIR in the apple mixture and most of the pecans. Garnish with the remaining pecans and cilantro.

Serve it with Tortilla Chips (page 229).

This guacamole is best served right away.

SEAFOOD GUACAMOLE

GUACAMOLE CON MARISCOS

My classic guacamole is sensational. But add a little crab and shrimp marinated in orange juice and chipotle and you have a modern version worthy of the most elegant restaurant but simple enough for a weeknight dinner at home. This is guacamole that has graduated from snack or condiment to proper appetizer.

MAKES ABOUT 3½ CUPS   **ACTIVE TIME: 35 MINUTES**   **START TO FINISH: 35 MINUTES**

4 ounces jumbo lump crabmeat, picked over

3 ounces cooked shrimp or lobster, cut into small pieces (½ cup)

3 tablespoons freshly squeezed orange juice

2 tablespoons chopped cilantro

1 tablespoon minced fresh jalapeño or serrano chile, including seeds, or more to taste

1 tablespoon mild olive oil

2 teaspoons minced canned chipotles in adobo, including sauce, or 1 teaspoon Chipotle Chile Powder (page 21)

¼ teaspoon fine salt, or ½ teaspoon kosher salt

1 recipe Classic Guacamole (page 104)

MIX the seafood together with the orange juice, cilantro, fresh chile, oil, chipotle, and salt and let the mixture marinate for about 20 minutes.

MAKE the Classic Guacamole, reserving the sprinkled cilantro.

With a slotted spoon, transfer about half of the seafood mixture into the guacamole, and stir. Season to taste with additional salt, then garnish with the remaining seafood mixture and the reserved cilantro.

Serve it with Corn Tortillas (page 39), Tortilla Chips (page 229), rice, beans, or any other side you like (pages 246–256).

The seafood mixture and the guacamole (with a piece of plastic wrap pressed against the surface) can be stored separately in the refrigerator for up to an hour. Let the guacamole come to room temperature and let the seafood mixture stand at room temperature just long enough to take some of the chill off before you assemble and serve the guacamole.

BLUE CHEESE GUACAMOLE

GUACAMOLE CON QUESO AZUL

You might think I came up with this recipe just to make Diana Kennedy cringe. But blue cheese and avocado do make a truly delicious union that, as any fan of the Cobb salad understands, is not as odd as it sounds. I typically use the best stuff I can find at the cheese counter, such as Roquefort, Cabrales, or Danish Blue, but even the already crumbled blue cheese you find in a good grocery store will be delicious.

MAKES ABOUT 2½ CUPS   **ACTIVE TIME: 20 MINUTES**   **START TO FINISH: 20 MINUTES**

2 tablespoons finely chopped white onion

1 tablespoon minced fresh jalapeño or serrano chile, including seeds, or more to taste

1 teaspoon kosher salt, or ½ teaspoon fine salt

¼ cup chopped cilantro, divided

1 tablespoon freshly squeezed lime juice, or more to taste

1 large or 2 small ripe Mexican Hass avocados, halved and pitted

¼ cup coarsely chopped smoked almonds, divided

3 tablespoons crumbled blue cheese, divided

MASH the onion, chile, salt (the coarseness of kosher salt will help you make the paste), and half of the cilantro to a paste in a molcajete or mortar. You can also mince and mash the ingredients together on a cutting board with a large knife or a fork, and then transfer the paste to a bowl. Stir in the lime juice.

SCORE the flesh in the avocado halves in a crosshatch pattern (not through the skin) with a knife and then scoop it with a spoon into the mortar or bowl. Add the rest of the cilantro and most of the almonds and blue cheese, toss well, and mash coarsely with a pestle or fork. Season to taste with additional lime juice and salt.

GARNISH with the rest of the almonds and blue cheese.

Serve it with Tortilla Chips (page 229).

This guacamole is best served right away.

GUACAMOLE WITH CHICHARRÓN

GUACAMOLE CHAMACUERO

In the *carnicerias* of Mexico, you'll find four-foot-long sheets of chicharrones, pork skins cooked slowly until all the fat renders. And if you're like me, you have a terrible time resisting these crackling crunchy treats. We Mexicans love them so much that we use pieces to scoop up guacamole. And in the state of Guanajuato, where, like the rest of the north of Mexico, the people are known for having a particular affinity for pork, cooks skip the dipping and combine the two. Of the many versions from this region I've eaten and made—some with a sprinkle of chicharrón and some with a handful—this recipe from my dear friend Ricardo Muñoz Zurita, a food historian and chef, is my favorite.

MAKES ABOUT 4 CUPS   **ACTIVE TIME: 25 MINUTES**   **START TO FINISH: 25 MINUTES**

¼ cup finely chopped white onion

2 tablespoons chopped cilantro

1 tablespoon minced fresh serrano or jalapeño chile, including seeds, or more to taste

½ teaspoon coarse salt, or ¼ teaspoon fine salt

1 large or 2 small Mexican Hass avocados, halved and pitted

1 large tomato, cored, seeded, and finely diced

2 cups crumbled pork chicharrón (2 ounces)

MASH the onion, cilantro, chile, and salt (coarse salt helps you make the paste) to a paste in a molcajete or other mortar. You can also mince and mash the ingredients together on a cutting board with a large knife or fork, and then transfer the paste to a bowl.

SCORE the flesh in the avocado halves in a crosshatch pattern (not through the skin) with a knife, and then scoop it into the mortar or bowl, toss well, and coarsely mash. Season to taste with additional chile and salt.

JUST before you serve it, gently stir in the tomatoes and half of the crumbled chicharrón and garnish with the remaining chicharrón.

Serve it with Carnitas (page 240), Corn Tortillas (page 39), Tortilla Chips (page 229), rice, beans, or any other side you like (pages 246–256).

This guacamole is best served right away.

PICKING YOUR PORK SKIN

You can find chicharrones in many Mexican grocery stores. For this recipe, look for thin, almost translucent sheets with only a little, if any, meat attached. And please, don't use the overly salty bagged pork rinds you see in gas stations and supermarkets.

TACO-SHOP GUACAMOLE

GUACAMOLE TAQUERO

Before you start gobbling delicate corn tortillas topped with salty, tasty meat in the taquerias of central Mexico, you get to crown your snack with your choice of several salsas, often including what might be my favorite taco condiment of all: guacamole taquero. Blurring the line between guacamole and salsa, this smooth blend of creamy avocado and tart tomatillos packs a spicy punch from serrano chiles and a hint of pungent epazote (many cooks add cilantro instead and so can you). I'll put this on just about any imaginable taco, but it's especially amazing spooned over those filled with Carnitas (page 240), steak, and grilled cactus.

MAKES 2 CUPS   **ACTIVE TIME: 15 MINUTES**   **START TO FINISH: 15 MINUTES**

½ pound tomatillos (5 or 6), husked, rinsed, and coarsely chopped

6 large (about 3½ inches long) fresh epazote or cilantro leaves

2 small garlic cloves, peeled and coarsely chopped

¼ cup coarsely chopped white onion

2 fresh serrano or jalapeño chiles, coarsely chopped, including seeds, or more to taste

1 tablespoon freshly squeezed lime juice, or more to taste

½ teaspoon fine salt, or 1 teaspoon kosher salt

1 small ripe Mexican Hass avocado, halved and pitted

PUT the tomatillos into the blender jar first, then add the epazote, garlic, onion, chiles, lime juice, and salt. Blend until very smooth, at least a minute (be patient; see note on page 50). Scoop the avocado flesh with a spoon into the blender jar and blend until smooth. Add a little water, if necessary, to achieve a pourable texture. Season to taste with additional chile, lime juice, and salt, and blend once more.

Serve it with Grilled Adobo-Marinated Skirt Steak (page 135), Adobo-Marinated Chicken (page 133), Tacos (page 212–214), Tortilla Chips (page 229), Carnitas (page 240), rice, beans, or any other side you like (pages 246–256).

This salsa tastes best the day it's made, but the acidity from the tomatillos will keep it from discoloring as quickly as most guacamoles. It'll still be delicious the next day if you store it in the refrigerator with a piece of plastic wrap pressed against the surface. Let it come to room temperature before you serve it.

CREAMY GUACAMOLE-TOMATILLO DIP GUACAMOLE CREMOSO

This tangy avocado dip requires no Iron Chef knife skills. The blades of your blender do all the work, turning the fruit, mayonnaise, and tomatillo salsa into a smooth, creamy sauce. To make this dish really easy, you can use jarred tomatillo salsa, as many Mexican cooks do, but make it yourself and the result will be even more delicious. I serve this with chips or crudités, on a simple turkey or ham sandwich, or as a sauce for grilled meat and fish. If you're itching for some heat, add half a jalapeño chile before you blend this guacamole.

MAKES 2 CUPS   ACTIVE TIME: **30 MINUTES**   START TO FINISH: **1¼ HOURS**

1 cup Cooked Green Salsa (page 99), cooled

1 large ripe Mexican Hass avocado, halved and pitted

3 tablespoons mayonnaise

1 teaspoon freshly squeezed lime juice

½ small garlic clove, peeled

¼ teaspoon fine salt, or ½ teaspoon kosher salt

POUR the Cooked Green Salsa into the blender jar. Use a spoon to scoop the avocado flesh into the blender jar, then add the mayonnaise, lime juice, garlic, and salt, and blend until smooth. Add water (1 tablespoon at a time) if the mixture is too thick to blend, but keep in mind it should be thick enough for dipping. Season to taste with additional salt.

Serve it with Corn Tortillas (page 39), Adobo-Marinated Fish (page 130), Grilled Adobo-Marinated Skirt Steak (page 135), Adobo-Marinated Chicken (page 133), Tacos (pages 212–214), Tortilla Chips (page 229), rice, beans, or any other side you like (pages 246–256).

This salsa tastes best the day it's made, but the acidity from the Cooked Green Salsa will keep it from discoloring as quickly as most guacamoles. It'll still be delicious the next day if you store it in the refrigerator with a piece of plastic wrap pressed against the surface. Let it come to room temperature before you serve it.

AVOCADO SAUCE SALSA DE AGUACATE

My aunt used to drizzle this pastel-green sauce on turkey that was left over after holiday dinners, its richness and silkiness turning the mild meat into something fantastic. Of course, you can use it on just about any sandwich you can think of, as well as on rotisserie chicken, pork loin, and grilled steak. The key is acheiving the right consistency: Because the fat and water content of avocados can vary, you might need to add a little more milk to achieve a thick sauce that will creep slowly forward when you tip the blender.

MAKES 3 CUPS   **ACTIVE TIME: 10 MINUTES**   **START TO FINISH: 10 MINUTES**

1 ripe Mexican Hass avocado, halved and pitted

1 cup whole milk

1 cup water, or more if necessary

¼ cup chopped cilantro

1 fresh jalapeño or serrano chile,
coarsely chopped, including seeds

1 very small garlic clove

1 teaspoon fine salt, or 2 teaspoons kosher salt

USE a spoon to scoop the avocado flesh into the blender jar and add all the remaining ingredients. Blend the mixture until smooth, adding more water, if necessary, to obtain a thick but still pourable consistency. Season to taste with additional salt.

Serve it with Adobo-Marinated Fish (page 130), Grilled Adobo-Marinated Skirt Steak (page 135), Adobo-Marinated Chicken (page 133), rice, beans, or any other side you like (pages 246–256).

You can make this guacamole up to two hours in advance. Store it in the refrigerator with a piece of plastic wrap pressed against the surface to prevent discoloration. Let it come to room temperature before you serve it.

ADOBOS

SIMPLE PUREES WITH SOULFUL APPLICATIONS

IN MEXICO CITY, YOU MIGHT STOP SHORT AT A TAQUERIA, HYPNOTIZED BY GYRO-LIKE HUNK OF PORK ROTAT-ING ON A VERTICAL SPIT, THE CHARRED MASS LICKED AT BY FLAMES AND BEGGING TO BE TUCKED INSIDE A TORTILLA. IN OAXACA, YOU MIGHT BE EQUALLY TRANSFIXED BY A BOWL OF DEEP RED STEW WITH CHUNKS OF TENDER CHICKEN AND A FAINT AROMA OF SPICE—*WHAT IS THAT WONDERFUL SMELL,* YOU WONDER, *CLOVE? CUMIN?* THESE TWO DISHES APPEAR IRRECONCILABLY DIFFERENT—A HUNK OF MEAT, A SOUPY STEW—BUT APPEARANCES CAN BE DECEIVING.

Both dishes make use of a thick, boldly flavored chile puree that's either used as a marinade to make grilled or roasted meat unforgettable or turned into a sauce or braising liquid. And both the chile-puree marinade and the long-simmered stew made from the puree are called adobos. Here's what nobody tells you: No matter their purpose, the purees are all essentially the same. They contain dried chiles, garlic, spices, sometimes a little vinegar, and occasionally a little achiote paste. You whir these ingredients in the blender and you're ready to go. Once you learn how easy they are to make, adobos will become a trusty part of your culinary arsenal (they freeze fantastically!), a simple way to turn a few ingredients into something spectacular.

The delicious adobos we know now are a relatively recent invention. Surely Mexican cooks had been rubbing meat with chiles before the sixteenth century, but it was the garlic and spices, like clove, cumin, and cinnamon, that the Spanish brought that made adobos so rich with complex flavors. These foreign ingredients caught on quickly, perhaps because similar flavors, such as pungent, almost spicy bulbs like wild onions and herbs, already had a place in Mexican cooking. Still, in adobos, the chile always takes center stage. Whatever type it is—ancho or guajillo, pasilla or mulato—it's always a large, dried chile that's chosen for its color, flavor, and body rather than its heat. If you're itching for some added spiciness, you can do what many Mexican cooks do and incorporate some smaller, spicier chiles, like chiles de árbol, puyas, and piquines.

The recipes in this chapter are broken into four categories. First, I provide recipes for several electrifying chile purees that can be used as marinades and turned into braising liquids or sauces. Next, you'll find specific recipes for using those purees as marinades, recipes for using them (and a few other special purees) as braising liquids, and finally, the simple steps that turn them into sauces.

ADOBOS: MAKING THE PASTE

It's such a simple and gratifying process: toasting chiles to release their aroma, soaking them to soften their texture, and blending them with garlic, spices, maybe a little vinegar, and water until you have an intensely flavored paste. But there are a few pieces of advice that will make it even easier and ensure that you do it just right.

First, most adobos require that you seed and devein large chiles. It's an important step, but don't drive yourself crazy trying to remove every last seed and vein. As long as you get rid of most of them, you're in great shape. And if you can find only chiles that are brittle, making seeding and deveining difficult, remember this trick to make them pliable: Put them in a resealable bag with a square of just-damp paper towel and refrigerate them overnight.

Second, once you've toasted and soaked the chiles, you'll have some leftover chile-infused water flecked with debris. Some cooks pour it into the blender jar with the chiles and the rest of the ingredients. I don't, because I find using fresh water gives the adobos a better, cleaner flavor.

Third, and I can't stress this enough: Although you may be tempted to make the adobos in the food processor, only the blender will create the finely textured puree you're looking for, effectively mimicking the original method of mashing ingredients in a molcajete, metate, or even between two stones.

Finally, because guajillos, which, along with anchos, are the most popular chiles used in adobos, have particularly tough skins, I always pour adobos made with guajillos through a medium sieve, easing it through with a spoon, before using it to marinate or turning it into a braising liquid or sauce. I suggest you do, too. I often strain adobos made with other chiles as well because I'm a stickler for a perfectly smooth texture without little bits of chile skins, but you'll still achieve a fabulous result even if you choose not to take this extra step.

> ## A HELPFUL ADOBO-TO-MEAT RATIO
>
> 1½ cups of adobo puree is enough to marinate 4 to 6 pounds of meat or fish, or to use as a sauce to cook 2 to 3 pounds of meat.

Chiles soaking

BASIC GUAJILLO ADOBO

ADOBO DE GUAJILLO

Depending on where they live, Mexican cooks build on this simple recipe by adding cloves or cinnamon or oregano, so feel free to tweak the recipe yourself by adding just a hint of spices—a clove or a few peppercorns, for instance. But first, try it at its most basic and see how just a few ingredients can add up to such great flavor. I love to marinate fish and shrimp in this adobo, but it's also delicious with meats like chicken and steak.

MAKES 1½ CUPS   **ACTIVE TIME: 15 MINUTES**   **START TO FINISH: 45 MINUTES**

3 ounces guajillo chiles (12), wiped clean, stemmed, slit open, seeded, and deveined

¾ cup water for blending, or more if necessary

2 garlic cloves, peeled

1½ teaspoons apple cider vinegar

¾ teaspoon fine salt, or 1½ teaspoons kosher salt

¾ teaspoon sugar

Rounded ¼ teaspoon ground cumin

HEAT a comal, griddle, or heavy skillet over medium-low heat, and toast the chiles 2 or 3 at a time, turning them over and pressing down on them with tongs frequently, until they're fragrant and their insides have changed color slightly, about 1 minute per batch. Soak the chiles in enough cold water to cover until they're soft, about 30 minutes. Drain and discard the soaking water.

PUT the ¾ cup of fresh water in the blender jar with the chiles and the remaining ingredients. Blend until smooth, at least 3 minutes, adding a little more water if necessary to puree. If you'd like a silky texture, strain the adobo through a medium-mesh sieve.

Now you can use this highly flavored puree as a marinade for seafood and meat (page 130). Or turn it into a fabulous cooking liquid (page 136) or sauce for eggs, beans, and enchiladas (page 147).

This adobo keeps in the refrigerator for up to five days or in the freezer for up to one month.

Beef in Adobo
(page 140)

BASIC ANCHO ADOBO
ADOBO DE CHILE ANCHO

Ancho chiles have a slightly sweeter, fruitier flavor than the guajillos that headline the previous recipe, and they add a thrilling spark to just about everything from shrimp to pork. Because this adobo is nice and tangy—I call for the classic acidic addition, Seville orange juice, but vinegar works, too—it goes especially well with rich cuts of meat.

MAKES 1½ CUPS   **ACTIVE TIME: 15 MINUTES**   **START TO FINISH: 45 MINUTES**

2½ ounces ancho chiles (5), wiped clean, stemmed, slit open, seeded, and deveined

½ cup water for blending, or more if necessary

¼ cup Seville orange juice or distilled white vinegar

2 garlic cloves, peeled

½ teaspoon fine salt, or 1 teaspoon kosher salt

½ teaspoon sugar

⅛ teaspoon dried oregano, preferably Mexican

⅛ teaspoon ground cumin

HEAT a comal, griddle, or heavy skillet over medium-low heat, and toast the chiles 2 at a time, turning them over and pressing down on them with tongs frequently, until they're fragrant and they've developed light-colored brown blisters, about 1½ minutes per batch. Soak the chiles in enough cold water to cover until they're soft, about 30 minutes. Drain and discard the soaking water.

PUT the ½ cup of fresh water in the blender jar with the chiles and the remaining ingredients. Blend until smooth, at least 3 minutes, adding a little more water if necessary to puree. If you like a silky, smooth texture, strain the adobo through a medium-mesh sieve.

Now you can use this highly flavored puree as a marinade for seafood and meat (page 130). Or turn it into a fabulous cooking liquid (page 136) or sauce for eggs, beans, and enchiladas (page 147).

This adobo keeps in the refrigerator for up to five days or in the freezer for up to one month.

When selecting ancho chiles, the redder (left), the better.

ADOBO D.F. ADOBO DE CHILE ANCHO ESTILO D.F.

It's amazing how complex and delicious this five-ingredient adobo becomes after a little simmering, the cinnamon-laced Mexican chocolate playing so beautifully off the sweet, fruity notes of the ancho chiles. And no, you don't even have to toast them here! This recipe is my riff on an adobo you see often in D.F., aka Mexico City (thank you, Laura Caraza, for introducing me to it), that has caught on in Texas, where many cooks turn it into a sauce for enchiladas. I understand why, but I also love using the deep dark liquid to stew pork and chicken.

MAKES 1½ CUPS   ACTIVE TIME: **10 MINUTES**   START TO FINISH: **40 MINUTES**

3½ ounces ancho chiles (7), wiped clean, stemmed, slit open, seeded, and deveined

1 cup water for blending, or more if necessary

1 ounce Mexican chocolate (3 small triangles of one disk)

1 (2-inch) piece canela (Mexican cinnamon), or ½ teaspoon ground cinnamon

1 garlic clove, peeled

1 tablespoon sugar

2 teaspoons apple cider vinegar

½ teaspoon fine salt, or 1 teaspoon kosher salt

SOAK the chiles (there's no need to toast them) in enough cold water to cover until they're soft, about 30 minutes. Drain and discard the soaking water.

PUT the 1 cup of fresh water in the blender jar with the chiles and the remaining ingredients. Blend until smooth, at least 3 minutes, adding a little more water if necessary to puree. If you like a silky, smooth texture, strain the adobo through a medium-mesh sieve.

Now you can turn it into a fabulous cooking liquid (page 136) or sauce for eggs, beans, and enchiladas (page 147). I don't recommend using this adobo as a marinade because its mellow flavor doesn't provide the right intensity.

This adobo keeps in the refrigerator for up to five days or in the freezer for up to one month.

VINEGAR: THE SPARK

Vinegars have long been used in Mexican cuisine. Early on they were made from fermented fruits like pineapple. Today, cooks often use mildly flavored apple cider, rice, and distilled white vinegars to add a touch of acidity. People often ask me how stewy adobos differ from certain simple moles—this acidity from vinegar is one way. And merely a few teaspoons can contribute just the spark you're looking for.

PASILLA-GUAJILLO ADOBO
ADOBO DE PASILLA Y GUAJILLO

Introducing a second chile into the mix takes just a few extra minutes, but rewards you by providing a well-rounded, sophisticated flavor. A splash of beer adds serious depth. Pasillas and guajillos go beautifully together, but once you get the hang of adobos, you'll find yourself experimenting with other combinations as well. Perhaps you'll do what my mom does, peeking into the cupboard, grabbing a few bags of whatever chiles you've had around for a while, and whipping up something incredible. This recipe gives you enough adobo to make Lamb Shanks Braised in Parchment (page 142)—with some left over for Lamb Adobo Enchiladas with Cooked Green Salsa (page 220) later in the week.

MAKES 3 CUPS   ACTIVE TIME: 30 MINUTES   START TO FINISH: 1 HOUR

2 ounces pasilla chiles (6), wiped clean, stemmed, slit open, seeded, and deveined

2 ounces guajillo chiles (8), wiped clean, stemmed, slit open, seeded, and deveined

¼ cup distilled white vinegar

¼ cup light Mexican beer

½ cup chopped white onion

4 garlic cloves, peeled

1 teaspoon fine salt, or 2 teaspoons kosher salt

½ teaspoon dried oregano, preferably Mexican

¼ teaspoon cumin seeds

5 whole cloves

HEAT a comal, griddle, or heavy skillet over medium-low heat, and toast the chiles 2 or 3 at a time, turning them over and pressing down on them with tongs frequently, until the chiles are fragrant, about 1 minute per batch. Soak the chiles in enough cold water to cover until they're soft, about 30 minutes. Drain and discard the soaking water.

PUT the vinegar and beer in the blender jar with the chiles and the remaining ingredients. Blend until smooth, at least 3 minutes, adding a little water if necessary to puree. If you like a silky, smooth texture, strain the adobo through a medium-mesh sieve.

Now you can use this highly flavored puree as a marinade for seafood and meat (page 130). Or turn it into a fabulous cooking liquid (page 136) or sauce for eggs, beans, and enchiladas (page 147).

This adobo keeps in the refrigerator for up to five days or in the freezer for up to one month.

THREE-CHILE ADOBO ADOBO DE TRES CHILES

Three chiles means three exciting flavors merging. But it's garlic galore and the roster of spices—cumin, peppercorns, and cloves—that make those chiles truly shine. Use this as a marinade, and your guests won't know why their steaks, lamb chops, or chicken breasts taste so good. Braise meat in it, and the result will be something so complex-tasting and delicious that some of your guests might start raving about your "mole." You don't have to tell them it's really an adobo—or how easy it was to make. If you can't find dried cascabel chiles, substitute 6 dried árbol chiles or 3 chipotle mora chiles, which will give you a different but equally delicious adobo.

MAKES ABOUT 1½ CUPS   **ACTIVE TIME: 20 MINUTES**   **START TO FINISH: 50 MINUTES**

1 ounce cascabel chiles (5), wiped clean and stemmed

1 ounce pasilla chiles (3), wiped clean, stemmed, slit open, seeded, and deveined

¾ ounce guajillo chiles (3), wiped clean, stemmed, slit open, seeded, and deveined

¾ cup water for blending, or more if necessary

8 garlic cloves, peeled

15 whole black peppercorns

8 whole allspice berries

3 whole cloves

1 (½-inch) piece canela (Mexican cinnamon), or ⅛ teaspoon ground cinnamon

1½ teaspoons cumin seeds

¾ teaspoon fine salt, or 1½ teaspoons kosher salt

BREAK each cascabel chile into about 3 pieces for easier toasting, discarding the seeds. Heat a comal, griddle, or heavy skillet over medium-low heat, and toast all the chiles, 2 or 3 at a time, turning them over and pressing down on them with tongs frequently, until fragrant, about 1 minute per batch. Soak the chiles in enough cold water to cover until they're soft, about 30 minutes. Drain and discard the soaking water.

PUT the ¾ cup of fresh water in the blender jar with the chiles and the remaining ingredients, and blend until smooth, at least 3 minutes, adding a little more water if necessary to puree. If you like a silky, smooth texture, strain the adobo through a medium-mesh sieve.

Now you can use this highly flavored puree as a marinade for seafood and meat (page 130). Or turn it into a fabulous cooking liquid (page 136) or sauce for eggs, beans, and enchiladas (page 147).

This adobo keeps in the refrigerator for up to five days or in the freezer for up to one month.

ADOBOS AS MARINADES

ADOBOS AS MARINADES If you're planning to grill, roast, pan sear, or broil tender proteins like pork chops, chicken breasts, fish, or skirt steak, adobo marinades are what you want. Your goal is to make a puree that's the texture of very thick barbecue sauce rather than that of thin, liquidy European-style marinades. It should be so thick that if you tip your blender, it barely pours, instead inching forward like cooling lava. The recipes instruct you to add some water in order to blend it to a smooth, thick puree, and occasionally, you will have to add a little more water than my recipes call for. The key is to add this extra water gradually, starting with a tablespoon, trying to blend, and if you need to, adding another. Doing it incrementally will keep you from making your adobo too loose—from which there's no going back.

Once you've made the puree, marinating is simple: You lightly salt your meat, slather on your adobo, and let it marinate. Then, when you're ready to cook, you put your adobo-slathered meat on a grill or in a hot pan with a bit of oil. I've experimented with adobos on both thick and thin cuts of meat, and I've found that thin cuts take better advantage of the flavorful puree. The high ratio of adobo-seasoned surface area to the luscious but unseasoned center of the meat means more flavor per bite.

ADOBO-MARINATED FISH

PESCADO ADOBADO

What a way to turn a piece of fish into something spectacular! The adobo never overwhelms the fish's flavor—instead, the chile and garlic recede into the background, making the fish taste better than ever. Don't forget to add a squeeze of lime just before you serve it.

SERVES 6   **ACTIVE TIME:** 35 MINUTES (INCLUDES MAKING THE ADOBO)   **START TO FINISH:** 1 HOUR 35 MINUTES (INCLUDES MAKING THE ADOBO)

6 (6-ounce) fish fillets or steaks, such as red snapper, black bass, striped bass, bluefish, or salmon

1 teaspoon fine salt, or 2 teaspoons kosher salt

½ cup Basic Guajillo Adobo (page 124), Basic Ancho Adobo (page 126), or Three-Chile Adobo (page 129)

2 tablespoons mild olive oil or vegetable oil

1 lime, cut into wedges

IF you're using fillets, score the skin in a crosshatch pattern with a sharp knife. Pat the fillets or steaks dry and season them with the salt, then coat both sides with the adobo and let them marinate in the refrigerator for 30 minutes. Meanwhile, preheat the oven to 200°F.

HEAT a large heavy skillet over medium heat, then add 1 tablespoon of oil and cook 2 to 3 pieces of fish, flesh side down, for 2 minutes. Turn the fish over and cook, pressing down on the fish to stop the fillets from curling (the scored skin will help), until just cooked through, 2 to 3 minutes. Transfer the pieces to a baking sheet and keep them warm in the oven while you cook the remaining batches of fish with more oil as necessary.

SQUEEZE the lime over the fish before serving.

Serve it with Corn Tortillas (page 39), Salsa (pages 46–89), rice, beans, or any other side dish you like (pages 246–256).

This dish is best served right away.

Add plenty of adobo paste when you're marinating.

ADOBO-MARINATED SHRIMP
CAMARONES ADOBADOS

Just one bite of these shrimp electrified by chiles and garlic takes my mind to the coastal cities and towns of Mexico. Leaving the shells on keeps the flesh succulent—if I can find them, I love to cook shrimp with the legs and heads attached, too, so I get to eat the crispy legs and suck at the tasty heads—ensuring that this will be one of the best dishes to come off your grill.

SERVES 3 TO 4   ACTIVE TIME: **45 MINUTES (INCLUDES MAKING THE ADOBO)**   START TO FINISH: **1 HOUR 45 MINUTES (INCLUDES MAKING THE ADOBO)**

1 pound large shrimp with shells (about 24)

About 1 teaspoon mild olive oil or vegetable oil

¾ teaspoon fine salt, or 1½ teaspoons kosher salt

½ cup Basic Guajillo Adobo (page 124), Basic Ancho Adobo (page 126), or Three-Chile Adobo (page 129)

1 lime, cut into wedges

BUTTERFLY the shrimp with the shells on by cutting through the shrimp lengthwise with a knife, starting with the flesh between the legs and cutting to (but not through) the shells. Open the shrimp flat and devein them. Alternatively, shell the shrimp and devein them by cutting each one along its back with a knife all the way to the tail, going just far enough into the flesh to access the vein.

LIGHTLY oil a large shallow baking pan, and arrange the shrimp in a single layer on the pan. Pat the shrimp dry and season them with the salt, then coat them with the adobo and arrange them flesh side up (if butterflied). Let them marinate in the refrigerator for 15 to 30 minutes.

PREHEAT the broiler and position the rack 8 inches from the heat source. Broil the shrimp until just cooked through, 5 to 7 minutes.

SQUEEZE the lime over the shrimp before serving.

Serve it with Corn Tortillas (page 39), Salsa (pages 46–89), rice, beans, or any other side dish you'd like (pages 246–256). Or turn it into Tacos (page 212–214).

This dish is best served right away.

ADOBO-MARINATED CHICKEN
POLLO ADOBADO

Never serve a boring chicken dinner again! The adobo infuses its flavor into the meat and gives it a beautiful reddish color. Your guests won't be able to control themselves when you pull this dish from the grill or oven.

SERVES 4   ACTIVE TIME: **30 MINUTES (INCLUDES MAKING THE ADOBO)**   START TO FINISH: **2½ HOURS (INCLUDES MAKING THE ADOBO)**

2 pounds chicken pieces

1 teaspoon fine salt, or 2 teaspoons kosher salt

**½ cup Basic Guajillo Adobo (page 124)
or Basic Ancho Adobo (page 126)**

About 1 tablespoon mild olive oil or vegetable oil

PAT the chicken pieces dry, season them with the salt, then coat them generously with the adobo. Let them marinate in the refrigerator for 1 to 2 hours.

TO GRILL: Heat a charcoal grill, banking the coals on one side. Or for a gas grill, set the burners on one side to high heat and the burners on the other side to medium-low heat. Oil the grill rack and sear the chicken directly over the coals (or over the high-heat burners on the gas grill) for about 3 minutes per side. Move the chicken to the side that's not above the coals (or to the side above the medium-low heat on the gas grill) and cook, covered, until done, 20 to 30 minutes.

TO COOK INDOORS: Preheat the oven to 350°F. Heat a grill pan or heavy skillet over medium-high heat. Lightly oil the grill pan and brown the chicken, about 3 minutes on each side. Transfer the chicken to the oven and cook until done, 20 to 30 minutes.

LET the meat rest for 5 minutes before serving.

Serve it with Corn Tortillas (page 39), Salsa (pages 46–89), rice, beans, or any other side dish you like (pages 246–256). Or turn it into Tacos (pages 212–214) or Quesadillas (page 225).

This dish is best served right away.

GRILLED ADOBO-MARINATED SKIRT STEAK CARNE ADOBADA

This heavenly steak is the kind of treat you'd get in tacos at the little stands in Mexican markets, tucked into warm tortillas and topped with spicy salsa. I love the beefy flavor, the chew, and the low price of skirt steak, but you can use any type of steak you'd like. If it's a thick cut, just sear it in a hot pan, then finish it in an oven preheated to 350°F.

SERVES 4   ACTIVE TIME: 30 MINUTES (INCLUDES MAKING THE ADOBO)   START TO FINISH: 2½ HOURS (INCLUDES MAKING THE ADOBO)

2 pounds skirt steak, cut into four 8- to 9-inch pieces

1 teaspoon fine salt, or 2 teaspoons kosher salt

½ cup Three-Chile Adobo (page 129) or Pasilla-Guajillo Adobo (page 128)

About 1 tablespoon mild olive oil or vegetable oil

PAT the steaks dry, season them with the salt, then coat them generously with adobo. Let them marinate in the refrigerator for 1 to 2 hours.

HEAT a grill or grill pan over medium-high heat. Lightly oil the grill or grill pan and cook the steaks, 3 to 5 minutes on each side for medium-rare, depending on their thickness. Let the steaks rest for 5 minutes before slicing for tacos or serving as whole steaks.

Serve it with Corn Tortillas (page 39), Salsa (pages 46–89), rice, beans, or any other side dish you like (pages 246–256). Or turn it into Tacos (pages 212–214).

This dish is best served right away.

VARIATION: ADOBO-MARINATED CHICKEN PAILLARDS

Flatten four 6-ounce chicken breast halves so they are about ¼ inch thick, sprinkle them with ¾ teaspoon salt, and coat them with Basic Guajillo Adobo (page 124) or Basic Ancho Adobo (page 126). Marinate and grill as you would the steaks, until just cooked through, 2 to 3 minutes per side.

ABOVE: Marinated skirt steak
OPPOSITE: Grilled and sliced

ADOBOS AS COOKING SAUCES

When you want to stew meat like pork shoulder, lamb shank, or any other cut that benefits from slow cooking, the adobos on the next few pages are the ones you're after. More of an everyday dish than moles or pipianes, these adobos result in spoon-tender meat wading in a tasty, slightly soupy sauce. Fairly mild but with a little spark of spice, these cooking sauces have some of the satisfying complexity of those more complicated sauces but take half the effort. These adobos are something you'd dig into along with rice and beans in ultra casual *loncherías* or *comida corrida* restaurants in Mexico.

Once you make the puree, you fry it along with sizzling pieces of browned meat, add water or stock, cover your pot, and let the adobo simmer away until the flavors of those spices and chiles and garlic give up their individuality and become one unified flavor. When it happens you'll notice little pools of oil forming on the surface of the adobo. That means, as we say, *la salsa está sazonada* ("the sauce is seasoned"). Your simple task as the meat transforms from tough to meltingly tender is to make sure the simmer is gentle and to keep the adobo's consistency the texture of thin gravy, adding a little water or stock whenever it threatens to get too thick. Note that adobos tend to splatter as they simmer, which can make a mess of your stove—and your shirt. But fear not: Slightly lower heat, a splatter screen, or even a partially covered pot will let you give your sponge a rest.

Adobos are great the next day, though the heat level will dip slightly. Any meat you've braised in adobo will keep in the refrigerator for several days or in the freezer for a month, so these are phenomenal make-ahead dishes. Any leftovers make great fillings for Tacos (pages 212–214), Enchiladas (pages 216–224), and Tamales (page 227).

I'll serve these adobos with rice and beans, or even mashed potatoes, which will soak up that sauce. Or I'll make a one-pot meal, adding a combination of chayote, green beans, zucchini, potato chunks, and peas to the pot when the meat is almost finished cooking. (Just add a touch more stock if your adobo looks too thick.)

CHICKEN IN ADOBO POLLO EN ADOBO

Since you can refrigerate adobo purees for five days or freeze them for a month, I'm always prepared to stop by the market on the way home, pick up some chicken, and make this tremendously easy and delicious dish.

SERVES 4   **ACTIVE TIME: 35 MINUTES (INCLUDES MAKING THE ADOBO)**   **START TO FINISH: 1³/₄ HOURS (INCLUDES MAKING THE ADOBO)**

2 pounds chicken pieces

1 teaspoon fine salt, or 2 teaspoons kosher salt

2 tablespoons mild olive oil or vegetable oil

1½ cups Basic Guajillo Adobo (page 124)

1½ cups water or chicken stock, plus more if necessary

Sugar and vinegar, if necessary

PAT the chicken dry and season it with the salt. Heat the oil in a 5- to 6-quart heavy pot over medium-high heat and brown the chicken, working in batches to avoid crowding the pot, 6 to 8 minutes per batch. Return all the chicken to the pot and carefully pour the adobo over it. If the adobo was in the blender, swish a little liquid around in the jar and add it to the pot. Simmer, stirring to coat the chicken and fry the sauce, until the sauce thickens slightly, about 5 minutes.

STIR in the water or stock, cover the pot, and simmer gently until the chicken is cooked through, about 40 minutes. Add more water, if necessary, to maintain a silky texture. If you prefer, you can cook the chicken, covered, in an ovenproof pot in a 350°F oven for the same length of time. Season to taste with sugar, vinegar, and additional salt.

Serve it with Corn Tortillas (page 39), rice, beans, or any other side dish you like (pages 246–256). Or turn it into Tacos (pages 212–214), Enchiladas (pages 216–224), or Tamales (page 227).

Chicken in adobo keeps in the refrigerator for up to three days or in the freezer for up to one month.

SWISH!

When your adobo is ready for the pot and you're about to add water or stock, try swishing some of that liquid around in the blender jar. That way, you won't leave behind any adobo that may have clung to it.

PORK IN ADOBO CERDO EN ADOBO

As browned chunks of pork shoulder simmer away in chocolate-brown liquid, they virtually melt into some of the most tender, luscious bites you will ever eat. The sauce becomes equally impressive, even richer and silkier than it was when it first hit the pan. By the time the pork is done, the adobo will have acquired amazing depth of flavor, especially when made with Adobo D.F. Make sure to tinker with the salt, sugar, and vinegar levels to reignite its spark.

SERVES 6   **ACTIVE TIME: 45 MINUTES (INCLUDES MAKING THE ADOBO)**   **START TO FINISH: 2¾ HOURS (INCLUDES MAKING THE ADOBO)**

2 pounds pork shoulder or other pork stewing meat, cut into 1½-inch cubes

½ teaspoon fine salt, or 1 teaspoon kosher salt

2 tablespoons mild olive oil or vegetable oil

1½ cups Adobo D.F. (page 127), Basic Ancho Adobo (page 126), or Basic Guajillo Adobo (page 124)

2 cups water or chicken stock, or more if necessary

Sugar and vinegar, if necessary

PAT the pork dry and season it with the salt. Heat the oil in a 4- to 5-quart heavy pot over medium-high heat. Brown the pork, in two batches if necessary (you want to avoid crowding the pot, though a little crowding is OK in this case), turning occasionally, 8 to 10 minutes per batch.

REDUCE the heat to medium and return all the pork to the pot. Carefully pour the adobo over the pork. If the adobo is in the blender, swish a little liquid around in the jar and add it to the pot. Simmer, stirring to coat the pork and fry the sauce, until the sauce is slightly thicker, about 5 minutes. Add the 2 cups of water or stock and return the sauce to a simmer.

REDUCE the heat to low, cover the pot, and gently simmer the pork, adding a couple of tablespoons of water from time to time to maintain a silky texture (you don't want it to be gloppy), until the pork is fork-tender, 1½ to 2 hours. If you prefer, you can cook the pork, covered, in an ovenproof pot in a 350°F oven for the same length of time. Season to taste with sugar, vinegar, and additional salt.

Serve it with Corn Tortillas (page 39), rice, beans, or any other side dish you like (pages 246–256). Or turn it into Tacos (pages 212–216), Enchiladas (page 216–224), or Tamales (page 227).

Pork in adobo keeps in the refrigerator for up to five days or in the freezer for up to one month.

BEEF IN ADOBO CARNE EN ADOBO

This hearty stew of tender beef, meaty mushrooms, and deep red sauce is a fantastic way to celebrate fall—and to use Basic Guajillo Adobo. You'll notice that the process is almost identical to making pork and chicken in adobo. The lesson again is that once you can make a simple puree, you're ready to make so many wonderful dishes.

SERVES 6   **ACTIVE TIME: 45 MINUTES (INCLUDES MAKING THE ADOBO)**   **START TO FINISH: 3¼ HOURS (INCLUDES MAKING THE ADOBO)**

2 pounds boneless beef chuck, cut into 1½-inch cubes

½ teaspoon fine salt, or 1 teaspoon kosher salt

2 tablespoons mild olive oil or vegetable oil

1½ cups Basic Guajillo Adobo (page 124), Basic Ancho Adobo (page 126), or Three-Chile Adobo (page 129)

2 cups water or chicken stock, or more if necessary

1 teaspoon sugar

½ pound mixed mushrooms, such as shiitake, button, and oyster, trimmed (stems removed from shiitakes) and thickly sliced

1 sprig epazote, optional

Vinegar, if necessary

PAT the beef dry and season it with the salt. Heat the oil in a 4- to 5-quart heavy pot over medium-high heat. Brown the beef, in batches if necessary (you want to avoid crowding the pot), turning occasionally, about 10 minutes per batch.

REDUCE the heat to medium and return all the beef to the pot. Carefully pour the adobo over the beef. If the adobo is in the blender, swish a little liquid around in the jar and add it to the pot. Simmer, stirring to coat the beef and fry the sauce, until the sauce is slightly thicker, about 5 minutes. Add the 2 cups of water or stock and the sugar, and return the sauce to a simmer.

REDUCE the heat to low, cover the pot, and gently simmer the beef, adding a couple of tablespoons of water from time to time to maintain a silky texture (you don't want it to be gloppy), until the beef is fork-tender, about 2 hours. If you prefer, you can cook the beef, covered, in an ovenproof pot in a 350°F oven for the same length of time. About 30 minutes before the beef is finished, stir in the mushrooms and epazote, and continue cooking until the beef is very tender and the mushrooms are cooked through. Season to taste with vinegar and additional salt.

Serve it with Corn Tortillas (page 39), rice, beans, or any other side dish you like (pages 246–256). Or turn it into Tacos (pages 212–214), Enchiladas (pages 216–224), or Tamales (page 227).

Beef in adobo keeps in the refrigerator for up to five days or in the freezer for up to one month.

THE BIG CHILL

Before refrigerating or freezing finished adobos, let them cool at room temperature. If you must refrigerate or freeze them before they've cooled, put them in uncovered, then cover them once they've chilled.

BEEF SHANK IN MULATO ADOBO
CHAMBARETE EN ADOBO DE MULATO

When my partner's aunt Susana Diaz was still with us and I'd visit her at her ranch in Coatepec Harinas, just outside of Mexico City, she'd make this stunning stew with hauntingly sweet mulato chiles. I remember scooping up that deep brown sauce with a spoon and using the same eating implement to cut the tender meat. Making the effort to find beef shin (shank sliced through the bone, which includes some lovely, wobbly marrow) and mulato chiles will pay off big time, but you'll have a great meal even if you substitute cubes of beef chuck and ancho chiles. The leftovers make particularly great tacos.

SERVES 4 TO 6   ACTIVE TIME: 30 MINUTES   START TO FINISH: 4¾ HOURS

2 (½-inch-thick) round slices large white onion

3 ounces mulato chiles (6), wiped clean, stemmed, slit open, seeded, and deveined

3 to 4 cups chicken stock or water, divided

2 garlic cloves, peeled

1 (2½-inch) piece canela (Mexican cinnamon), or ½ teaspoon ground cinnamon

2 whole cloves

1 tablespoon apple cider vinegar, or more to taste

1 tablespoon sugar

1 teaspoon dried oregano, preferably Mexican

2 teaspoons fine salt, or 4 teaspoons kosher salt, divided

4½ pounds beef shin slices (about four 1½-inch-thick slices), or 3½ pounds beef chuck, cut into 2-inch pieces

1 teaspoon freshly ground black pepper

2 tablespoons mild olive oil or vegetable oil

HEAT a comal, griddle, or heavy skillet over medium-low heat. Roast the onion slices, turning once, until they're softened and charred on both sides, 15 to 20 minutes.

MEANWHILE, put the chiles (there's no need to toast them) in a small pot with enough water to cover. Bring the water to a boil, reduce the heat, and simmer the chiles for 8 minutes. Drain them and discard the cooking liquid. Put 2 cups of the chicken stock or fresh water in the blender jar with the drained chiles, roasted onion, garlic cloves, cinnamon, cloves, vinegar, sugar, oregano, and 1 teaspoon of the salt and blend until smooth, at least 3 minutes. If you like a silky texture, strain the adobo through a medium-mesh sieve.

PAT the meat dry and season with the pepper and the remaining 1 teaspoon of salt. Heat the oil in a large braising casserole (about 12 inches wide) set over medium-high heat and brown the slices of meat in one layer, turning once, about 3 minutes on each side. (You may need to do this in 2 batches so as not to crowd the pot, but all the shin slices should fit snugly in one layer once browned. You can use a pot that's not as wide if you're using beef chuck). Pour the mulato adobo over the browned beef slices, then shake the casserole a couple of times to evenly distribute the sauce and meat. Cover, reduce the heat to low, and let the adobo simmer for approximately 4 hours, or until the meat is fork-tender. Add more water, if necessary, to maintain a silky texture. If you prefer, you can cook the beef, covered, in an ovenproof pot in a 350°F oven for the same length of time. Season to taste with additional vinegar, sugar, and salt.

Serve it with Corn Tortillas (page 39), rice, beans, or any other side dish you like (pages 246–256). Or turn it into Tacos (pages 212–214), Enchiladas (pages 216–224), or Tamales (page 227).

Beef Shank in adobo keeps in the refrigerator for up to three days or in the freezer for up to one month.

LAMB SHANKS BRAISED IN PARCHMENT MIXIOTE DE BORREGO

I have fond memories of driving from Mexico City to my family's country house and getting uncontrollably hungry whenever we came to a certain group of ladies selling *mixiotes*. The word originally meant the thin-as-parchment skin of the maguey plant (a colossal succulent that you see just about everywhere in Mexico), but came to refer to the delicious meats braised inside maguey-skin packages. Today, the use of the skins has been banned after its popularity threatened the survival of the maguey plant, but cooks substitute parchment paper for the mixiote. My dear friend Josephina Howard turned me on to the concept of using whole lamb shanks instead of the small pieces of meat you'd find in Mexico. The result is fantastic, makes a stunning presentation, and still takes me back to those country roads. Use any leftovers from the lamb shanks to make Lamb Adobo Enchiladas with Cooked Green Salsa (page 220).

SERVES 4 GENEROUSLY   ACTIVE TIME: 1 HOUR (INCLUDES MAKING THE ADOBO)   START TO FINISH: 4 HOURS (INCLUDES MAKING THE ADOBO)

8 avocado leaves, either fresh or dried

4 (14- to 16-ounce) lamb shanks

1 teaspoon fine salt, or 2 teaspoons kosher salt

2 cups Pasilla-Guajillo Adobo (page 128)

8 (15 × 30-inch) pieces parchment paper

4 cotton strings

HEAT a comal, griddle, or heavy skillet over medium-low heat, and toast the avocado leaves, a few at a time, turning frequently with tongs, until lightly browned and fragrant, 1 to 2 minutes.

PAT the lamb dry and season it with the salt.

ARRANGE two pieces of parchment on top of each other so that they form a cross. Holding the bone with one hand, stand a lamb shank in the middle, pour ½ cup of adobo over the meaty part (keep the bone clean), and rest 2 whole avocado leaves against the shank. Gather the parchment up around the bone with the other hand, then tie the top with string to close the parchment around the bone. Repeat with the remaining lamb shanks, adobo sauce, and avocado leaves.

BRING about 1 inch of water to a boil in the bottom of a deep steamer pot (a pasta pot with a deep steamer insert works well) and arrange the lamb packages, standing up, in the deep steamer basket. Cover and steam over the boiling water, adding more boiling water as necessary, until the lamb is so tender that it's falling off the bone, 2½ to 3 hours. Because you're steaming for such a long time, use this trick to tell when you need to add more water: Put a clean coin in the boiling water. As long as there's water left, you'll hear the coin jiggle. If it stops, it's time to add more water.

SERVE the lamb shanks in the packages and let your guests open them, or open them yourself and serve them in large bowls.

Serve it with Corn Tortillas (page 39), rice, beans, or any other side dish you like (pages 246–256). Or turn it into Tacos (pages 212–214), Enchiladas (pages 216–224), or Tamales (page 227).

You can prepare the packages a day ahead and keep them in the refrigerator until you're ready to cook them. Cooked lamb shanks in adobo keep in the refrigerator for up to three days or in the freezer for up to one month.

RIBS FROM LA HUASTECA VERACRUZANA

ADOBO DE LA HUASTECA VERACRUZANA

I have my friend Ricardo Muñoz Zurita, an author and the owner of Café Azul y Oro in Mexico City, to thank for this gorgeous adobo that almost crosses the line into mole territory. It's a glimpse into the Huasteca region in Veracruz, featuring two chiles and, unlike most adobos, roasted garlic, onion, and tomatoes. As it bubbles away, bobbing with meaty ribs, whip up rice and beans and you'll have a meal you won't soon forget.

SERVES 6 TO 8   **ACTIVE TIME: 1¾ HOURS**   **START TO FINISH: 3¼ HOURS**

FOR THE MEAT
4 quarts water

4½ pounds country-style pork ribs

1 small white onion, quartered

8 garlic cloves, peeled and halved

2 teaspoons fine salt, or 4 teaspoons kosher salt

FOR THE SAUCE
6 ounces guajillo chiles (24), wiped clean, stemmed, slit open, seeded, and deveined

1 ounce ancho chiles (2), wiped clean, stemmed, slit open, seeded, and deveined

3 (½-inch-thick) round slices white onion

15 large garlic cloves, peeled

1½ pounds tomatoes (about 4 medium-large)

2 teaspoons cumin seeds

1 teaspoon dried oregano, preferably Mexican

½ teaspoon whole black peppercorns

4 whole cloves

1 teaspoon fine salt, or 2 teaspoons kosher salt

3 tablespoons pork lard, mild olive oil, or vegetable oil

½ cup distilled white vinegar

COOK THE RIBS

PUT the water, ribs, onion, garlic, and salt in a large (8- to 10-quart) heavy pot, and bring the water to a simmer. Skim the surface, as necessary, and simmer, uncovered, until the meat is tender, about 1½ hours. Transfer the ribs to a plate, then strain the broth into a bowl (discarding the onion and garlic), and set both aside.

PREPARE THE SAUCE

MEANWHILE, heat a comal, griddle, or heavy skillet over medium-low heat, and toast the chiles 2 or 3 at a time, turning them over and pressing down on them with tongs frequently, until they're fragrant, 1 to 1½ minutes total per batch. Soak the chiles in enough cold water to cover until they're soft, about 30 minutes. Drain and discard the soaking water.

ROAST the onion and garlic on the comal, turning the garlic frequently, until the garlic is just tender and golden brown with some blackened spots, 8 to 10 minutes, and carefully turning the onion rounds once, until they're softened and charred on both sides, 15 to 25 minutes.

SET the oven to broil and preheat. Alternatively, you can preheat the oven to 500°F. If you're using the oven broiler, position the rack 8 inches from the heat source. Core the tomatoes and cut a small "X" through the skin on the opposite ends. Put the tomatoes, cored sides up, on a shallow baking pan and roast them, without turning, until they're blackened on their tops and cooked to the core, 20 to 30 minutes.

SLIP the skins from the tomatoes, then put the tomatoes in the blender jar with the onion, garlic, cumin, oregano, peppercorns, cloves, and salt and blend until smooth, at least

3 minutes. Be careful when you're blending hot ingredients: Cover the top with a kitchen towel, and hold the top firmly in place with your hand. Work in batches to avoid blending with a full jar. Transfer the puree to a bowl.

BLEND the drained chiles in the same blender jar with just enough water (about 2 cups) to make a thick puree.

PREHEAT the oven to 350°F.

CLEAN and dry the pot the pork ribs were cooked in and heat the lard or oil in the pot over medium-low heat until it shimmers. Add the chile puree and simmer, stirring frequently, until it thickens to a paste, about 15 minutes. Add the other puree and bring to a boil. Reduce the heat and simmer for 5 minutes, stirring. Then stir in the vinegar and

just enough reserved broth (2 to 3 cups) to achieve a silky (not gloppy) texture; reserve the remaining broth for another use. Return the pork ribs to the pot in one layer and bring the liquid to a simmer. Cover and simmer gently until the meat is fork-tender, about 1 hour. If you prefer, you may put the pot in a 350°F oven to braise for the same length of time. Season to taste with additional salt and vinegar.

Serve it with Corn Tortillas (page 39), rice, beans, or any other side dish you like (pages 246–256).

You can cook the pork ribs and the purees and keep them in the refrigerator a day or two before you assemble the dish. The finished dish keeps in the refrigerator for up to three days.

Guajillo chiles

BRAISED SHORT RIBS IN ADOBO
COSTILLAS DE RES EN ADOBO

If you've ever braised short ribs, you know how unbelievably luscious the meat becomes and how impressive the ribs are to bring to the table. This adobo takes them to the next level, matching their supremely beefy flavor with the deep flavor of anchos and chipotles. The method is a little different from the typical adobo in that the blending happens after the meat is cooked with the chiles and garlic.

SERVES 8   ACTIVE TIME: 45 MINUTES   START TO FINISH: 3¾ HOURS

2 ounces ancho chiles (4), wiped clean, stemmed, slit open, seeded, and deveined

6 pounds bone-in beef short ribs

2 tablespoons dried oregano, preferably Mexican

2 teaspoons fine salt, or 4 teaspoons kosher salt

1 teaspoon whole black peppercorns

½ teaspoon ground cumin

3 celery stalks, sliced

2 carrots, peeled and sliced

1 large white onion, halved lengthwise and sliced

1½ heads garlic, cloves separated and peeled (½ cup)

½ ounce chipotle mora chiles (4 or 5, purplish-red color), wiped clean and stemmed

8 bay leaves

2 cups water

PREHEAT the oven to 350°F.

HEAT a comal, griddle, or heavy skillet over medium-low heat, and toast the ancho chiles 2 at a time, turning them over and pressing down on them with tongs frequently, until they're fragrant and have developed light-colored brown blisters, 1½ minutes per batch. Tear the chiles into large pieces.

IN a very large bowl, toss the short ribs with the oregano, salt, peppercorns, and cumin to season evenly.

SCATTER the celery, carrots, onions, and garlic on a large roasting pan to create a bed. Arrange the short ribs on top (it's fine if you can't do it in one layer), then tuck the toasted torn ancho chiles, chipotle chiles, and bay leaves among the ribs. Add the water to the pan and cover tightly with 2 layers of foil. Bake the short ribs until the meat is fork-tender, about 3 hours.

REMOVE the bones and the bay leaves with tongs, then transfer the meat to a bowl. Pour the contents of the pan through a large sieve set over another bowl, reserving both the broth and the solids. Spoon off any fat that has risen to the surface of the broth, then put the broth in the blender jar with the solids and blend them together until smooth, 2 to 3 minutes. Be careful when you're blending hot ingredients: Cover the top with a kitchen towel, and hold the top firmly in place with your hand. Work in batches to avoid blending with a full jar. Season the sauce to taste with additional salt, then pour the sauce over the meat. Reheat in the oven, if necessary.

Serve it with Corn Tortillas (page 39), rice, beans, or any other side dish you like (pages 246–256). Or turn it into Tacos (pages 212–214), Enchiladas (pages 216–224), or Tamales (page 227).

The adobo keeps in the refrigerator for up to three days.

ADOBO-BRAISED LAMB
BARBACOA DE BORREGO

Barbacoa is in the pantheon of Mexican meats, right next to Carnitas (page 240). Traditionally, massive hunks of lamb or goat, even whole animals, get wrapped in banana leaves or maguey leaves and cooked underground until the meat is ultra tender. In the northern regions of Mexico, some cooks make lamb in this style, but they add a fantastic chile paste to the meat before they cook it and call it birria. This recipe merges the two dishes—no outdoor cooking pit required. The result is one of the most amazing taco or enchilada fillers you can imagine. Serve it with Jalisco-Style Guajillo Salsa (page 77).

SERVES 6 TO 8   ACTIVE TIME: 30 MINUTES   START TO FINISH: 4 HOURS

or stock

1 ounce guajillo chiles (4), wiped clean, stemmed, slit open, seeded, and deveined

4 dried árbol chiles, wiped clean and stemmed

½ cup water or chicken stock

2 tablespoons apple cider vinegar, or more to taste

5 large garlic cloves, peeled

2 teaspoons finely grated peeled fresh ginger

1 teaspoon cumin seeds

1 teaspoon dried oregano, preferably Mexican

1 teaspoon fine salt, or 2 teaspoons kosher salt

4 whole cloves

1 (2½-pound) piece boneless lamb leg or shoulder roast, or 1 (3-pound) piece including bone

---

PREHEAT the oven to 350°F.

HEAT a comal, griddle, or heavy skillet over medium-low heat. Toast the guajillo and árbol chiles, turning them over and pressing down on them with tongs frequently, until the guajillos are fragrant and the insides have changed color slightly, about 1 minute, and the árbol chiles are browned all over with some blackened spots, 3 to 4 minutes. Soak the chiles in enough cold water to cover until they're soft, about 30 minutes. Drain and discard the soaking water.

PUT the chiles in the blender jar along with the ½ cup of fresh water or stock, vinegar, garlic, ginger, cumin, oregano, salt, and cloves and blend until smooth, at least 3 minutes.

PUT the lamb in a deep casserole just large enough to hold it and rub the adobo thickly on all sides, pouring any remaining adobo over the lamb. Cover the casserole tightly with a lid or a double layer of heavy-duty foil and cook in the oven until the meat is fork-tender, 2 to 3 hours.

LET the lamb cool slightly, then shred the meat with two forks and return it to the sauce (discard any bones). If you're not using it right away, you can cool the lamb completely, then shred it with your fingers. Season to taste with additional vinegar and salt.

Serve it with Corn Tortillas (page 39), rice, beans, or any other side dish you like (pages 246–256). Or turn it into Tacos (pages 212–214), Enchiladas (pages 216–224), or Tamales (page 227).

The finished lamb keeps in the refrigerator for up to three days or in the freezer for up to one month.

ADOBOS AS FINISHING SAUCES Once you've made the adobo puree, you're
a few easy steps away from a silky, aromatic sauce that you can use to make Enchiladas (see page 216–224) and Chilaquiles (page 231), or pour over beans, eggs, or anything you can think of. Just like the puree from which it's made, the sauce freezes successfully, so don't worry if you make more than you need for tonight's dinner. The process is the same for any adobo, but the serving possibilities are endless.

ADOBO SAUCE

MAKES 2½ TO 3 CUPS   **ACTIVE TIME: 10 MINUTES (DOES NOT INCLUDE MAKING THE ADOBO)**
START TO FINISH: 50 MINUTES (DOES NOT INCLUDE MAKING THE ADOBO)

2 tablespoons mild olive oil or vegetable oil

1½ cups adobo, such as Basic Guajillo Adobo (page 124), Basic Ancho Adobo (page 126), or Adobo D.F. (page 127)

About 2½ cups water

Salt, sugar, and vinegar to taste

HEAT the oil in a 3- to 4-quart heavy saucepan over medium heat until it shimmers. Carefully pour in the adobo (it may splatter) and cook, stirring frequently, until it thickens slightly, about 5 minutes.

ADD 2 cups of the water and return the sauce to a simmer. Partially cover the saucepan to prevent splattering. Cook the sauce for 35 to 45 minutes more. Add a couple of tablespoons of water from time to time, if necessary, to maintain a silky texture (you don't want it to be gloppy). When the sauce is nearly ready, you'll see little pools of oil forming on the surface. Season to taste with salt, sugar, and vinegar.

Spoon it over fried eggs, grilled meat, or Enchiladas (pages 216–224).

Adobo sauce keeps in the refrigerator for up to five days or in the freezer for up to one month.

MEXICO'S ICONIC SAUCES

MOLES HAVE BECOME SYNONYMOUS WITH TIME-CONSUMING, COMPLICATED COOKING. IT'S EASY TO SEE WHY. THE BEST-KNOWN VERSION IN THE UNITED STATES. IS MOLE POBLANO, A WONDERFUL DEEP BROWN SAUCE THAT CAN TAKE HOURS OF EFFORT AND 22 INGREDIENTS, INCLUDING, FAMOUSLY, A LITTLE CHOCOLATE. NO WONDER THE NOTION OF MAKING MOLE AT HOME SEEMS AS ABSURD AS RESURFACING YOUR OWN KITCHEN COUNTERS. BUT I'LL LET YOU IN ON A WELL-KNOWN SECRET IN MEXICO: WHILE SOME HOME COOKS DO MAKE MOLE POBLANO AND A FEW OF THE OTHER COMPLICATED MOLES FOR CELEBRATIONS, OFTEN WITH HELP FROM FAMILY MEMBERS, THE REST OF THE WIDE RANGE OF UNBELIEVABLY DELICIOUS MOLES ARE NOT DIFFICULT AT ALL.

Most likely derived from the ancient Nahuatl word *molli*—which means, essentially, "a bunch of ingredients ground up"—mole is simply a mixture of ingredients that typically includes some combination of chiles, spices or herbs, tomatoes or tomatillos, and sometimes seeds (sesame, pumpkin, or, in rare cases, melon) or nuts (almonds, peanuts, or hazelnuts). If these mixtures are made mostly with nuts or seeds, they're technically called pipianes (or pepianes), though as I explain below, I've merged this category with moles because their preparations are so similar and isolating them exaggerates their differences rather than encouraging home cooks to make them all.

Moles and pipianes are served in the fanciest restaurants; in the humblest comidas corridas, where four-course meals cost just a few pesos; and of course, in millions of homes. They can be brothy or soupy or thick, and their color can range from deep red to vibrant green to midnight black. They are made throughout Mexico, from the mountains of Puebla and the central high plains to the northern deserts down to the villages of Oaxaca and to the sunny seaside states of Veracruz and Jalisco. You even see pipián-like dishes (called *sikil-pac,* in the Mayan language) in the Yucatán, where the food is so different from the rest of Mexico's that you'd think it were from another country.

Yet my fear is that emphasizing this dramatic regional diversity has overwhelmed American cooks rather than exciting them with options. So instead of organizing this vast array of dishes by location, I have first broken it into three major categories— thin moles, thick moles, and pipianes—and then further by color or, in the case of pipianes, by main ingredient. Not only will my groupings guide you to recipes based on what you have in your refrigerator or what you crave, but they will also help ease you into these sauces, because those of the same color or texture share certain ingredients and techniques—green moles tend to feature fresh green chiles, while red ones tend to get their color from anchos and guajillos. That way, cooking just one mole will put you on a path to mastering many more.

PREVIOUS PAGES *148–149, CLOCKWISE FROM TOP LEFT: Green Mole from Oaxaca, Mole Amarillo from Oaxaca, White Almond Sauce, Pistachio Sauce, Mole Poblano, Soupy Red Mole*

What's fascinating about moles is that all of their ingredients combine in such a way that they give up their individual identities and create one entirely new flavor. And most important for the home cook, making them can be as simple as blending chiles, peanuts, and garlic, or chiles, onion, garlic, and herbs. Whatever the case, they require no esoteric skills or equipment—a sturdy blender and a heavy saucepan will get you through most of the recipes—and many take only a bit more effort than salsas and adobos.

In fact, the line between adobos and certain simple moles is a thin one indeed. As long as you follow my instructions for toasting, roasting, and frying the ingredients, then all you have to do is puree these ingredients in your blender, cook the result (either by frying the mixture in a little oil before thinning it with water or stock or by adding it directly to simmering liquid), and bask in the praise that comes with serving your friends a plate of something they thought they'd have to travel well south of the border to find.

In some of the recipes, I'll ask you to fry ingredients in oil, a technique common to moles that might seem intimidating at first. But you'll quickly get the hang of it. All you have to do is set a metal sieve over a small heatproof bowl. Then you'll fry the ingredients one by one, pouring them into the sieve as they finish frying and returning the oil to the pan. And as long as you follow my instructions, you won't have to change the oil.

As you'll learn, there are no hard-and-fast rules to moles and pipianes. For centuries, cooks have been creating these sauces using infinite combinations of ingredients from markets and gardens. I'm not going to give you recipes for every mole from every region, but rather a carefully chosen selection, from the time-tested to the remarkably modern, that will get you comfortable with the ways all moles and pipianes are made.

TIPS FOR MOLES AND PIPIANES

DON'T WASTE A DROP: Like adobos, moles and pipianes begin with a puree of chiles and other ingredients. Once you've poured the puree into the pot and my recipes tell you to add water or stock, try swishing some of that liquid around in the blender jar. That way, you won't leave behind any mole that may have clung to it.

REDUCING SPLATTER: Because making many moles and pipianes requires you to fry and simmer blended mixtures of chiles, nuts, and spices, I recommend buying a splatter screen, which is an inexpensive way to keep your stove (and shirt) clean while you're cooking. Alternatives include using a particularly deep pot (one advantage of the traditional cazuela), partially covering the pot, or reducing the heat slightly when the sauce begins to splatter.

NUTTY GARNISH: If you have any extra of the nuts or seeds you used to make a thick mole, chop them and sprinkle them on top of your finished dish.

COOL DOWN: Before refrigerating or freezing moles, let them cool, uncovered, at room temperature. If you must refrigerate or freeze moles before they've cooled, refrigerate them, uncovered, then cover them once they've chilled.

HOW TO SERVE MOLES AND PIPIANES

Some of the sauces that follow go so well with a certain meat or fish that I've included that protein in the recipe, but you can serve many of these moles with whatever meat or vegetables you'd like. Of course, I've given you some suggestions and provided basic recipes for Poached Chicken (page 242) and Cooked Pork (page 243), which also yield stock that you can use to make the sauce. The traditional accompaniments are Corn Tortillas (page 39), Mexican White Rice (page 251), and beans, like my Chipotle-Avocado Leaf Black Beans (page 249)—but anything works as long as it helps you soak up the delicious sauce. Leftovers make a very tasty filling for Tacos (pages 212–214) and thick moles and pipianes can be used for Enchiladas (pages 216–224).

THIN MOLES

This category of moles is made from a mixture of ingredients that typically does not include seeds, and if it does, not enough to thicken the sauce beyond a soupy consistency. In general, they're less elaborate than thicker moles, and in comparison, the flavors of spices tend to keep a low profile.

THIN RED MOLES

Perhaps the most common kind of thin mole and a staple of everyday cooking in Mexico, this family of thin moles—often called *moles de olla* (or "moles in a pot"), or occasionally *clemoles* or *tlemoles*—reveal themselves as a single dish taken in many directions. The color always comes from dried chiles, like anchos, guajillos, and pasillas, but the combination a particular cook uses depends on what he has on hand or what result he aims for. That's why I've only included one recipe. These moles beg for an herbaceous note, so I often use epazote or cilantro, while my grandmother always used a little bundle of mint, parsley, and cilantro. It's really up to you. Whatever the cook chooses, on restaurant and home tables, bowls of *moles de olla* bring ruddy broths packed with tender beef and vegetables like corn and chayote. Lime wedges are almost always served alongside for you to squeeze into the mole before the slurping begins.

SOUPY RED MOLE "IN A POT" WITH BEEF MOLE DE OLLA

This homey, Central Mexican mole requires no frying and no endless list of ingredients, which makes it the kind of dish you'll find in just about any *fonda* or busy mom's kitchen. The brothy, murky mole bobbing with meat and vegetables, like corn and chayote, gets its flavor from a simple chile and garlic paste that's dissolved in the liquid you used to cook your beef, and it's served with warm tortillas, chopped white onion, cilantro, and lime on the side. Plenty of lime juice is essential, especially if you don't use xoconostles, which can be hard to find. Keep in mind that the combination of ancho and pasilla chiles is just one of many possibilities, a general blueprint that you can build on.

MAKES 8 SERVINGS   **ACTIVE TIME: 45 MINUTES**   **START TO FINISH: 2 HOURS**

4½ pounds beef shank (or shin) slices (four to six 1- to 1½-inch-thick slices), or 4½ pounds stewing beef with some bones

8 cups water, or more to cover

1½ teaspoons fine salt, or 1 tablespoon kosher salt, divided

4 medium xoconostles (tart prickly pears), peeled (see note) and cut into ¼-inch-thick slices (optional)

1½ ounces ancho chiles (3), wiped clean, stemmed, slit open, seeded, and deveined

⅔ ounce pasilla chiles (2), wiped clean, stemmed, slit open, seeded, and deveined

2 (½-inch-thick) round slices white onion

5 garlic cloves, peeled

1 pound tomatoes (about 3 medium)

5 large sprigs fresh epazote

1 large chayote (about 10 ounces), peeled, quartered lengthwise, and cut crosswise into ½-inch-thick slices

2 ears corn, cut crosswise into 2- to 3-inch-thick rounds

1 pound zucchini, halved lengthwise and cut crosswise into ½-inch-thick slices

¼ pound green beans, trimmed and cut into 1-inch lengths

GARNISH
Finely chopped white onion

Chopped cilantro

Lime wedges

IF you're using beef shanks, cut the beef off the bone and into 1½-inch pieces and put them in a 6- to 7-quart heavy pot along with the bones, water, 1 teaspoon of the salt, and the xoconostles, if you're using them. Bring the water to a simmer over high heat, skimming the surface as necessary. Reduce the heat, then cover and simmer for 1 hour. (You'll cook the beef more when you add the sauce.)

MEANWHILE, prepare the sauce: Heat a comal, griddle, or heavy skillet over medium-low heat, and toast the chiles 2 or 3 at a time, turning them over and pressing them down with tongs until they're fragrant and the insides have changed color slightly, 1 to 1½ minutes per batch. Soak the chiles in enough cold water to cover until they're softened, about 30 minutes. Drain and discard the soaking water.

ROAST the onion slices and garlic on the comal, turning the garlic over once or twice, until it's just tender and golden brown with some blackened spots, 8 to 10 minutes; and carefully turning the onion slices over once, until they're softened and charred on both sides, 15 to 20 minutes.

SET the oven or toaster oven to broil and preheat. Alternatively, you can preheat the oven to 500°F. If you're using the oven broiler, position the rack 8 inches from the heat source. Core the tomatoes and cut a small "X" through the skin on the opposite ends. Put the tomatoes, cored sides up, on a foil-lined baking pan, and roast them (without turning them) until they're blackened on the tops and cooked to the core, 20 to 30 minutes.

SLIP the skins from the tomatoes, then put the tomatoes in the blender jar along with the onion, garlic, chiles, ½ teaspoon of the salt, and ½ cup of the broth from the simmered beef. Blend the mixture until it's smooth, about 3 minutes. Be careful when you're blending hot ingredients: Cover the top with a kitchen towel, and hold the top firmly in place with your hand. Work in batches to avoid blending with a full jar.

POUR the sauce into the pot with the beef and add the epazote sprigs. Swish a little liquid around in the blender and add it to the pot. Continue to simmer, covered, until the beef is fork-tender, about 30 minutes. Add the chayote to the pot and cook, covered, for 10 minutes. Add the corn, zucchini, and green beans to the pot and cook, covered, until the vegetables are tender, about 10 minutes more. Remove the epazote sprigs and season the mole to taste with additional salt.

Serve the mole in large soup bowls with plenty of broth. Sprinkle each serving with chopped onion and cilantro and pass lime wedges for guests to squeeze into their bowls.

This mole keeps in the refrigerator for up to three days or in the freezer for up to a month.

NOTE: To peel xoconostles, slice off both ends of the fruit. Make one lengthwise cut through the thick skin (but not into the flesh). Using your fingers, grab the skin of one side of the lengthwise cut and pull, turning the fruit with your other hand. The skin should pull off in one piece.

Mole de olla with the requisite garnishes.

THIN GREEN MOLES To make these striking moles, cooks employ some combination of green chiles (like serranos, jalapeños, chilacas, and poblanos), herbs (like cilantro, epazote, and hoja santa), tomatillos, lettuces, and many other edible greens. This all adds up to a sauce with a sharper spiciness compared with the warm heat of moles de olla, a touch of acidity, and a pungency from those herbs.

GREEN MOLE FROM OAXACA

MOLE VERDE OAXAQUEÑO

This is one of Oaxaca's best known moles and the epitome of Mexican soul food: A simple broth, some pork and vegetables, made into something fantastic thanks to a puree of pungent herbs like *hoja santa* and epazote. Your first bite of this bright green mole delivers a fresh hit of herbaceous flavor, a little lovely tartness from the tomatillos, and the sneaky heat of fresh chiles. This is my favorite version, adapted from the author (and my dear friend) Marilyn Tausend.

MAKES 6 SERVINGS　　**ACTIVE TIME: 1 HOUR**　　**START TO FINISH: 2¼ HOURS**

FOR THE PORK

2½ pounds pork shoulder, cut into 1½-inch pieces, or 3 pounds meaty country-style pork ribs, or a combination of both

8 cups water

1 medium white onion, quartered

2 large garlic cloves, peeled and roughly chopped

1 teaspoon fine salt, or 2 teaspoons kosher salt

1 small chayote (6 ounces), peeled, quartered lengthwise, and cut crosswise into ½-inch-thick slices

¼ pound green beans, trimmed and cut into 1-inch lengths

2 cups cooked white or navy beans, or 1 (19-ounce) can, drained and rinsed

FOR THE MOLE

½ pound tomatillos (5 or 6), husked, rinsed, and roughly chopped

3 large romaine lettuce leaves, torn into pieces

1 packed cup chopped cilantro

1 packed cup coarsely chopped flat-leaf parsley

1 medium white onion, coarsely chopped

⅓ cup coarsely chopped hoja santa (holy leaf), stems discarded

3 fresh serrano or jalapeño chiles, coarsely chopped, including seeds

2 garlic cloves, peeled

2 tablespoons corn tortilla flour (masa harina)

1 tablespoon dried oregano, preferably Mexican

2 sprigs fresh epazote, coarse bottom stem removed

1 teaspoon fine salt, or 2 teaspoons kosher salt

½ teaspoon freshly ground black pepper

Pinch of ground clove

Pinch (or more) of grated piloncillo (see note) or light brown sugar, if necessary

2 tablespoons mild olive oil or vegetable oil

COOK THE PORK

PUT the pork in a 5- to 6-quart heavy pot with the water, along with the onion, garlic, and salt. Bring the water to a simmer over high heat, skimming the surface as necessary.

Reduce the heat, then cover and simmer until the meat is fork-tender, about 1½ hours. Discard the onion, then add the chayote and cook, covered, for 10 minutes. Add the green beans and navy beans and cook, partially covered, until the green beans are tender, about 5 minutes.

PREPARE THE MOLE

WORKING in 2 batches, if necessary, put the tomatillos, lettuce, cilantro, parsley, onion, hoja santa, chiles, garlic, tortilla flour, oregano, epazote, salt, pepper, ground clove, and 2 cups of the broth from the pork into the blender jar. Puree the mixture until it's smooth, about 3 minutes per batch. Add a pinch or more of the piloncillo if the mole tastes too tart.

HEAT the oil in a 3- to 4-quart heavy pot over medium heat until it shimmers. Carefully add the mole and simmer,

stirring frequently, until it has thickened slightly, about 10 minutes. As it's simmering, swish a little liquid around in the blender and add it to the pot.

POUR the mole into the pot with the pork and vegetables, and simmer together for 10 minutes. Season the mole to taste with additional salt.

Serve it with Corn Tortillas (page 39), rice, beans, or any other side you like (pages 246–256).

This mole is best eaten the day it's made.

NOTE: Piloncillo is a type of Mexican raw sugar that has a lovely molasses-like flavor and comes in a pestle-shape block. It is available at Mexican grocery stores or by mail order (see Sources, page 258).

RED SNAPPER PAPILLOTES IN GREEN MOLE HUACHINANGO EN MOLE VERDE

Inside packets of parchment paper, a fresh, vibrant—and best of all, simple—mole cooks fillets of red snapper, leaving them so flavorful and lovely.

MAKES 6 SERVINGS   ACTIVE TIME: **35 MINUTES**   START TO FINISH: **45 MINUTES**

FOR THE MOLE

½ pound tomatillos (5 or 6), husked, rinsed, and roughly chopped

1 cup water

2 packed cups chopped cilantro

1 packed cup chopped flat-leaf parsley

4 large mint sprigs, leaves only

¼ cup finely chopped white onion

3 fresh jalapeño or serrano chiles, coarsely chopped, including seeds

3 large garlic cloves, peeled

1 teaspoon fine salt, or 2 teaspoons kosher salt

½ teaspoon aniseed

½ teaspoon coriander seeds

½ teaspoon cumin seeds

FOR THE FISH

6 (5- to 6-ounce) red snapper fillets, with or without skin (see note)

About 1 teaspoon fine salt, or 2 teaspoons kosher salt

About 2 tablespoons mild olive oil or vegetable oil

6 (12 × 15-inch) pieces parchment paper or foil

PREHEAT the oven to 500°F and position the racks in the upper and lower thirds of the oven. Put a large baking sheet on each rack to heat in the oven.

MAKE THE MOLE

COMBINE all the mole ingredients in the blender jar and blend until very smooth, about 3 minutes.

PREPARE THE FISH

SEASON the fish with the salt and rub or brush it with the oil.

WORKING with one sheet of parchment paper at a time, fold the sheet in half to make a 12 × 7½-inch rectangle, creasing the edge, then unfold the paper. Spoon about 1 tablespoon of the mole on the bottom half of the sheet, top with a fillet, then top the fillet with about ⅓ cup of mole.

FOLD the top half of the sheet over the fillet. Starting at one corner of the crease, fold the edges of the sheet over, forming small triangular folds and following a semicircular path around the fillet (each fold should overlap the previous one), smoothing out the folds as you go and tucking the last fold under, until the fish is completely enclosed and the papillote is completely sealed. Repeat the procedure with the remaining fillets. Alternatively, you can put the fish and mole in simpler rectangular packages, making sure to leave a little room between the fish and the top of the package.

PUT the papillotes on the hot baking sheets, and bake until the packages are puffed and trembling, about 10 minutes. Open one package to check that the fish is done, then close again and serve the papillotes for guests to open themselves.

Serve it with Corn Tortillas (page 39), rice, beans, or any other side you like (pages 246–256).

This mole is best eaten the day it is made. You can make the packages and chill them on trays in the refrigerator up to four hours before you bake them. If you do this, use foil rather than parchment paper, which may become too wet and tear.

NOTE: You can substitute 2 pounds peeled large shrimp for the red snapper.

THIN YELLOW MOLES

These moles are not as widely made as thin green and red moles, but they are just as tasty. In some cases, their color comes from a yellow chile, like the famous mole amarillo from Oaxaca, or another ingredient, like the root called *azafranillo* (turmeric, in English) that gives a mole from the state of Querétaro its golden hue. But more often, it comes from the combination of a reddish ingredient, like guajillos, and a green one, like hoja santa, that's diluted with stock and cooked.

OAXACAN YELLOW MOLE
MOLE AMARILLO DE OAXACA

This mole is really special, and eating it is one of my first orders of business when I'm in Oaxaca. I adore the soupy yellowish broth, sometimes bobbing with little masa dumplings called *chochoyotes* (actually they're called many things, including *chochoyones* and *orejitas*) or hearty vegetables, and almost always containing some tasty meat. The unique flavor of this mole comes from a combination of pungent herbs, like hoja santa and epazote, and the local chile chilhuacle (either yellow or red ones), which looks like a cross between the rattle-shaped chile cascabel and a bell pepper. This chile doesn't often wind up in the United States, but even in Oaxaca, where the chile can be quite pricey, cooks will use guajillos instead. You can, too. The mole's velvety texture and background of acidity come from tomatillos and just a bit of fresh masa to thicken the sauce slightly. Of course, you can also use dried masa or even a cooked tortilla blended with the rest of the ingredients.

SERVES 8 TO 10　　**ACTIVE TIME: 1 HOUR**　　**START TO FINISH: 2 HOURS**

FOR THE BEEF

4 pounds stewing beef, such as shin or chuck, cut into 1½-inch pieces

8 cups water

1 medium white onion, coarsely chopped

4 garlic cloves, peeled

1 bay leaf

2 teaspoons dried oregano, preferably Mexican

1 teaspoon fine salt, or 2 teaspoons kosher salt

FOR THE MOLE

1 ounce ancho chiles (2), wiped clean, stemmed, slit open, seeded, and deveined

1 ounce dried chilhuacles amarillos or guajillo chiles (4), wiped clean, stemmed, slit open, seeded, and deveined

½ pound tomatoes (about 2 small)

½ pound tomatillos (5 or 6), husked and rinsed

6 garlic cloves, peeled

2 whole cloves

5 whole black peppercorns

½ teaspoon cumin seeds

½ teaspoon fine salt, or 1 teaspoon kosher salt

2 large fresh *hojas santa* (holy leaves), stems discarded, or 4 toasted avocado leaves

2 tablespoons mild olive oil or vegetable oil

FOR THE VEGETABLES

1 large chayote, peeled, quartered lengthwise, and cut crosswise into ½-inch-thick slices

1 large zucchini, halved lengthwise and cut crosswise into ½-inch-thick slices

6 ounces green beans, trimmed and cut into 1½-inch lengths

FOR THE CHOCHOYOTES (MASA DUMPLINGS)

1 cup corn tortilla flour (masa harina)

¾ cup warm water

3 tablespoons lard, mild olive oil, or vegetable oil

½ teaspoon fine salt, or 1 teaspoon kosher salt

GARNISH

Chopped white onion

Lime wedges

COOK THE BEEF

PUT the beef in a 6- to 8-quart pot along with the water, onion, garlic, bay leaf, oregano, and salt. Bring to a simmer over high heat, skimming the surface as necessary. Reduce the heat, then cover and simmer until the beef is just tender, about 1¼ hours. Discard the bay leaf.

MAKE THE MOLE

WHILE the beef is simmering, heat a comal, griddle, or heavy skillet over medium-low heat, and toast the chiles, 2 or 3 at a time, turning them over and pressing them down with tongs until they're fragrant and the insides have changed color slightly, 1 to 1½ minutes per batch.

CORE the tomatoes and cut a small "X" through the skin on the opposite ends. Put the chiles, tomatoes, and tomatillos into a 3-quart saucepan with enough cold water to cover and bring to a boil over high heat. Reduce the heat and simmer gently, uncovered, until the tomatoes and tomatillos are tender but still intact, about 15 minutes. Using a slotted spoon, remove the chiles, tomatoes, and tomatillos from the cooking liquid and discard the cooking liquid. Transfer the tomatoes to a cutting board and remove their skins. Combine the skinned tomatoes along with the tomatillos and chiles in the blender jar. Add the garlic, whole spices, salt,

and hoja santa (or avocado leaves) and blend until the mixture is very smooth, about 3 minutes. Be careful when you're blending hot ingredients: Cover the top with a kitchen towel, and hold the top firmly in place with your hand. Work in batches to avoid blending with a full jar.

HEAT the oil in a 3-quart heavy saucepan over medium heat until it simmers. Carefully add the mole and simmer, stirring frequently, until it has thickened slightly, 8 to 10 minutes. As the mole is simmering, swish a little liquid around in the blender and add it to the pot.

COMBINE THE BEEF, VEGETABLES, AND MOLE

WHEN the beef is just tender, add the mole and chayote to the pot with the beef and cook over medium heat, partially covered, for 10 minutes. Add the zucchini and green beans and cook, partially covered, until the vegetables are just tender, about 10 minutes more. Season with salt to taste.

MAKE THE CHOCHOYOTES

COMBINE the tortilla flour, water, lard, and salt in a bowl, and mix with your hands until you have a soft dough that leaves a very light film on your hands as you mix it. Knead it a few times with your palms so you can be sure there are no spots of dry flour. Form a small amount of dough into a marble-size ball, then press your thumb into the ball to create a deep dimple. If the dough cracks around the edges of the dimple, add a little more water to the mixture and try again. If the dough is too soft to hold its shape well, gradually add a little more tortilla flour.

UNCOVER the mole. Form the chochoyotes with the remaining dough, gently dropping them into the simmering mole as they are made. Once all the chochoyotes are in the pot, continue to cook until they float to the top and are tender in the center, about 5 minutes more. Season to taste with additional salt.

Serve the mole in bowls and garnish with chopped onion. Pass lime wedges to be squeezed into the mole. Serve it with Corn Tortillas (page 39).

This mole keeps in the refrigerator for up to two days. If you're making the mole ahead of time, make and cook the chochoyotes just before serving.

LAMB IN MODERN YELLOW MOLE

BORREGO EN MOLE AMARILLO

It's the daily mission of every immigrant far from home to take the ingredients he can find and try to re-create the flavors he longs for, the flavors of home. That's what inspired me to create a sauce that evokes the moles amarillos of Oaxaca and Querétaro without the hard-to-find chiles chilhuacles and hoja santa.

SERVES 6   **ACTIVE TIME: 45 MINUTES**   **START TO FINISH: 1¾ HOURS**

FOR THE LAMB

2½ pounds boneless lamb shoulder or leg, cut into 2-inch pieces, including some fat, or 3½ pounds lamb pieces with bone

6 cups water, or just enough to cover lamb

1 cup thinly sliced white onion

6 garlic cloves, peel and minced

2 teaspoons dried oregano, preferably Mexican

1 large sprig fresh mint

1 teaspoon fine salt, or 2 teaspoons kosher salt

FOR THE MOLE

1 ounce guajillo chiles (4), wiped clean, stemmed, slit open, seeded, and deveined

4 dried árbol chiles, wiped clean and stemmed

½ pound tomatillos (5 or 6), husked, rinsed, and roughly chopped

1 packed cup chopped cilantro

⅓ cup corn tortilla flour (masa harina)

3 large garlic cloves, peeled

1 teaspoon aniseed

1 teaspoon cumin seeds

12 small whole black peppercorns

3 whole cloves

½ teaspoon fine salt, or 1 teaspoon kosher salt

FOR THE VEGETABLES

½ pound carrots (2 medium), cut diagonally into ½-inch slices

½ pound small red potatoes (about 5), quartered

½ pound zucchini (1 medium), halved lengthwise and cut crosswise into ½-inch slices

¾ cup shelled fresh or frozen peas

GARNISH

Chopped white onion

Chopped cilantro

Lime wedges

COOK THE LAMB

PUT the lamb in a 5- to 6-quart heavy pot with the remaining ingredients for cooking the lamb and bring the water to a simmer over high heat, skimming the surface as necessary. Reduce the heat, then cover and simmer until the lamb is tender, about 1¼ hours.

MAKE THE MOLE

SOAK the guajillo chiles (there's no need to toast them) with enough cold water to cover for 30 minutes. Drain the guajillos and discard the soaking water.

MEANWHILE, heat a comal, griddle, or heavy skillet over low heat, and toast the árbol chiles, turning them over and pressing them down frequently, until the chiles are browned all over and blackened in spots, about 8 minutes.

PUT the guajillos and árbol chiles in the blender jar with the tomatillos, cilantro, tortilla flour, garlic, aniseed, cumin, peppercorns, cloves, and salt. Add 2 cups of the broth from the lamb and blend to form a smooth puree, about 3 minutes. Be careful when you're blending hot ingredients: Cover the top with a kitchen towel, and hold the top firmly in place with your hand. Work in batches to avoid blending with a full jar. Strain the mole through a medium-mesh sieve, if desired, to remove any tough bits of guajillo skin.

FINISH THE MOLE WITH THE VEGETABLES

POUR the mole into the pot with the lamb, stirring to incorporate. Swish a little liquid around in the blender and add it to the pot. Bring the mixture to a simmer. Add the carrots and potatoes, cover the pot, and simmer for 10 minutes. Add the zucchini and peas, and simmer, covered, until all the vegetables are tender, about 10 minutes more. Season to taste with additional salt.

Lamb in Modern Yellow Mole has a yellow-orange hue.

Serve bowls of the mole topped with chopped onion and cilantro, and pass lime wedges for guests to squeeze into their bowls, as well as warm Corn Tortillas (page 39) to roll and dip into the sauce.

This mole keeps in the refrigerator for up to two days.

VARIATION WITH BEEF SHANK OR OXTAIL:

Instead of lamb, use 3 pounds of beef shank, cut into 2-inch pieces, including pieces with bone, or 3½ pounds of crosscut oxtail.

YELLOW MOLE FROM QUERÉTARO
MOLE AMARILLO DE QUERÉTARO

This one is not nearly as well known as Oaxaca's yellow mole, but perhaps it should be. It comes from Querétaro, a city in El Bajio—the lowlands that mark the geographical center of the country where my friend Sergio Remolina lived and investigated this recipe. Most of the food in this wealthy area of the country is of the obviously mestizo sort—a mingling of indigenous and colonial influences—and this is a great example: the tomatoes and tomatillos are cooked in lard or oil and the sauce is finished with a sweet-salty combination of pineapple, olives, and capers.

MAKES 4 CUPS SAUCE (ENOUGH FOR 4 TO 6 SERVINGS)   ACTIVE TIME: 40 TO 55 MINUTES   START TO FINISH: 1¾ TO 2¾ HOURS

½ cup pork lard, mild olive oil, or vegetable oil, divided

⅔ pound tomatoes (about 2 medium), cored, seeded, and coarsely chopped

⅓ pound tomatillos (about 4), husked, rinsed, and coarsely chopped

1½ cups coarsely chopped white onion

2 large garlic cloves, chopped

3 tablespoons blanched almonds

2 tablespoons raisins

1 (1-inch) piece canela (Mexican cinnamon)

5 whole black peppercorns

2 whole cloves

¼ teaspoon cumin seeds

3 fresh serrano or jalapeño chiles, coarsely chopped, including seeds

½ teaspoon fine salt, or 1 teaspoon kosher salt

¼ teaspoon ground turmeric

½ recipe Poached Chicken (page 242), including 3 to 4 cups of stock, divided

2 tablespoons corn tortilla flour (masa harina)

1 cup finely diced fresh pineapple

½ cup cooked chickpeas (if using canned beans, rinse and drain them)

12 pitted green olives, halved

2 tablespoons capers, drained and rinsed

1 tablespoon chopped flat-leaf parsley

HEAT ¼ cup of the lard or oil in a medium heavy skillet over medium heat, and cook the tomatoes, tomatillos, onion, and garlic, stirring, until all the vegetables are softened and the tomatillos have turned a khaki-green color, 10 to 15 minutes. Transfer the mixture to the blender jar.

WIPE the skillet clean and heat the remaining ¼ cup of the lard or oil over medium heat. Fry the almonds, stirring, until golden, about 2 minutes. Transfer them with a slotted spoon to the blender. Fry the raisins in the same skillet, stirring, until they puff, about 1 minute. Transfer them with a slotted spoon to the blender.

TRANSFER any of the lard or oil remaining in the skillet to a 3- to 4-quart heavy pot and reserve. Wipe the skillet clean and toast the canela, peppercorns, cloves, and cumin over medium heat, stirring, until fragrant, about 30 seconds. Transfer the spices to the blender.

ADD the chiles, salt, and turmeric to the blender jar along with ½ cup of the chicken stock. Blend until the mixture is smooth, about 3 minutes. Be careful when you're blending hot ingredients: Cover the top with a kitchen towel, and hold the top firmly in place with your hand.

HEAT the reserved lard or oil in the pot over medium heat until it shimmers. Carefully add the mole and simmer, stirring frequently, until it has thickened slightly, about 10 minutes. As it's simmering, swish a little liquid around in the blender and add it to the pot.

ADD just enough stock (about 1 cup) to thin the mole to a velvety consistency that thinly coats a wooden spoon. Simmer gently, partially covered, adding more stock to maintain the velvety consistency and stirring occasionally, until pools of oil appear on the surface, about 30 minutes.

DISSOLVE the corn tortilla flour in 1 cup of the chicken stock, and stir the mixture into the mole. Simmer, uncovered, stirring occasionally and adding more stock as necessary, for 20 minutes.

ADD the chicken, pineapple, chickpeas, olives, and capers to the mole. Reduce the heat to low and warm the mixture until just heated through, 15 to 20 minutes. Season to taste with additional salt.

Serve bowls of the mole sprinkled with the parsley. Serve it with Corn Tortillas (page 39), rice, beans, or any other side you like (pages 246–256).

This mole keeps in the refrigerator for up to two days.

THICK MOLES

Texture is not the only thing that distinguishes these moles from their soupier siblings. The addition of seeds and nuts brings rich, satiny body but also healthy oils that make the flavor of the rest of the ingredients fuller than those moles that mainly use stock. Other tasty thickening agents reflect cooks' resourcefulness—some use masa, charred tortillas, even animal crackers!

Still, achieving the right texture is essential to mastering these moles. Rather than the soupy or brothy textures of thin moles, you want a velvety liquid, just thick enough so that it thickly coats a wooden spoon, but is never, ever gloppy. As the mole bubbles away in the pot, keep an eye on the consistency, adding a little more water or stock whenever it threatens to get too thick.

It may sound as obvious as reminding you to brush your teeth twice a day, but when you're making complicated dark moles, it helps to have all of your ingredients measured and prepped before you start cooking. This will make the cooking process go quickly and smoothly and will ensure that when you're frying multiple ingredients one after the other, the oil will never have a chance to overheat while you're scrambling to seed chiles or measure nuts.

THICK RED MOLES These exhilaratingly delicious moles tend to involve more ingredients—seeds, nuts, or both, maybe a little masa, and spices—than their thin counterparts. Plus, many of them are slightly sweet, like the ones from Veracruz that incorporate ripe plantains. But despite the complex-tasting result, they take only a bit more effort. Cooks who have ancho and guajillo chiles in the cupboard can make one of these moles tonight!

MEXICO CITY-STYLE "LITTLE" RED MOLE MOLITO ROJO CHILANGO

You call these *molitos* ("little moles") because they don't have an endless list of ingredients. These come from urban areas, where nowadays cooks often don't have time to make more involved moles. In fact, you probably won't find this particular mole, which I've adapted from the great Sergio Remolina, outside of Mexico City—unless you count your home kitchen, of course.

MAKES 8 CUPS SAUCE (ENOUGH FOR 8 TO 10 SERVINGS)   **ACTIVE TIME: 1¼ TO 1½ HOURS**   **START TO FINISH: 2 TO 3 HOURS**

3 garlic cloves, peeled

2 ounces ancho chiles (4), wiped clean, stemmed, slit open, seeded (reserve the seeds), and deveined

2 ounces guajillo chiles (8), wiped clean, stemmed, slit open, seeded (reserve the seeds), and deveined

1⅓ ounces pasilla chiles (4), wiped clean, stemmed, slit open, seeded (reserve the seeds), and deveined

3½ ounces hulled raw (green) pumpkin seeds (⅔ cup)

1⅔ ounces unhulled sesame seeds (⅓ cup)

3 whole black peppercorns

2 whole allspice berries

2 whole cloves

1 (1-inch) piece canela (Mexican cinnamon)

3 cups water

¼ cup lard, mild olive oil, or vegetable oil

1 corn tortilla

1 cup chopped white onion

2 teaspoons fine salt, or 4 teaspoons kosher salt

1 recipe Cooked Pork (page 243) or Poached Chicken (page 242), including 3½ to 4½ cups of stock, divided

HEAT a medium heavy skillet over medium-low heat, and roast the garlic and toast the chiles, a few at a time, turning the chiles over and pressing them down with tongs frequently, until they are fragrant and the insides have changed color slightly, 1 to 1½ minutes per batch. Transfer the chiles to a bowl and cover them with cold water. Continue roasting the garlic cloves, turning them over once or twice, until they are tender and golden brown with some blackened spots, 8 to 10 minutes total. Set the garlic aside.

TOAST the reserved chile seeds in the skillet, stirring constantly, until fragrant and a shade darker, 1 to 2 minutes. Add the seeds to the bowl with the chiles and soak for 30 minutes. Drain and discard the soaking water.

WHILE the chiles are soaking, toast the pumpkin seeds in the skillet over medium heat, stirring constantly, until puffed and only slightly browned, 5 to 8 minutes. Transfer them to another bowl.

TOAST the sesame seeds, peppercorns, allspice, cloves, and canela in the skillet, stirring constantly, until the sesame seeds are a shade darker and the spices are fragrant, about 4 minutes. Add them all to the bowl with the pumpkin seeds.

BLEND the drained chiles with the 3 cups of fresh water in a blender, working in batches if necessary, until the mixture is very smooth, about 3 minutes.

HEAT the lard or oil in a 6- to 7-quart heavy pot over medium heat until it shimmers, and fry the tortilla, turning once with tongs, until it's golden and crisp, about 2 minutes. Transfer it to a paper towel and blot the surface.

FRY the onion in the same pot, stirring, until softened, about 5 minutes. Using a slotted spoon, transfer the onion to the bowl containing the pumpkin seeds. Crumble the tortilla into the pumpkin seed mixture and add the roasted garlic. Set aside.

CAREFULLY pour the chile puree into the pot and simmer, stirring frequently (use a splatter screen so the sauce doesn't make a mess of the stove), until the sauce is slightly thicker, about 10 minutes. As the sauce is simmering, swish a little liquid around in the blender and add it to the pot. Turn the heat to low.

PUT the pumpkin seed mixture in the blender jar (there's no need to clean it first), along with the salt and 2 cups of the pork or chicken stock. Blend until it's smooth, about 3 minutes.

STIR the pumpkin seed puree into the chile puree and bring to a simmer, stirring occasionally and adding enough stock (about 1½ cups) to obtain a velvety consistency that thickly coats a wooden spoon, but isn't gloppy. Simmer, partially covered, adding more stock as necessary to maintain the consistency, until pools of oil appear on the surface, about 30 minutes. Season to taste with additional salt.

ADD the pork or chicken to the mole, reduce the heat to low, and cook until it's just heated through, 15 to 20 minutes.

Serve it with Corn Tortillas (page 39), rice, beans, or any other side you like (pages 246–256). Or turn it into Tacos (pages 212–214), Enchiladas (pages 216–224), or Tamales (page 227).

This mole actually improves after a day in the refrigerator. It keeps in the refrigerator for up to three days or in the freezer for up to a month.

In my recipes for thick moles and pipianes, remember that I call for unhulled sesame seeds, which are a bit darker and larger than the pearly white ones you see on your hamburger bun. Look for unhulled sesame seeds (see page 33) at natural foods stores and Mexican markets. If you use the hulled seeds, your sauce is more likely to break.

RED PEANUT MOLE
MOLE COLORADO DE CACAHUATE

Making mole with fruits is common practice, particularly in Veracruz, but don't think that that means only sweetness. The plantains, apples, and prunes in this version provide a luxurious, silky body, and the chiles and spices keep the sweetness in perfect balance.

MAKES 6 CUPS SAUCE (ENOUGH FOR 6 TO 8 SERVINGS)   **ACTIVE TIME: 1½ TO 1¾ HOURS**   **START TO FINISH: 2½ TO 3½ HOURS**

¼ cup mild olive oil or vegetable oil

4 garlic cloves, peeled

1 cup shelled skinless peanuts (5 ounces), preferably raw

1 ripe (brown or black) plantain, peeled and cut crosswise in ½-inch slices

1 large sweet apple, such as McIntosh, Gala, or Red Delicious, cored and cut into 8 wedges

½ medium white onion, thinly sliced

1⅓ ounces guajillo chiles (6), wiped clean, stemmed, slit open, seeded, and deveined

⅓ ounce pasilla de Oaxaca chiles (2), wiped clean, stemmed, slit open, seeded, and deveined, or 3 dried chipotles moras (purplish-red color), wiped clean and stemmed

⅓ cup pitted prunes

4 whole allspice berries

4 whole cloves

1 (1-inch) piece canela (Mexican cinnamon), or ¼ teaspoon ground cinnamon

Rounded ¼ teaspoon aniseed

Rounded ¼ teaspoon coriander seeds

Rounded ¼ teaspoon cumin seeds

1 corn tortilla

1 teaspoon fine salt, or 2 teaspoons kosher salt

1 recipe Poached Chicken (page 242) or Cooked Pork (page 243), including 5 to 6 cups of stock, divided

2 teaspoons apple cider vinegar, or more to taste

HAVE ready a large bowl and a metal sieve set over a small heatproof bowl.

HEAT the oil in a small skillet over medium heat until it shimmers and fry the following ingredients one by one. As they're fried, use a slotted spoon to transfer them to the large bowl (for ingredients that are difficult to scoop, empty the contents of the skillet into the sieve to drain first, then return the oil to the skillet and put the fried ingredient in the larger bowl).

FRY the garlic cloves, turning them over occasionally, until they're golden brown, about 3 minutes.

FRY the peanuts, stirring, until they're deep golden brown and very aromatic, about 2 minutes.

FRY the plantain slices, turning once, until they're soft and lightly browned, about 3 minutes.

FRY the apple wedges, turning occasionally, until they're lightly browned and semi-soft, about 5 minutes.

FRY the onion, stirring, until it's soft and lightly browned, about 3 minutes.

FRY the chiles, 2 or 3 at a time, turning them once, 10 to 20 seconds per batch; be very careful not to burn the chiles.

FRY the prunes, turning once, until they blister and puff slightly, about 1 minute.

AT this point, there should be only a little oil left for quickly frying the spices. Mix together the allspice, cloves, cinnamon, aniseed, coriander, and cumin and add them to the skillet, stirring for a few seconds to release their aromas. Then transfer the spices and any remaining oil to the bowl of fried ingredients.

USING tongs, hold the tortilla directly over a burner set to medium, turning it over frequently, until it's dark golden brown and some burned spots appear on both sides. Crumble it into the fried ingredients.

ADD 3 cups of the stock to the fried ingredients, and soak for 20 minutes.

WORKING in 2 batches, puree the contents of the bowl in the blender jar, adding half of the salt and 1 cup of the remaining stock to each batch, until very smooth, 3 to 5 minutes per batch.

POUR the mole into a heavy 5- to 6-quart pot and bring it to a simmer over medium heat, stirring occasionally. As it's simmering, swish a little liquid around in the blender jar and add it to the pot. Reduce the heat to low and simmer the mole (use a splatter screen so the sauce doesn't make a mess of the stove), until small pools of oil appear on the surface, about 30 minutes. As the mole simmers, stir it frequently and add more stock as necessary to maintain a velvety consistency that thickly coats a wooden spoon, but isn't gloppy.

ADD the chicken or pork to the mole and cook over low heat until it's just heated through, 15 to 20 minutes. Season to taste with vinegar and additional salt.

Serve it with Corn Tortillas (page 39), rice, beans, or any other side you like (pages 246–256). Or turn it into Tacos (pages 212–214), Enchiladas (pages 216–224), or Tamales (page 227).

This mole actually improves after a day in the refrigerator. It keeps in the refrigerator for up to five days without the meat or up to three days with the meat, or in the freezer for up to one month.

OAXACAN RED MOLE MOLE COLORADITO

Three cloves, a little oregano, a couple of peppercorns, and canela—it's amazing that this seemingly inconspicuous combination of spices just screams to me, "Red mole from Oaxaca!" In fact, I swear I can sniff the air within a hundred feet of this very traditional version, adapted from my friend Iliana de la Vega, and tell you exactly what's simmering away in the pot. Some cooks add some fried sweet plantains or chocolate as a sweetener, so that's up to you.

MAKES 5 CUPS SAUCE (ENOUGH FOR 6 SERVINGS)   ACTIVE TIME: **40 TO 55 MINUTES**   START TO FINISH: **1½ TO 2½ HOURS**

1⅓ pounds tomatoes (about 4 medium)

4 garlic cloves, peeled

4 ounces ancho chiles (8), wiped clean, stemmed, slit open, seeded, and deveined

1 ounce guajillo chiles (4), wiped clean, stemmed, slit open, seeded, and deveined

6 tablespoons mild olive oil or vegetable oil, divided

2 (1-inch-thick) slices baguette

2½ ounces unhulled sesame seeds (½ cup)

10 whole black peppercorns

3 whole cloves

1 (1-inch) piece canela (Mexican cinnamon)

1 teaspoon dried marjoram

1 teaspoon dried oregano, preferably Mexican

2 tablespoons sugar

1 teaspoon fine salt, or 2 teaspoons kosher salt

½ recipe Cooked Pork (page 243) or Poached Chicken (page 242), including 3 to 4 cups of stock, divided

SET the oven to broil and preheat. Alternatively, you can preheat the oven to 500°F. If you're using the oven broiler, position the rack 8 inches from the heat source. Core the tomatoes and cut a small "X" through the skin on the opposite ends. Roast the tomatoes, cored sides up, on a foil-lined pan until their tops are blackened and the tomatoes are cooked to the core, 20 to 30 minutes total. Slip the skins off the tomatoes.

MEANWHILE, heat a comal, griddle, or heavy skillet over medium-low heat and toast the chiles, 2 or 3 at a time, turning them over and pressing them down frequently with tongs, until they are fragrant and the insides have changed color slightly, 1 to 1½ minutes per batch. Roast the garlic, turning it once or twice, until it is just tender and golden brown with some blackened spots, 8 to 10 minutes. Soak the chiles in enough cold water to cover until they're softened, about 30 minutes. Drain and discard the soaking water.

HEAT 3 tablespoons of the oil in a small heavy skillet over medium heat until it shimmers, then fry the bread on both sides until golden. Transfer it to the blender jar.

MIX together the sesame seeds, peppercorns, cloves, and canela and cook them in the oil remaining in the skillet (if the bread has soaked up all the oil, just cook them in the dry pan), stirring, until they're fragrant and the sesame seeds are a shade darker, about 3 minutes. Add the marjoram and oregano and cook a few seconds more, then transfer the mixture to the blender.

ADD the drained chiles to the blender along with the tomatoes, garlic, sugar, salt, and 2 cups of the stock, and blend until the mixture is very smooth, about 3 minutes. Be careful when you're blending hot ingredients: Cover the top with a kitchen towel, and hold the top firmly in place with your hand. Work in batches to avoid blending with a full jar.

HEAT the remaining 3 tablespoons of oil in a 5- to 6-quart heavy pot over medium heat until it simmers. Carefully add the mole and shimmer, stirring frequently, until it has thickened slightly, about 10 minutes. As it's simmering, swish a little liquid around in the blender and add it to the pot.

ADD just enough stock (about 1 cup) to thin the sauce to a velvety consistency that thickly coats a wooden spoon, but isn't gloppy. Reduce the heat and simmer, partially covered, adding more stock as necessary to maintain the consistency, until pools of oil appear on the surface, about 30 minutes. Season to taste with additional salt.

ADD the pork or chicken to the mole, reduce the heat to low, and cook until it's just heated through, 15 to 20 minutes.

Serve it with Corn Tortillas (page 39), rice, beans, or any other side you like (pages 246–256). Or turn it into Tacos (pages 212–214), Enchiladas (pages 216–224), or Tamales (page 227).

This mole actually improves after a day in the refrigerator. It keeps in the refrigerator for up to five days without the meat or up to three days with the meat, or in the freezer for up to one month.

THICK GREEN MOLES Pumpkin seeds go particularly well with the ingredients that dominate green moles, so even versions that include several seeds and nuts tend to have more pumpkin seeds by proportion. These moles range from the simple—perhaps a few green chiles and tomatillos, a couple handfuls of pumpkin seeds, and some peppercorns—to the conspicuously elaborate, a 20-plus-ingredient dish full of almonds and peanuts and sesame seeds and parsley and hoja santa (I'll spare you the complete list) dreamt up to demonstrate wealth. In this section, there's only one thick green mole, because I've chosen to put other sauces that might fit here in the Pipianes section beginning on page 189. Remember, if the sauce breaks, which can happen to sauces made with pumpkin seeds, just blend it again.

GUANAJUATO-STYLE GREEN MOLE
MOLE VERDE ESTILO GUANAJUATO

Unlike the thin mole verde from Oaxaca (page 156), this version from Guanajuato requires no hoja santa or epazote, which should encourage those of you who might not have access to these ingredients. Fortunately, you won't have to sacrifice that lively, verdant flavor profile. Pumpkin seeds give the sauce some added body and a bit of lovely fat to carry all that flavor.

MAKES 8 CUPS SAUCE (ENOUGH FOR 8 TO 10 SERVINGS)   ACTIVE TIME: 40 TO 55 MINUTES   START TO FINISH: 1 TO 2 HOURS

½ pound hulled raw (green) pumpkin seeds (1½ cups)

1 pound tomatillos (10 or 12), husked, rinsed, and roughly chopped

2 cups chopped lettuce, such as romaine (4 large outer leaves) or green leaf

½ cup finely chopped white onion

⅓ cup chopped radish leaves (about 15 large) or spinach leaves

¼ cup chopped cilantro

3 ounces fresh serrano chiles (10), coarsely chopped, including seeds

2 large garlic cloves, peeled

1 teaspoon fine salt, or 2 teaspoons kosher salt

1 recipe Cooked Pork (page 243) or Poached Chicken (page 242), including 6 to 7 cups of stock, divided

¼ cup pork lard, mild olive oil, or vegetable oil

HEAT a heavy skillet over medium heat and toast the pumpkin seeds until they're puffed and just slightly browned, 5 to 8 minutes. Transfer them to the blender jar.

ADD the tomatillos, lettuce, onion, radish leaves, cilantro, chiles, garlic, and salt to the jar. Pour in 1½ cups of stock, or more if necessary to blend, and blend until the mixture is very smooth, about 3 minutes.

HEAT the lard or oil in a 6- to 7-quart heavy pot over medium heat and carefully pour in the blended mixture. Cook, stirring, until the mixture thickens (it will look a bit like scrambled eggs), about 10 minutes. As it's cooking, swish a little liquid around in the blender and add it to the pot. Add just enough stock (about 3 cups) to thin the sauce to a velvety consistency that thickly coats a wooden spoon, but isn't gloppy. Return the mixture to a simmer. Simmer gently, uncovered, stirring occasionally and adding more stock as necessary to maintain the velvety consistency, until dark green pools of oil appear on the surface, about 20 minutes. Season to taste with additional salt.

IF the sauce separates, blend it again (in batches) in the blender until it's smooth, then return it to the pot. Add the pork or chicken to the mole, reduce the heat to low, and cook until it's just heated through, 15 to 20 minutes.

Serve it with Corn Tortillas (page 39), rice, beans, or any other side you like (pages 246–256). Or turn it into Tacos (pages 212–214), Enchiladas (pages 216–224), or Tamales (page 227).

This mole keeps in the refrigerator for up to two days.

THICK DARK MOLES

THICK DARK MOLES These are the moles, mole poblano in particular, that have captured international imagination: the slightly sweet, deep brown or midnight black sauces charged with seemingly endless lists of ingredients. Their complexity was, at the time of their invention, likely a conspicuous demonstration of wealth, a show of colonial superiority that scoffed at the indigenous peoples and their "unsophisticated" moles made from just a handful of ingredients. (Of course, the folks concerned with flaunting their status probably left the task of preparing those elaborate dishes to their cooks.) Now, of course, these dishes are as Mexican as I am. Because these moles are time-consuming to make, cooks today either make them for special occasions; buy the ingredients in paste form at the market, where vendors display the pastes in great heaps; or soup-up jars of premade commercial mole, which can make for tasty sauces. But making them yourself is not as hard as it seems, and the product is unbeatable. Expect to use several varieties of dark-colored chiles like mulatos and pasillas, a bunch of spices, nuts, seeds, and even sweeteners like sugar, apples, plantains, or Mexican chocolate. Sure, these take some effort, but it's the kind of effort that fills your kitchen with the aromas of toasting chiles and frying nuts, the kind of effort you'll want to make again soon.

MOLE FROM PUEBLA MOLE POBLANO

It's ironic that the mole that has served as the ambassador for all others in the United States is also one of the most misunderstood. Whenever I hear this sophisticated mole casually referred to as "chocolate sauce," I'm saddened, because it's so much more! While a little Mexican chocolate does contribute to its sweetness, so do a host of nuts and, sometimes, a plantain, an apple, or animal crackers. In fact, I'd bet there are as many recipes for it as there are cooks in Puebla, and everyone seems convinced that their version is the best. Me? I'm in love with this one, straight from Ana Elena Martinez's kitchen to yours.

MAKES **ABOUT 10 CUPS SAUCE (ENOUGH FOR 10 TO 12 SERVINGS)**   ACTIVE TIME: 1½ TO 1¾ HOURS   START TO FINISH: 2½ TO 3½ HOURS

3 ounces tomato (about 1 small)

3 ounces tomatillos (2 medium), husked and rinsed

1 (½-inch-thick) round slice white onion

5 garlic cloves, peeled

1 cup mild olive oil or vegetable oil, divided

4 ounces mulato chiles (8), wiped clean, stemmed, slit open, seeded (reserve the seeds), and deveined

2 ounces ancho chiles (4), wiped clean, stemmed, slit open, seeded (reserve the seeds), and deveined

2 ounces pasilla chiles (6), wiped clean, stemmed, slit open, seeded (reserve the seeds), and deveined

½ ounce chipotle meco chiles (2 to 3, tobacco-color), wiped clean, stemmed, slit open, seeded (reserve the seeds), and deveined

1 corn tortilla

½ cup blanched almonds

3 tablespoons hulled raw (green) pumpkin seeds

¼ cup packed raisins

1 (1-inch) slice baguette

½ small ripe (brown or black) plantain, peeled and cut crosswise into ½-inch slices

Scant ¼ cup unhulled sesame seeds

1 (1-inch) piece canela (Mexican cinnamon)

6 whole cloves

¼ teaspoon aniseed

¼ teaspoon coriander seeds

¼ teaspoon whole allspice berries (5 large)

¼ teaspoon whole black peppercorns

1 recipe Poached Chicken (page 242) or Poached Turkey (page 242), including 6 to 8 cups of stock, divided

6 ounces Mexican chocolate (2 disks)

1 tablespoon sugar

1½ teaspoons fine salt, or 1 tablespoon kosher salt

GARNISH
¼ cup toasted unhulled sesame seeds

SET the oven or toaster oven to broil and preheat. Alternatively, you can preheat the oven to 500°F. If you're using the oven broiler, position the rack 8 inches from the heat source. Core the tomato and cut a small "X" through the skin on the opposite end. Roast the tomato, cored side up, and tomatillos on a foil-lined pan, turning the tomatillos over once halfway through, until their tops and bottoms have blackened and they are a khaki-green color and cooked to the core, 20 to 30 minutes; and the tomato (without turning) until its top is blackened and it's cooked to the core, 20 to 30 minutes total. Slip the skin off the tomato.

MEANWHILE, heat a comal, griddle, or heavy skillet over medium-low heat, and roast the onion and garlic on the comal, turning the garlic over occasionally, until it is just tender and golden brown with some blackened spots, 8 to 10 minutes; and carefully turning the onion slice over once, until it's softened and charred on both sides, 15 to 20 minutes.

HEAT ½ cup of the oil in a medium heavy skillet over medium heat until it simmers. Fry the chiles, a few of the same variety at a time, turning them over with tongs, until puffed and slightly changed in color, 30 to 45 seconds per batch of mulato and ancho chiles, 45 seconds to 1 minute for pasilla chiles, and about 1½ minutes for chipotle meco chiles. As the chiles are fried, transfer them to a large bowl. When all the chiles are fried, add enough cold water to cover them and let them soak for 30 minutes. Discard the remaining oil from frying the chiles and set the skillet aside.

The thick, velvety texture of the finished mole

USING tongs, hold the tortilla directly over a burner set to medium, turning it over frequently, until it's dark, golden brown and some burned spots appear on both sides. Crumble it into the soaking fried chiles.

HAVE ready a medium bowl and a metal sieve set over a small heatproof bowl.

HEAT the remaining ½ cup of oil in the reserved skillet over medium heat until it shimmers and fry the following ingredients one by one. As they're fried, use a slotted spoon to transfer them to the medium bowl (for ingredients that are difficult to scoop, empty the contents of the skillet into the sieve to drain first, then return the oil to the skillet and put the fried ingredient into the medium bowl).

FRY the almonds, stirring, until they are golden, about 2 minutes.

FRY the pumpkin seeds, stirring, until they are puffed and only slightly browned, about 1 minute.

FRY the raisins, stirring, until they are puffed, about 1 minute.

FRY the bread, turning over once, until golden on both sides, about 3 minutes.

FRY the plantain slices, turning over once, until golden, about 3 minutes.

TRANSFER the remaining oil (2 to 4 tablespoons) in the skillet to a 7- to 8-quart heavy pot and set aside.

WIPE the skillet clean and heat it over medium heat until it's hot. Toast 3 tablespoons of the reserved chile seeds (save the remainder for another use) in the skillet, stirring, until fragrant and a shade darker, about 2 minutes. Transfer the chile seeds to the medium bowl. Toast the sesame seeds, canela, cloves, aniseed, coriander, allspice, and peppercorns in the skillet, stirring, until the sesame seeds are a shade darker, about 1½ minutes. Transfer the mixture to the medium bowl.

DRAIN the chiles and discard the soaking water, and puree them in the blender jar with about 2 cups of the stock.

HEAT the reserved oil in the pot over medium heat until hot, then add the chile puree and cook (use a splatter screen so the sauce doesn't make a mess of the stove), stirring occasionally, until thickened slightly, about 10 minutes.

MEANWHILE, working in 2 batches, combine the fried and toasted ingredients (from the medium bowl) with the roasted tomato, tomatillos, onion, and garlic in the blender jar, along with 2 more cups of the stock per batch, and blend until smooth, about 3 minutes per batch. Be careful when you're blending hot ingredients: Cover the top with a towel, and hold the top firmly in place with your hand. Add the mixture to the chile puree in the pot as you blend it, and once you're done, swish a little liquid around in the blender and add it to the pot.

ADD the chocolate, sugar, and salt to the mole, stirring until the chocolate melts. Simmer, partially covered, stirring occasionally and adding more stock as needed to maintain a velvety consistency that thickly coats a wooden spoon, but isn't gloppy, about 45 minutes. Season to taste with additional sugar and salt.

ADD the chicken or turkey to the mole, reduce the heat to low, and cook until it's just heated through, 15 to 20 minutes.

Spoon the mole into bowls and garnish with the toasted sesame seeds. Serve it with Corn Tortillas (page 39), rice, beans, or any other side you like (pages 246–256). Or turn it into Tacos (pages 212–214), Enchiladas (pages 216–224), or Tamales (page 227).

This mole actually improves after a day in the refrigerator. It keeps in the refrigerator for up to five days without the meat or up to three days with the meat, or in the freezer for up to one month.

Enchiladas made with Mole Poblano (page 218)

BLACKBERRY MOLE MOLE DE ZARZAMORAS

When I opened La Circunstancia many years ago, I had the bright idea to open in one of the worst neighborhoods in Mexico City. But against all odds, the restaurant was a hit—I like to think that it might not have been filled night after night with happy customers had it not been for this mole. My sister Mayan came up with the idea of incorporating blackberries, which you don't often see inside a mole pot. But the sweetness, that acidic backbone, and the deep, dark fruity flavor are right in line with the flavor profile of traditional dark moles. I paired it with duck at the restaurant, but you'll also love it with pork and chicken.

MAKES 6 CUPS SAUCE (ENOUGH FOR ABOUT 6 SERVINGS)   **ACTIVE TIME: 1 TO 1¼ HOUR**   **START TO FINISH: 1½ TO 2½ HOURS**

6 tablespoons mild olive oil or vegetable oil, divided

2 heaping tablespoons shelled skinless peanuts, preferably raw

2 tablespoons whole raw almonds (about 15)

2 heaping tablespoons hulled raw (green) pumpkin seeds

2 heaping tablespoons raw pecan pieces

1 ounce ancho chiles (2), wiped clean, stemmed, slit open, seeded (reserve the seeds), and deveined

1 ounce mulato or ancho chiles (2), wiped clean, stemmed, slit open, seeded (reserve the seeds), and deveined

1 ounce pasilla chiles (3), wiped clean, stemmed, slit open, seeded (reserve the seeds), and deveined

1 (½-inch-thick) round slice white onion

2 garlic cloves, peeled

3 tablespoons unhulled sesame seeds

1 (1½-inch) piece canela (Mexican cinnamon)

⅛ teaspoon aniseed

⅛ teaspoon coriander seeds

Pinch of dried oregano, preferably Mexican

Pinch of ground cloves

Pinch of ground cumin

1 corn tortilla

1 recipe Poached Chicken (page 242) or Cooked Pork (page 243), including 5 to 6 cups of stock, divided

12 ounces ripe blackberries (2 cups)

3 to 4 tablespoons sugar

¾ teaspoon fine salt, or 1½ teaspoons kosher salt

GARNISH
Lightly toasted unhulled sesame seeds (optional)

HAVE ready a large bowl and a metal sieve set over a small heatproof bowl.

HEAT 4 tablespoons of the oil in a small (7- to 8-inch) skillet over medium heat until it shimmers and fry the following ingredients one by one. As they're fried, use a slotted spoon to transfer them to the large bowl (for ingredients that are difficult to scoop, empty the contents of the skillet into the sieve to drain first, then return the oil to the skillet and put the fried ingredient in the larger bowl).

FRY the peanuts and almonds together until the peanuts are golden, about 30 seconds.

FRY the pumpkin seeds just until they swell and stop making noise, 15 to 30 seconds.

FRY the pecans until lightly colored, 15 to 30 seconds.

FRY each chile on both sides, turning with tongs, just until the inside flesh has turned a lighter color, 10 to 15 seconds. Be careful not to burn them.

FRY the onion and garlic together until they are lightly browned, about 3 minutes.

MIX together 1½ tablespoons of the reserved chile seeds, sesame seeds, canela, aniseed, and coriander, and fry them in the oil, stirring constantly, just until the sesame seeds are lightly toasted, about 1 minute (be careful not to burn the sesame seeds or the chile seeds). Stir in the oregano, cloves, and cumin, then transfer the mixture, including the oil, to the large bowl of fried ingredients.

USING tongs, hold the tortilla directly over a burner set to medium, turning it over frequently, until it's dark, golden brown and some burned spots appear on both sides. Crumble it into the fried ingredients.

WORKING in 2 batches, transfer the fried ingredient mixture to the blender jar and pour in 2 cups of the stock per batch (4 cups total). Blend until smooth, 3 to 5 minutes per batch.

HEAT the remaining 2 tablespoons of oil in a heavy 5- to 6-quart saucepan over medium heat until it shimmers, then carefully pour in the blended sauce and stir. Swish a little liquid around in the blender and add it to the pot. Reduce the heat to low.

ADD the blackberries, 3 tablespoons of the sugar, and ¼ cup of the stock to the blender jar (there's no need to clean it first), and blend until the mixture is smooth. Strain the blackberry puree through a medium-mesh sieve into the sauce, discarding the seeds.

BRING the sauce to a simmer (use a splatter screen so the sauce doesn't make a mess of the stove). Cook over low heat, uncovered, stirring frequently and adding more stock as necessary to maintain a velvety consistency that thickly coats a wooden spoon but isn't gloppy, until you see small pools of oil on the surface of the mole, about 30 minutes. Season to taste with additional sugar and salt. The sauce should taste only slightly sweet.

ADD the chicken or pork to the mole, reduce the heat to low, and cook until it's just heated through, 15 to 20 minutes. Serve, sprinkled with the sesame seeds, if you like.

Serve it with Corn Tortillas (page 39), rice, beans, or any other side you like (pages 246–256).

This mole keeps in the refrigerator for up to two days or in the freezer for up to one month.

Pasilla chiles

MOLES & PIPIANES: MEXICO'S ICONIC SAUCES

PASILLA AND APPLE MOLE
MOLE DE MANZANA CON PASILLA

Usually, the silky body of a mole is supplied by chiles and tomatoes or tomatillos. But in this modern version, I've included apples for that purpose, a common addition to dark moles but not typically the headliner. The perfumey sweetness of the apples—be sure you give them some color when you sauté them in the skillet—makes for a fabulously fruity sauce.

MAKES 6 CUPS SAUCE (ENOUGH FOR 6 TO 8 SERVINGS)   **ACTIVE TIME: 1 TO 1¼ HOUR**   **START TO FINISH: 1½ TO 2½ HOURS**

3½ ounces pasilla chiles (10), wiped clean, stemmed, slit open, seeded, and deveined

3 (½-inch-thick) round slices white onion (about ½ large onion)

⅓ pound tomato (about 1 medium)

2 tablespoons mild olive oil or vegetable oil

1 pound sweet red apples (3), such as McIntosh, Gala, or Red Delicious, cored and cut into 8 wedges each

½ cup shelled skinless peanuts, preferably raw

5 garlic cloves, peeled

1 (2½-inch) piece canela (Mexican cinnamon), or ½ teaspoon ground cinnamon

¾ teaspoon cumin seeds

4 whole cloves

1 teaspoon fine salt, or 2 teaspoons kosher salt

1 recipe Cooked Pork (page 243) or Poached Chicken (page 242), including 6 to 7 cups of stock, divided

1 to 2 tablespoons apple cider vinegar, if necessary

1 to 2 tablespoons sugar, if necessary

HEAT a comal, griddle, or heavy skillet over medium-low heat and toast the chiles, 2 or 3 at a time, turning them over and pressing them with tongs frequently, until they're slightly blistered and the insides are tobacco colored, 1 to 1½ minutes per batch. As the chiles are toasted, transfer them to a bowl and soak them in enough cold water to cover until they're soft, about 30 minutes. Drain and discard the soaking water.

WHILE the chiles are soaking, roast the onion slices on the comal, turning them over once, until they're softened and charred on both sides, 15 to 20 minutes.

SET the oven to broil and preheat. Alternatively, you can preheat the oven to 500°F. If you're using the oven broiler, position the rack 8 inches from the heat source. Core the tomato and cut a small "X" through the skin on the opposite end. Put the tomato, cored side up, on a foil-lined baking pan, leaving room for the apple wedges. Roast the tomato (without turning it) until it's blackened on the top and cooked to the core, 20 to 30 minutes.

ONCE the tomato is roasting, heat the oil in a medium heavy skillet over medium heat until it shimmers. Add the apples and sauté, turning over once, until golden, about 6 minutes. Using tongs, transfer the sautéed apples to the baking pan with the roasting tomato, and roast the apples until they're tender, 10 to 20 minutes.

ONCE the apples are roasting in the oven, put the peanuts in the oil remaining in the skillet and cook, stirring, until golden, about 2 minutes.

TRANSFER the onion slices, tomato, apples, and peanuts to a bowl as they finish roasting, then add the drained chiles, garlic, canela, cumin, cloves, and salt. Stir well.

WORKING in 2 batches, combine the apple mixture with about 3 cups of stock (1½ cups per batch) in the blender jar and blend until the mixture is smooth, about 3 minutes per batch. Be careful when you're blending hot ingredients: Cover the top with a kitchen towel, and hold the top firmly in place with your hand.

AS the mole is blended, transfer it to a 5- to 6-quart heavy pot and bring it to a simmer over medium heat, stirring. Swish a little liquid around in the blender and add it to the pot. Simmer, uncovered (use a splatter screen so the sauce doesn't make a mess of the stove), stirring frequently, until the mole has thickened slightly, about 10 minutes. Add just enough of the remaining stock (about 3 cups) to obtain a velvety consistency that thickly coats a wooden spoon, but isn't gloppy. Reduce the heat and simmer gently, uncovered, adding more stock as necessary to maintain the consistency, about 20 minutes. Season to taste with the vinegar, sugar, and additional salt.

ADD the pork or chicken to the mole, reduce the heat to low, and cook until it's just heated through, 15 to 20 minutes.

Serve it with Corn Tortillas (page 39), rice, beans, or any other side you like (pages 246–256).

This mole actually improves after a day in the refrigerator. It keeps in the refrigerator for up to five days without the meat or up to three days with the meat, or in the freezer for up to one month.

The sticks on the left are regular cinnamon, and the larger two on right are Mexican cinnamon (canela).

MOLES & PIPIANES: MEXICO'S ICONIC SAUCES

HAZELNUT MOLE MOLE DE AVELLANAS

The idea for this modern mole struck me when a friend mentioned that he grows hazelnuts near his home in Xalapa, the capital of Veracruz. It's not a nut many cooks in Mexico use, so I started experimenting, pairing it with vanilla, which is native to the state. Surely, cooks have made something like it before, but what I came up with is really special—a savory, velvety sauce that puts the incredibly aromatic nut front and center. You'd never know that I add vanilla and chipotle if I didn't tell you, but the mole wouldn't be as great without them. It's great with chicken, but I also adore pairing it with lobster, shrimp, and scallops (see Shrimp and Scallop Enchiladas with Hazelnut Mole, page 224).

MAKES 6 CUPS SAUCE (ENOUGH FOR 6 TO 8 SERVINGS)   **ACTIVE TIME: 45 MINUTES**   **START TO FINISH: 1½ HOURS**

1½ cups raw hazelnuts (8 ounces)

¼ pound tomatillos (about 3), husked and rinsed

1 head garlic, cloves separated and peeled

1 (½-inch-thick) round slice white onion

⅓ cup mild olive oil or vegetable oil

¾ ounce chipotle mora chiles (6 to 7, purplish-red color), wiped clean and stemmed

1 guajillo chile (¼ ounce), wiped clean, stemmed, slit open, seeded, and deveined

1½ teaspoons sugar

1 teaspoon fine salt, or 2 teaspoons kosher salt

½ teaspoon ground cumin

3½ to 4½ cups chicken stock

1 vanilla bean, split lengthwise

2 bay leaves

GARNISH
Additional finely chopped skinned hazelnuts, toasted (optional)

PREHEAT the oven to 350°F. Toast the hazelnuts on a small foil-lined baking pan in the oven until the skins have split and the nuts are golden, 10 to 12 minutes. Transfer the nuts to a kitchen towel and wrap them with it. Let the nuts stand for 10 minutes to steam, which will help remove the skins. Then, gathering up the edges of the towel with one hand, rub the nuts against each other through the cloth with the other hand to loosen the skins. Lay the towel open on a flat surface and separate the nuts from their skins with your hands (it'll be easy). Transfer the nuts to a bowl, and discard the skins.

ONCE the hazelnuts are wrapped in the towel, heat a comal, griddle, or heavy skillet over medium-low heat, and roast the tomatillos, garlic, and onion, turning them all over once, until the garlic is just tender and golden brown with some blackened spots, 8 to 10 minutes, and the tomatillos and the onion are cooked through and blackened on both sides, 15 to 20 minutes.

HEAT the oil in a medium skillet over medium heat, then add the hazelnuts and fry until they are a deep golden color, 3 to 5 minutes. Pour the oil and the nuts into a metal sieve set over a heatproof bowl to drain. Transfer the nuts to a large bowl.

RETURN the oil to the skillet and put the skillet back on the heat. Fry the chipotles, turning them with tongs until they're puffed and slightly lighter in color, about 45 seconds. Using tongs or a slotted spoon, transfer them to the bowl with the hazelnuts, then fry the guajillo chile, about 30 seconds. Transfer it to the bowl.

TRANSFER the oil from the skillet to a 5- to 6-quart heavy pot (this will give you enough room to add the meat later; if you're making just the sauce, a 3- to 4-quart pot is fine) and set it aside.

WORKING in 2 batches, blend the hazelnuts, tomatillos, garlic, onion, and chiles with the sugar, salt, cumin, and 1½ cups of the stock per batch (3 cups total) in the blender jar until smooth, about 5 minutes.

Hazelnut Mole with seared scallops

HEAT the oil in the pot over medium heat until it shimmers, then carefully pour in the sauce (it may splatter). Swish a little stock around in the blender and add it to the pot. Bring the sauce to a simmer, stirring frequently, until it has thickened slightly, about 10 minutes. Add just enough additional stock to obtain a velvety texture that is just thick enough to coat a wooden spoon, but not gloppy. Scrape the seeds from the vanilla bean into the mole, then drop in the vanilla pod along with the bay leaves. Simmer the mole, uncovered (use a splatter screen so the sauce doesn't make a mess of the stove), stirring frequently and adding more stock as needed to maintain a velvety texture, about 45 minutes. Season to taste with additional sugar and salt.

Serve it with seared scallops or Poached Chicken (page 242), and Corn Tortillas (page 39), rice, beans, or any other side you like (pages 246–256). Or turn it into Enchiladas (pages 216–224).

This mole actually improves after a day in the refrigerator. It keeps in the refrigerator for up to five days without the chicken or up to two days with the chicken or seafood, or in the freezer for up to one month.

XICO-STYLE MOLE MOLE ESTILO XICO

This full-bodied, slightly fruity sauce from Xico, a town in the highlands of Veracruz, is one of those amazingly complex dishes that has given moles their reputation as impossible to make at home. But because I've streamlined this recipe, you'll be able to make it for friends without sacrificing an entire day to fussing and frying.

MAKES 8 CUPS SAUCE (ENOUGH FOR 8 TO 10 SERVINGS)   **ACTIVE TIME: 1¼ TO 1½ HOURS**   **START TO FINISH: 2 TO 3 HOURS**

4½ ounces mulato chiles (9), wiped clean, stemmed, slit open, seeded, and deveined

1 ounce pasilla chiles (3), wiped clean, stemmed, slit open, seeded, and deveined

½ cup raw hazelnuts

⅓ pound tomato (about 1 medium)

½ cup mild olive oil or vegetable oil

¾ cup coarsely chopped white onion

4 garlic cloves, peeled

1½ teaspoons fine salt, or 1 tablespoon kosher salt

1 recipe Poached Chicken (page 242) or Poached Turkey (page 242), including 5 to 6 cups of stock, divided

¼ cup raw almonds (1¼ ounces)

¼ cup raw pecans (1 ounce)

½ cup raw pine nuts (2¼ ounces)

1 small or ½ large ripe (brown or black) plantain, peeled and cut into ½-inch-thick slices

½ cup raisins

½ cup pitted prunes

1 (½-inch-thick) slice baguette

3 tablespoons unhulled sesame seeds

1 (1-inch) piece canela (Mexican cinnamon), or ¼ teaspoon ground cinnamon

5 whole black peppercorns

2 whole cloves

1 corn tortilla

½ cup grated piloncillo (see note), or light brown sugar

1½ ounces Mexican chocolate (4 small triangles)

GARNISH
Lightly toasted unhulled sesame seeds (optional)

PREHEAT the oven or toaster oven to 350°F.

SOAK the chiles in cold water to cover for 30 minutes. (There's no need to toast them.) Drain and discard the soaking water.

TOAST the hazelnuts on a foil-lined baking pan in the oven until the skins have split and the nuts are golden, 10 to 12 minutes. Transfer the nuts to a kitchen towel and wrap them with it. Let the nuts stand for 10 minutes to steam, which will help remove the skins. Then, gathering up the edges of the towel with one hand, rub the nuts against each other through the cloth with the other hand to loosen the skins. Lay the towel open on a flat surface and separate the nuts from their skins with your hands (it'll be easy). Transfer the nuts to a bowl and discard the skins.

ONCE the hazelnuts are wrapped in the towel, increase the oven temperature to 500°F. Core the tomato and cut a small "X" through the skin on the opposite end. Put the tomato, cored side up, on the baking pan and roast, without turning it over, until the top is blackened and the tomato is cooked to the core, 20 to 30 minutes. Slip the skin from the tomato and transfer the tomato to a bowl.

HEAT 2 tablespoons of the oil in a small heavy skillet over medium heat and cook the onion and garlic, stirring frequently, until softened, 3 to 5 minutes. Transfer the onion and garlic to the blender jar along with the drained chiles, salt, and about 1 cup of the stock. Blend the mixture until it's very smooth, about 3 minutes. Transfer the puree to a bowl.

HAVE ready a large bowl and a metal sieve set over a small heatproof bowl.

HEAT ¼ cup of the oil in the skillet over medium heat until it shimmers and fry the following ingredients one by one. As they're fried, use a slotted spoon to transfer them to the large bowl (for ingredients that are difficult to scoop, empty the contents of the skillet into the sieve to drain first, then return the oil to the skillet and put the fried ingredient in the larger bowl).

The ingredients for
Xico-Style Mole

MOLES & PIPIANES: MEXICO'S ICONIC SAUCES

FRY the hazelnuts, stirring, until they are deep golden, about 3 minutes.

FRY the almonds, stirring, until they are golden, about 2 minutes.

FRY the pecans, stirring, until they get slightly darker, about 2 minutes.

FRY the pine nuts, stirring, until they are golden, about 2 minutes.

FRY the plantain slices, turning them over once, until they're golden, about 3 minutes.

FRY the raisins, stirring, until they are puffed, about 1 minute.

FRY the prunes, turning them over once, until they blister and puff slightly, about 1 minute.

FRY the bread, turning it over once, until it is golden and has absorbed the remaining oil, about 2 minutes.

TOAST the sesame seeds, canela, peppercorns, and cloves, together in the now-dry skillet, stirring frequently, just until the sesame seeds are fragrant and a shade darker, about 4 minutes.

USING tongs, hold the tortilla directly over a burner set to medium, turning it over frequently, until it's dark, golden brown and some burned spots appear on both sides. Crumble it into the fried ingredients.

WORKING in 2 batches, put the fried and toasted ingredients in the blender jar along with the roasted tomato and 1¼ cups of the remaining stock per batch (2½ cups total). Blend until the mixture is very smooth, about 3 minutes. Be careful when you're blending hot ingredients: Cover the top with a kitchen towel, and hold the top firmly in place with your hand.

HEAT the remaining 2 tablespoons of oil in a 6- to 7-quart heavy pot over medium heat until it shimmers, then carefully pour in the chile puree and nut puree, stirring, and bring them to a simmer. Add the piloncillo and chocolate, and stir until the chocolate melts. Simmer the mole, uncovered (use a splatter screen so the sauce doesn't make a mess of the stove), stirring frequently, until it thickens slightly, about 10 minutes. Add enough of the remaining chicken stock (1 to 2 cups) to thin the mole to a velvety consistency that thickly coats a wooden spoon, but isn't gloppy. Simmer gently, uncovered, for 30 minutes longer, adding more stock as necessary to maintain the velvety consistency. Season to taste with additional salt.

ADD the chicken or turkey to the mole, reduce the heat to low, and cook until it's just heated through, 15 to 20 minutes.

Serve it with Corn Tortillas (page 39), rice, beans, or any other side you like (pages 246–256). Or turn it into Tacos (pages 212–214), Enchiladas (pages 216–224), or Tamales (page 227).

This mole actually improves after a day in the refrigerator. It keeps in the refrigerator for up to five days without the meat or up to three days with the meat, or in the freezer for up to one month.

NOTE: Piloncillo is a type of Mexican raw sugar that has a lovely molasses-like flavor and comes in a pestle-shape block. It is available at Mexican grocery stores or by mail order (see Sources, page 258).

BLACK MOLE FROM OAXACA
MOLE NEGRO OAXAQUEÑO

Mole poblano might be the most popular example in the United States, but mole negro from Oaxaca, the so-called king of moles, is surely one of the most intriguing. Seasoned with indigenous ingredients and newcomers, and probably originally executed by hired help, the midnight-black sauce has one of those lengthy ingredient lists that includes a few unexpected mole ingredients and a few familiar ones treated in a rather unfamiliar way: Chile seeds are charred almost beyond recognition, giving the mole its black color and a welcome bitterness that plays against the sweetness of ripe plantain and Mexican chocolate. The mole is typically made with black chilhuacle chiles, but you can use guajillos and give them a darker-than-usual toast, as I've instructed. And to mimic Oaxacan oregano, I've called for a combination of oregano and marjoram. This is probably the most complicated mole in this book, but once you cook a few others, you'll quickly graduate to this one.

MAKES 12 CUPS SAUCE (ENOUGH FOR 12 SERVINGS)   ACTIVE TIME: 1¾ TO 2 HOURS   START TO FINISH: 2¾ TO 3¾ HOURS

1¼ ounces guajillo chiles (5), wiped clean, stemmed, slit open, seeded (reserve the seeds), and deveined

1¼ ounces chilhuacle negro chiles (5), or an additional 5 guajillo chiles, wiped clean, stemmed, slit open, seeded (reserve the seeds), and deveined

2 ounces mulato chiles (4), wiped clean, stemmed, slit open, seeded (reserve the seeds), and deveined

1⅔ ounces pasilla chiles (5), wiped clean, stemmed, slit open, seeded (reserve the seeds), and deveined

1 pound tomatoes (about 3 medium)

½ pound tomatillos (5 or 6 medium), husked and rinsed

1 medium white onion, cut into ½-inch-thick round slices

6 garlic cloves, peeled

4 avocado leaves

2 corn tortillas

⅔ cup pork lard (5 ounces), mild olive oil, or vegetable oil

1 large ripe (brown or black) plantain, peeled and cut into ½-inch-thick slices

1 (2-inch) piece ginger, peeled and thinly sliced

2 (1-inch) slices baguette

2 ounces shelled skinless peanuts (rounded ⅓ cup), preferably raw

2 ounces blanched almonds (rounded ⅓ cup)

2 ounces raw pecans (½ cup)

2 ounces raisins (⅓ cup)

2 ounces unhulled sesame seeds (⅓ cup)

1 (2-inch) piece canela (Mexican cinnamon)

10 whole black peppercorns

4 whole allspice berries

4 whole cloves

1 teaspoon dried oregano

1 teaspoon dried marjoram

3 cups water

1 tablespoon sugar

2 teaspoons fine salt, or 4 teaspoons kosher salt

1 recipe Poached Chicken (page 242) or Poached Turkey (page 242), including 6 to 8 cups of stock, divided

6 ounces Mexican chocolate (2 disks), broken into wedges

PREHEAT the oven to 375°F.

SPREAD the guajillo and chilhuacle chiles, if you're using them, on a foil-lined baking pan and toast them in the middle of the oven, turning them over occasionally, until they are nice and dark, 10 to 12 minutes (they will have a charred rather than fruity taste). Transfer the chiles to a bowl. Spread the mulato and pasilla chiles on the baking pan, and toast them in the middle of the oven, turning them over occasionally, until they are nice and dark, 5 to 7 minutes. Add them to the bowl with the other chiles. Add enough water to cover the chiles and set aside to soak for 30 minutes.

SET the oven to broil and preheat. Alternatively, you can preheat the oven to 500°F. If you're using the oven broiler, position the rack 8 inches from the heat source. Core the tomatoes and cut a small "X" through the skin on the opposite ends. Roast the tomatoes, cored sides up, and tomatillos on a foil-lined baking pan, turning the tomatillos over once until the tomatillos turn a khaki-green color and are cooked to the core, 20 to 30 minutes; and the tomatoes are blackened on their tops and cooked to the core, 20 to 30 minutes. Slip the skins from the tomatoes.

MEANWHILE, heat a comal, griddle, or heavy skillet over medium-low heat, and roast the onion slices and garlic on the comal, turning the garlic over occasionally, until it is just tender and golden brown with some blackened spots, 8 to 10 minutes, and turning the onion slices over just once, until they are softened and charred on both sides, 15 to 20 minutes.

HEAT a medium heavy skillet over medium-high heat and have ready a small bowl of cold water. Toast all the reserved chile seeds in the skillet, stirring constantly, until they are completely black and shiny, 4 to 5 minutes total. Use a long kitchen lighter or match to ignite the seeds, shaking the pan gently to make sure they all catch fire. The flame will extinguish quickly and by itself. Add them to the bowl of cold water and soak for 10 minutes. Drain them, discarding the soaking liquid, and add the chile seeds to the bowl of toasted chiles.

TOAST the avocado leaves in the skillet over medium heat turning them over and pressing them down with tongs frequently, until they're lightly browned and fragrant, 1 to 2 minutes. Add the avocado leaves to the bowl of chiles. Set the skillet aside.

USING tongs, hold the tortilla directly over a burner set to medium. Toast on both sides, letting the tortilla catch fire and burn until it's completely black, about 4 minutes. Repeat the procedure with the remaining tortilla and crumble both tortillas into the bowl of chiles.

HAVE ready a large bowl and a metal sieve set over a small heatproof bowl.

HEAT the lard or oil in the reserved skillet over medium heat until it shimmers and fry the following ingredients one by one. As they're fried, use a slotted spoon to transfer them to the large bowl (for ingredients that are difficult to scoop, empty the contents of the skillet into the sieve to drain first, then return the oil to the skillet and put the fried ingredient in the larger bowl).

FRY the plantain slices, turning them over once, until they're brown on both sides, about 8 minutes.

FRY the ginger, turning the slices over once, until they're browned on both sides, about 1½ minutes.

FRY the baguette slices, turning them over once, until they're well browned, about 2 minutes.

FRY the peanuts, stirring, until golden, about 2½ minutes.

FRY the almonds, stirring, until golden, about 2 minutes.

FRY the pecans, stirring, until well browned, about 1½ minutes.

FRY the raisins, stirring, until puffed, about 30 seconds.

FRY the sesame seeds along with the canela, peppercorns, allspice, and cloves until golden brown, about 1 minute. Add the oregano and marjoram and cook until the herbs brown slightly, about 15 seconds. Transfer to the sieve and drain, reserving the oil.

DRAIN the chile mixture. Working in 2 batches, if necessary, blend the chile mixture in the blender jar with 3 cups of water until it's very smooth, about 3 minutes. Strain through a medium-mesh sieve into a bowl, discarding any solids.

WORKING in 2 batches, put the fried ingredients into the blender jar along with the roasted tomatoes, tomatillos, onion, garlic, sugar, salt, and about 2 cups per batch of the stock (4 cups total) and blend until the mixture is very smooth, about 3 minutes.

HEAT 3 tablespoons of the reserved oil (or add some fresh oil if there isn't enough) in a wide 7- to 8-quart heavy pot over medium heat until it shimmers. Carefully pour in the strained chile puree and simmer (use a splatter screen so the sauce doesn't make a mess of the stove), stirring frequently, until it has slightly thickened, 8 to 10 minutes. As the puree is simmering, swish a little liquid around in the blender and add it to the pot.

ADD the tomato-nut puree to the chile puree and cook, stirring constantly, for 5 minutes. Add enough of the remaining stock (1 to 2 cups) to thin the sauce to a velvety consistency that thickly coats a wooden spoon, but isn't gloppy. Bring the mole to a simmer. Gently simmer the mole, partially covered, over low heat for 30 minutes.

STIR in the chocolate and cook, stirring, until the chocolate is melted, then continue to simmer gently, partially covered, adding more stock, as necessary, to maintain the velvety consistency, about 30 minutes more. Season to taste with additional sugar and salt.

ADD the chicken or turkey to the mole, reduce the heat to low, and cook until it's just heated through, 15 to 20 minutes.

Serve it with Corn Tortillas (page 39), rice, beans, or any other side you like (pages 246–256). Or turn it into Tacos (pages 212–214), Enchiladas (pages 216–224), or Tamales (page 227).

This mole actually improves after a day in the refrigerator. It keeps in the refrigerator for up to five days without the meat or up to three days with the meat, or in the freezer for up to one month.

Some recipes for thick moles call for shelled, raw, skinless peanuts, which you can purchase at your local natural foods store. If you must, you can substitute roasted, peanuts for raw ones—in that case, you don't have to fry them as you would if they were raw.

PIPIANES

Many Mexican cooks will balk at the idea of grouping pipianes and moles in the same chapter. The big difference is that, in pipianes—history has muddied the word's origin, but it's thought to come from the word *pepita*, which means "seed"—the seeds, nuts, or both, are generally the main ingredient, while in moles, nuts and seeds share the spotlight more equally with other ingredients. In addition, pipianes tend to be slightly simpler than moles. But the fluidity of the definitions becomes apparent as you travel the country. For instance, what people from Central Mexico call a mole verde made with pumpkin seeds would be considered a pipián by people in the *sierra* of Puebla. In light of this, I've decided that it's time to group moles and pipianes together. They each use many of the same ingredients and are prepared in a very similar way. Keeping them separate just exaggerates their differences and overwhelms cooks. I've made another decision that might rankle traditionalists. In Mexico, when you say pipián, most people think of sauces made with pumpkin seeds. But when you explore a little, you find that a pipián is any sauce made of seeds, nuts, or grains, sometimes multiple varieties or a combination of seeds, nuts, and grains. Which means that two more categories of sauce could be considered subsets of pipianes: *encacahuatados* (sauces made mostly of peanuts) and *almendrados* (those made mostly of almonds). Neither category is popularly considered part of the pipián family—in fact, you might get funny looks if you refer to them as pipianes in Mexico—but again, the techniques used to make them are so similar, why pretend they're entirely different? I'd rather show you how similar they actually are than stick to strict definitions based on tradition.

Toasted pumpkin seeds (left) and raw pumpkin seeds (right)

PIPIANES MADE WITH PUMPKIN SEEDS

When you say the word *pipián*, these are the sauces that immediately pop into Mexican people's heads. These thick, rich sauces are made with pumpkin seeds, which frugal and clever Mexican cooks kept from the squashes in their gardens and put to delicious use. If they're paired with fresh chiles and herbs, the result is a pretty pastel green, while those made with anchos, guajillos, and puyas are pale red. And while they're quite smooth, they often have little bits of pumpkin seeds that don't blend all the way and provide a little soft crunch.

TIPS FOR PUMPKIN SEED PIPIANES

Remember, when my recipes call for pumpkin seeds, I always mean hulled raw pumpkin seeds, which are small and green. You'll find them at your local natural foods store.

Pumpkin seed sauces occasionally break while you're simmering them. It's common and has an easy solution: Just blend the sauce again, in a few batches, until it's smooth and return it to the pot.

SIMPLE PUMPKIN SEED SAUCE
PIPIÁN VERDE

If my mother or any other sophisticated eater tells me that he or she is dropping by for dinner with a few friends, I'll throw together a dish that doesn't take much time but still delivers great flavor—something like this pipián. A major wallop of heat from the serranos is essential to cut through the richness of those pumpkin seeds like a sharp knife through ripe tomato. If you're serving it with seafood, don't forget to squeeze on some lime juice.

MAKES 4 CUPS SAUCE (ENOUGH FOR 4 OR 5 SERVINGS)   **ACTIVE TIME: 25 TO 40 MINUTES**   **START TO FINISH: 50 MINUTES TO 2 HOURS**

5 ounces hulled raw (green) pumpkin seeds (1 cup)

⅓ cup chopped white onion

3 fresh serrano or jalapeño chiles, coarsely chopped, including seeds

1 small garlic clove, peeled

½ teaspoon dried oregano, preferably Mexican

¼ teaspoon ground cumin

½ teaspoon fine salt, or 1 teaspoon kosher salt

4 to 5 cups chicken stock, divided

2 tablespoons mild olive oil or vegetable oil

½ cup chopped cilantro

½ recipe Poached Chicken (page 242), ½ recipe Cooked Pork (page 243), or 1¼ pounds raw shrimp or fish fillets

GARNISH
Lime wedges, if you're using shrimp or fish

HEAT a skillet over medium heat and toast the pumpkin seeds, stirring and tossing constantly, until they're puffed and just slightly browned, 5 to 8 minutes.

PUT the pumpkin seeds in the blender jar along with the onion, chiles, garlic, oregano, cumin, salt, and 2 cups of the stock, and blend until the mixture is smooth, at least 3 minutes.

HEAT the oil in a 4- to 5-quart heavy pot (this will give you enough room to add the meat or fish later; if you're making just the sauce, a 3- to 4-quart pot is fine) over medium heat until it simmers, and carefully pour in the blended mixture. Cook (use a splatter screen so the sauce doesn't make a mess of the stove), stirring, until thickened, about 5 minutes. Add just enough stock to thin the sauce to a velvety consistency that thickly coats a wooden spoon, but isn't gloppy. Simmer, partially covered, for 20 minutes, adding more stock, as necessary, to maintain the velvety consistency.

RETURN some of the sauce, about 1 cup (or all if the sauce has broken and looks like scrambled eggs), to the blender, then add the cilantro and blend until smooth. Be careful when you're blending hot ingredients: Cover the top with a kitchen towel, and hold the top firmly in place with your hand. Work in batches to avoid blending with a full jar.

Return the sauce to the pot and simmer, uncovered, 5 minutes more. As the sauce is simmering, swish a little liquid around in the blender and add it to the pot. Season to taste with additional salt.

IF you're using chicken or pork, add it to the sauce now, reduce the heat to low, and cook until it's just heated through, 15 to 20 minutes. If you're using shrimp or fish, season it with salt, gently cook it in the sauce until just cooked through, about 10 minutes, and serve with lime wedges.

Serve it with Corn Tortillas (page 39), rice, beans, or any other side you like (pages 246–256). Or turn it into Enchiladas (pages 216–224).

This pipián tastes best the day it's made.

*Shrimp in Simple
Pumpkin Seed Sauce*

PUEBLA-STYLE PUMPKIN SEED SAUCE PIPIÁN VERDE DE PUEBLA

Straight from my friend Ana Elena Martinez's kitchen in Puebla, this bright, vibrant green sauce, packed with tangy tomatillos and herbs and lettuce, would be called a mole almost anywhere else in the country. But she and her compatriots call it a pipián, and who am I to argue when she makes something this good?

MAKES 8 CUPS SAUCE (ENOUGH FOR 8 TO 10 SERVINGS)   **ACTIVE TIME: 1 TO 1¼ HOURS**   **START TO FINISH: 1 TO 2 HOURS**

6 ounces tomatillos (about 4), husked, rinsed, and coarsely chopped

3 fresh serrano or jalapeño chiles, coarsely chopped, including seeds

1 teaspoon fine salt, or 2 teaspoons kosher salt

1 recipe Poached Chicken (page 242) or Cooked Pork (page 243), including 5 to 6 cups of stock, divided

6 ounces hulled raw (green) pumpkin seeds (1¼ cups)

2 ounces unhulled sesame seeds (rounded ⅓ cup)

2 tablespoons mild olive oil or vegetable oil

2 romaine lettuce leaves, torn

½ cup chopped cilantro

1 fresh hoja santa (holy leaf), stem discarded

_____

PUT the tomatillos, chiles, salt, and 2 cups of the stock in the blender jar.

HEAT a skillet over medium heat and toast the pumpkin seeds, stirring and tossing constantly, until they're puffed and just slightly browned, 5 to 8 minutes. Transfer the pumpkin seeds to the blender.

ADD the sesame seeds to the skillet and toast, stirring and tossing constantly, until they're fragrant and a shade darker, 3 to 4 minutes. Transfer the sesame seeds to the blender and blend the mixture until it is smooth, about 3 minutes.

HEAT the oil in a 6- to 7-quart heavy pot (this will give you enough room to add the meat later; if you're making just the sauce, a 3- to 4-quart pot is fine) over medium heat until it shimmers. Carefully pour the sauce into the oil (it may splatter), and let the sauce simmer, stirring often, until it has thickened slightly, 5 to 7 minutes (use a splatter screen so the sauce doesn't make a mess of the stove). Add 2 cups of the stock and bring to a simmer.

PUT 1 cup of the remaining stock in the blender along with the lettuce, cilantro, and hoja santa and blend until smooth, about 1 minute.

STIR the herb mixture into the sauce in the pot and bring the mixture back to a simmer. As it's simmering, swish a little liquid around in the blender and add it to the pot. Add more stock, if necessary, to maintain a velvety consistency that thickly coats a wooden spoon, but isn't gloppy. Season to taste with additional salt. If the sauce appears broken (like scrambled eggs), blend it again, in batches, until smooth, transferring the blended sauce to another pot.

ADD the chicken or pork to the sauce, reduce the heat to low, and cook until it's just heated through, 15 to 20 minutes.

Serve it with Corn Tortillas (page 39), rice, beans, or any other side you like (pages 246–256).

This pipián tastes best the day it's made.

TOTONAC-STYLE SAUCE
PIPIÁN VERDE TOTONACO

Like the previous pipián but unlike many others, you'll find no spices in this dish, shared with me by my friend Ricardo Muñoz Zurita. It's made in the style of the Totonacs, an indigenous people with a sophisticated language, culture, and cuisine who eschew many ingredients that are relatively new to Mexico. For that reason, a punch of heat is really important, even if you have to use six chiles!

MAKES 9 CUPS SAUCE (ENOUGH FOR 8 TO 10 SERVINGS)   ACTIVE TIME: **1 HOUR**   START TO FINISH: **1½ TO 2½ HOURS**

11 ounces hulled raw (green) pumpkin seeds (2 cups)

2½ ounces unhulled sesame seeds (½ cup)

1½ pounds tomatillos (15 to 18), husked, rinsed, and coarsely chopped

1½ packed cups chopped cilantro

½ cup coarsely chopped white onion

3 to 4 fresh serrano or jalapeño chiles, coarsely chopped, including seeds, or more to taste

4 large garlic cloves, peeled

2 teaspoon fine salt, or 4 teaspoon kosher salt

1 recipe Poached Chicken (page 242), 1 recipe Cooked Pork (page 243), including 6 to 7 cups of stock, divided, or 2½ pounds raw shrimp or fish fillets and 6 to 7 cups of fish, shrimp, or chicken stock

¼ cup mild olive oil or vegetable oil

GARNISH
Lime wedges, if you're using shrimp or fish

HEAT a skillet over medium heat and toast the pumpkin seeds, stirring and tossing constantly, until they're puffed and just slightly browned, 5 to 8 minutes. Transfer to a bowl. Toast the sesame seeds in the skillet over medium heat, stirring and tossing constantly, until they're fragrant and a shade darker, 3 to 4 minutes. Transfer to the bowl of pumpkin seeds.

WORKING in 2 batches, blend the pumpkin seeds and sesame seeds with the tomatillos, cilantro, onion, chiles, garlic, salt, and 1½ cups of the stock per batch (3 cups total) in the blender jar until the mixture is smooth, about 3 minutes per batch.

HEAT the oil in a 6- to 7-quart heavy pot (this will give you enough room to add the meat or fish later; if you're making just the sauce, a 4- to 5-quart pot is fine) set over medium-high heat. Carefully add the blended mixture and simmer over medium heat, uncovered (use a splatter screen so the sauce doesn't make a mess of the stove), stirring frequently, until the sauce has thickened slightly, about 10 minutes. As it's simmering, swish a little liquid around in the blender and add it to the pot. Stir in enough stock (about 3 cups) to thin the sauce to a velvety consistency that thickly coats a wooden spoon, but isn't gloppy. Lower the heat and simmer gently, uncovered, stirring occasionally, for 15 minutes more, adding more stock, as necessary, to maintain the velvety consistency. If the sauce separates, blend it again in the blender (in batches) until it's smooth again, then return it to the pot. Season to taste with additional salt.

IF you're using the chicken or pork, add the meat to the sauce, reduce the heat to low, and cook until it's just heated through, 15 to 20 minutes. If you're using shrimp or fish, season it with salt, then gently cook it in the sauce until it is just cooked through, about 10 minutes, and serve with lime wedges.

Serve it with Corn Tortillas (page 39), rice, beans, or any other side you like (pages 246–256).

This pipián keeps in the refrigerator for up to two days.

VERACRUZ-STYLE SESAME AND PUMPKIN SEED SAUCE TLATONILE

Expect a big punch of epazote and a beautiful brick-red color from this pipián from the highlands of Veracruz. I have adapted it from a recipe given to me by my friend Sergio Remolina. Two types of seeds—pumpkin and sesame—make for a complex flavor and rich texture. Because comapeño chiles, which are native to Veracruz, are very hard to find in the United States, you can substitute puya chiles, which are like smaller, hotter guajillos.

MAKES 8 CUPS SAUCE (ENOUGH FOR 8 TO 10 SERVINGS)   ACTIVE TIME: 45 MINUTES   START TO FINISH: 1½ HOURS

1 ounce ancho chiles (2), wiped clean, stemmed, slit open, seeded, and deveined

1 ounce comapeño or puya chiles (12 to 15), wiped clean, stemmed, slit open, seeded, and deveined

½ pound hulled raw (green) pumpkin seeds (1½ cups)

5 ounces unhulled sesame seeds (1 cup)

1 teaspoon fine salt, or 2 teaspoons kosher salt

1 recipe Poached Chicken (page 242), including 6 to 8 cups of stock, divided

¼ cup pork lard, mild olive oil, or vegetable oil

3 large epazote sprigs

HEAT a medium heavy skillet over medium-low heat and toast the chiles, a few at a time, turning them over and pressing them down with tongs frequently, until they are fragrant and the insides have changed color slightly, 1 to 1½ minutes per batch. Soak the chiles in enough cold water to cover for 30 minutes. Drain and discard the soaking water.

HEAT a skillet over medium heat and toast the pumpkin seeds, stirring and tossing constantly, until they're puffed and just slightly browned, 5 to 8 minutes. Transfer them to a bowl.

TOAST the sesame seeds in the same skillet over medium heat, stirring and tossing constantly, until they're fragrant and a shade darker, 3 to 4 minutes. Transfer them to the bowl of pumpkin seeds.

WORKING in 2 batches, blend the chiles, pumpkin seeds, sesame seeds, and salt in the blender jar with 4 cups of the stock (2 cups per batch), or enough stock to form a smooth puree, about 3 minutes per batch.

HEAT the lard or oil in a 6- to 7-quart heavy pot over medium heat until it shimmers. Carefully pour in the blended puree and simmer, stirring frequently, until the mixture thickens slightly, about 10 minutes. As it's simmering, swish a little liquid around in the blender and add it to the pot. Add just enough stock to thin the sauce to a velvety consistency that thickly coats a wooden spoon, but isn't gloppy. Add the epazote and simmer, partially covered, until small pools of oil appear on the surface of the sauce, about 20 minutes. As the sauce simmers, add chicken stock, as necessary, to maintain the velvety consistency. Discard the epazote. Season to taste with additional salt.

IF the sauce separates, blend it again (in batches) until it's smooth. Return the sauce to the pot. Add the chicken to the sauce, reduce the heat to low, and cook until it's just heated through, 15 to 20 minutes.

Serve it with Corn Tortillas (page 39), rice, beans, or any other side you like (pages 246–256).

This pipián keeps in the refrigerator for up to two days.

PUMPKIN SEED AND CASCABEL CHILE DIP PIPIÁN DE CASCABEL PARA BOTANA

Instead of duplicating the saucy texture of most pipianes, I created this thicker rendition, which makes a rich, spicy dip for chips or toasted bread.

MAKES **ABOUT 1 CUP**   ACTIVE TIME: **30 MINUTES**   START TO FINISH: **40 MINUTES**

3 ounces hulled raw (green) pumpkin seeds (about ½ cup)

3 large garlic cloves, peeled

2 ounces tomatillos (2 small), husked and rinsed

¾ ounce cascabel chiles (3 to 4), wiped clean and stemmed

½ cup chopped cilantro

½ cup water

1 small fresh serrano chile, finely chopped, including seeds

½ teaspoon fine salt, or 1 teaspoon kosher salt

¼ teaspoon cumin seeds

———————————

HEAT a heavy skillet (do not use cast iron) over medium heat and toast the pumpkin seeds, stirring and tossing constantly, until they're puffed and just slightly browned, 5 to 8 minutes. Put the seeds in a bowl and set aside.

HEAT the same skillet over medium-low heat. Roast the garlic, turning it over once or twice, until it's tender and golden brown with some blackened spots, 8 to 10 minutes. Roast the tomatillos, turning them over once, until their tops and bottoms have blackened and the tomatillos are a khaki-green color and cooked to the core, 20 to 30 minutes.

BREAK each cascabel chile into about 3 pieces for easier toasting, discarding the seeds and veins. Toast them in batches alongside the tomatillos and garlic, turning them over and pressing them down with tongs frequently, until fragrant, about 1 minute per batch.

PUT the tomatillos in the blender jar first, then add the pumpkin seeds, garlic, and cascabel chiles along with the cilantro, water, serrano chile, salt, and cumin. Blend until smooth, about 3 minutes. Season to taste with additional salt.

Serve it with Corn Tortillas (page 39) or Tortilla Chips (page 229).

This dip keeps in the refrigerator for up to five days.

PUMPKIN SEED AND PASILLA DE OAXACA PASTE CHINTEXTLE

When I serve this garlic-spiked paste of pumpkin seeds and the spectacular pasillas de Oaxaca to Mexican friends, I get a similar reaction. "Wow," they exclaim, "this tastes like the countryside!" Somehow, just from the particular flavor profile of this simple concoction, we Mexicans can tell that this is not something you often find in cities. Instead, it's what men who toil on farms buy in local street markets or get from their wives before they head to work, because it keeps well even in the high heat of the afternoon. When they need a snack, they break out tostadas (crunchy corn tortillas) and spread on chintextle, the potent paste turning even that simple snack into a real treat. Many versions are even simpler than this one, which I got from my friend Iliana de la Vega, sometimes made with just chiles, salt, and garlic—or even just chiles and salt. At home, I stir a little chintextle into soup and I smear it on pieces of bread or fresh corn tortillas, gobbling one after the other.

MAKES 1 CUP   ACTIVE TIME: 25 MINUTES   START TO FINISH: 1 DAY (TO LET THE FLAVORS DEVELOP)

1½ ounces pasilla de Oaxaca chiles (9), wiped clean and stemmed

4 ounces hulled raw (green) pumpkin seeds (¾ cup)

5 large garlic cloves, peeled

2 tablespoons rice vinegar

2 tablespoons distilled white vinegar, or more to taste

½ teaspoon fine salt, or 1 teaspoon kosher salt

1 to 2 tablespoons mild olive oil or vegetable oil, if necessary

HEAT a comal, griddle, or heavy skillet over medium-low heat, and toast the chiles a few at a time, turning them over and pressing them down with tongs frequently, until they become a lighter shade of brown and develop some blisters, about 2 minutes per batch. Set them aside to cool.

HEAT a skillet over medium heat and toast the pumpkin seeds, stirring and tossing constantly, until they're puffed and just slightly browned, 5 to 8 minutes. Transfer them to a plate to cool.

PUT the chiles, pumpkin seeds, and garlic in the food processor (there's not enough liquid to use the blender here) and process to form a paste, scraping the sides often. Add the vinegars and process again. Season to taste with the distilled vinegar and salt, and process again to blend. If necessary, add oil, a little at a time, to help blend the mixture into a very smooth paste. Processing will take at least 3 minutes total.

BEFORE you serve it, refrigerate the chintextle in an airtight container for one day to allow the flavors to develop.

Serve it with Corn Tortillas (page 39), Tortilla Chips (page 229), Tostadas (page 229), or any bean dish you like (pages 246–250).

The paste keeps in the refrigerator for up to two weeks or in the freezer for up to two months.

*The perfect snack—
Chintextle spread on a
warm tortilla*

PUMPKIN SEED AND JALAPEÑO DIP
PIPIÁN DE JALAPEÑO Y PEPITA PARA BOTANA

With the consistency of mayonnaise, this super-simple sauce makes a fabulous dip for chips, cucumber, and jicama, or condiment for sandwiches.

MAKES 1¼ CUPS   **ACTIVE TIME: 20 MINUTES**   **START TO FINISH: 25 MINUTES**

3½ ounces hulled raw (green) pumpkin seeds (⅔ cup)

4 fresh jalapeño chiles

2 tablespoons mild olive oil or vegetable oil

¾ cup water

1 small garlic clove, peeled

½ teaspoon fine salt, or 1 teaspoon kosher salt

HEAT a heavy skillet over medium heat and toast the pumpkin seeds, stirring and tossing constantly, until they're puffed and just slightly browned, 5 to 8 minutes. Put the seeds in the blender jar.

HOLD 1 jalapeño chile vertically by the stem, with the tip of the chile touching the cutting board. Cut the flesh off the chile in three or four long pieces (the seeds will still be attached to the stem and look like a lantern). Discard the stem and seeds. Repeat with the remaining chiles. If you want a higher level of spiciness, leave one of the chiles whole and remove the stem.

HEAT the oil in the skillet over medium-high heat until it shimmers, then add the chile pieces and sauté, stirring frequently, until they're blistered on all sides, but still bright green, about 3 minutes.

ADD the chiles, the chile cooking oil, water, garlic, and salt to the pumpkin seeds in the blender. Blend to form a smooth puree that has the texture of mayonnaise, about 3 minutes. Season to taste with additional salt.

Serve it with Corn Tortillas (page 39) or Tortilla Chips (page 229).

This dip keeps in the refrigerator for up to five days.

ENCACAHUATADOS

Mexican food novices are always enamored when I serve them encacahuatados, the smooth, savory, and sometimes very spicy peanut-spiked sauces that are eaten throughout Mexico. Their striking color makes the first impression, then the lovely richness and sweetness of the peanuts, tempered by the acidity of tomatillos, tomatoes, or vinegar, takes over, convincing anyone who tries them that this delicious category of sauces deserves much more celebration in the United States.

Most encacahuatados are made with raw skinless peanuts, which you can find shelled in your local natural foods store. But in two of my recipes, I've called for roasted peanuts to make things easier—that way, you don't have to fry them as you would if they were raw. Either way, store the peanuts in an airtight container in a cool, dark place for two months or in the freezer for six months.

CLASSIC PEANUT SAUCE
ENCACAHUATADO CLASSICO

Maria Dolores Torres Izabal is a wonderful cook with a whimsical spirit. I've eaten some truly epic meals at her home. Occasionally, I'd bring a modern dish that I'd thought up, and while some of my elders rolled their eyes, she would never fail to support my endeavors and always encouraged me to keep experimenting. This recipe is adapted from her fabulous encacahuatado. The pinkish sauce is perhaps the most recognizable version, and, as a tribute to her, I kept it true to tradition.

MAKES 4 CUPS SAUCE (ENOUGH FOR 4 TO 6 SERVINGS)   **ACTIVE TIME: 30 TO 45 MINUTES**   **START TO FINISH: 1½ TO 2½ HOURS**

1 pound tomatoes (about 3 medium)

2 fresh serrano chiles, stemmed

2 garlic cloves, peeled

1 cup (5 ounces) shelled roasted peanuts, such as cocktail peanuts

⅓ cup chopped white onion

1 (2-inch) piece canela (Mexican cinnamon), or ½ teaspoon ground cinnamon

2 whole cloves

½ teaspoon fine salt, or 1 teaspoon kosher salt

½ recipe Poached Chicken (page 242), including 3 to 4 cups of stock, divided

2 tablespoons mild olive oil or vegetable oil

SET the oven to broil and preheat. Alternatively, you can preheat the oven to 500°F. If you're using the oven broiler, position the rack 8 inches from the heat source. Have ready a large bowl to hold the ingredients that you'll remove from the oven as they finish roasting.

CORE the tomatoes and cut a small "X" through the skin on the opposite ends. Put the tomatoes, cored sides up, on a foil-lined baking pan, and cook until their tops have blackened and the tomatoes are cooked to the core, 20 to 30 minutes. Meanwhile, heat a comal, griddle, or heavy skillet over medium-low heat, and roast the chiles, turning them over occasionally, until they're tender, blistered all over, and blackened in spots, about 10 minutes; and the garlic, turning over occasionally, until it's just tender and golden brown with some blackened spots, 8 to 10 minutes. Slip the skins

from the tomatoes, and remove the skins from the chiles (you might have to use a paring knife).

PUT the tomatoes, chiles, and garlic in the blender jar with the peanuts, onion, cinnamon, cloves, salt, and 2 cups of the stock, and blend until smooth, about 3 minutes. Be careful when you're blending hot ingredients: Cover the top with a kitchen towel, and hold the top firmly in place with your hand. Work in batches to avoid blending with a full jar.

HEAT the oil in a 4- to 5-quart heavy pot (this will give you enough room to add the chicken later; if you're making just the sauce, a 3- to 4-quart pot is fine) over medium heat until it shimmers. Add the blended mixture and simmer, stirring frequently, until it has thickened slightly, about 10 minutes. Add enough stock to thin the sauce to a velvety consistency that thickly coats a wooden spoon but isn't gloppy. As it's simmering, swish a little liquid around in the blender and add it to the pot. Reduce the heat to low and simmer the sauce, uncovered (use a splatter screen so the sauce doesn't make a mess of the stove), stirring frequently, until small pools of oil appear on the surface, about 35 minutes. As the sauce simmers, add more stock, as necessary, to maintain the velvety consistency. Season to taste with additional salt.

ADD the chicken to the sauce, reduce the heat to low, and cook until it's just heated through, 15 to 20 minutes.

Serve it with Corn Tortillas (page 39), rice, beans, or any other side you like (pages 246–256).

This encacahuatado actually improves after a day in the refrigerator. It keeps in the refrigerator for up to five days without the chicken or up to three days with the chicken, or in the freezer for up to one month.

RED PEANUT SAUCE ENCACAHUATADO ROJO

A simple sauce with fabulous flavor—the zip of árbol chiles and the earthiness of guajillos perk up slightly sweet, roasted peanuts. The result is completely savory and satisfying.

MAKES 4 CUPS SAUCE (ENOUGH FOR 4 TO 6 SERVINGS)   **ACTIVE TIME: 30 TO 45 MINUTES**   **START TO FINISH: 1½ TO 2½ HOURS**

⅓ pound tomato (about 1 medium)

4 garlic cloves, peeled

½ ounce guajillo chiles (2), wiped clean, stemmed, slit open, seeded, and deveined

2 to 4 dried árbol chiles, wiped clean and stemmed

2 tablespoons mild olive oil or vegetable oil, divided

1 cup shelled skinless peanuts (5 ounces), preferably raw

⅛ teaspoon whole black peppercorns

2 whole cloves

¼ teaspoon dried thyme

¼ teaspoon dried oregano, preferably Mexican

½ recipe Poached Chicken (page 242) or Cooked Pork (page 243), including 4 to 5 cups of stock, divided

1 teaspoon apple cider vinegar, or more to taste

1 teaspoon sugar

½ teaspoon fine salt, or 1 teaspoon kosher salt

SET the oven to broil and preheat. Alternatively, you can preheat the oven to 500°F. If you're using the oven broiler, position the rack 8 inches from the heat source. Have ready a large bowl to hold the ingredients that you'll remove from the oven as they finish roasting.

CORE the tomato and cut a small "X" through the skin on the opposite end. Put the tomato, cored side up, on a foil-lined baking pan. Roast without turning, until it's blackened on top and cooked to the core, 20 to 30 minutes. Slip the skin from the tomato. Meanwhile, heat a comal, griddle, or heavy skillet over medium-low heat, and toast the guajillo chiles, árbol chiles, and garlic, turning them over frequently, until the guajillos are fragrant, about 1 minute, the árbol chiles are dark brown, 3 to 4 minutes, and the garlic is just tender and golden brown with some blackened spots, 8 to 10 minutes.

HEAT 1 tablespoon of the oil in a medium skillet over medium heat, and cook the peanuts, stirring constantly, until they're deep golden brown, about 2 minutes. Transfer the peanuts and oil to a medium bowl.

SOAK the peanuts, roasted chiles, peppercorns, cloves, thyme, and oregano in 2½ cups of the stock for 30 minutes. Soaking the ingredients will make blending easier, but if you're in a hurry and have a good blender, you can skip this step and just add the stock when you blend.

BLEND the peanut mixture along with the tomato, garlic, vinegar, sugar, and salt in the blender jar until very smooth, about 3 minutes.

HEAT the remaining 1 tablespoon of oil in a 4- to 5-quart heavy pot (this will give you enough room to add the chicken later; if you're making just the sauce, a 3- to 4-quart pot is fine) over medium heat until it shimmers, then add the blended mixture and simmer, stirring frequently, until it has thickened slightly, about 10 minutes. As it's simmering, swish a little liquid around in the blender and add it to the pot. Add enough stock to thin the sauce to a velvety consistency that thickly coats a wooden spoon but isn't gloppy. Cook, uncovered (use a splatter screen so the sauce doesn't make a mess of the stove), stirring occasionally, until small pools of oil appear on the surface of the sauce, about 35 minutes. As the sauce simmers, add more stock, as necessary, to maintain the velvety consistency. Season to taste with additional vinegar, sugar, and salt.

ADD the chicken or pork to the sauce, reduce the heat to low, and cook until it's just heated through, 15 to 20 minutes.

Serve it with Corn Tortillas (page 39), rice, beans, or any other side you like (pages 246-256).

This encacahuatado actually improves after a day in the refrigerator. It keeps in the refrigerator for up to five days without the meat or up to three days with the meat, or in the freezer for up to one month.

Pork loin with Red Peanut Sauce makes a fine substitute for chicken.

GREEN PEANUT SAUCE
ENCACAHUATADO VERDE

Green encacahuatados are not nearly as common as reddish ones, but I love the way that tangy tomatillos balance the richness of the peanuts. Plenty of cilantro gives the sauce a lovely herbaceous flavor and a bright green color, and a touch of cumin, like pixie dust, brings the flavors together. Since the peanuts are the only ingredient you'd have to fry, I saved you some effort by calling for salted roasted peanuts.

MAKES 4 CUPS SAUCE (ENOUGH FOR 4 TO 6 SERVINGS)   ACTIVE TIME: 30 TO 45 MINUTES   START TO FINISH: 1½ TO 2½ HOURS

½ pound tomatillos (5 to 6), husked and rinsed

2 to 3 fresh serrano chiles, stemmed

⅓ cup chopped white onion

1 cup shelled roasted peanuts (5 ounces), such as cocktail peanuts

1 garlic clove, peeled

½ teaspoon fine salt, or 1 teaspoon kosher salt

½ teaspoon ground cumin

⅔ cup chopped cilantro, divided

½ recipe Poached Chicken (page 242), including 2 to 3 cups of stock, divided

2 tablespoons mild olive oil or vegetable oil

_____

PUT the tomatillos, chiles, and onion in a small saucepan with enough water to cover and bring the water to a simmer. Lower the heat and simmer gently, turning the tomatillos and chiles occasionally, until the tomatillos have turned a khaki-green color and are tender, but still intact, about 15 minutes. If necessary, let them stand in the pan off the heat for up to 15 minutes to finish cooking the tomatillos throughout.

USING a slotted spoon, transfer the tomatillos, chiles, and onion to the blender jar, then add the peanuts, garlic, salt, cumin, ⅓ cup of the cilantro, and 2 cups of the stock. Blend until very smooth, about 3 minutes. Be careful when you're blending hot ingredients: Cover the top with a kitchen towel, and hold the top firmly in place with your hand. Work in batches to avoid blending with a full jar.

HEAT the oil in a 4- to 5-quart heavy pot (this will give you enough room to add the chicken later; if you're making just the sauce, a 3- to 4-quart pot is fine) over medium heat until it shimmers. Add the blended mixture and simmer, stirring frequently, until it has thickened slightly, about 10 minutes. As it's simmering, swish a little liquid around in the blender and add it to the pot. Add enough stock to thin the sauce to a velvety consistency that thickly coats a wooden spoon but isn't gloppy. Reduce the heat to low. Simmer, uncovered (use a splatter screen so the sauce doesn't make a mess of the stove), stirring frequently until small pools of oil appear on the surface, about 20 minutes. As the sauce simmers, add more stock, as necessary, to maintain the velvety consistency. Blend 1 cup of the sauce with the remaining ⅓ cup of cilantro until the mixture is speckled, then return it to the sauce and season to taste with additional salt.

ADD the chicken to the sauce, reduce the heat to low, and cook until it's just heated through, 15 to 20 minutes.

Serve it with Corn Tortillas (page 39), rice, beans, or any other side you like (pages 246–256).

This encacahuatado keeps in the refrigerator for up to two days.

ALMENDRADOS Because almonds came from abroad and were very expensive, they became a high-status nut, a staple in sauces in upper-class households. The nut is still quite expensive in Mexico, so you're more likely to find this array of fragrant sauces in central urban areas and in people's homes rather than the local comida corrida.

BRAISED CHICKEN IN RED ALMOND SAUCE ESTOFADO DE ALMENDRA

A cinnamon-scented sauce made from almonds and tomatoes, this almendrado is just like something my Oaxacan-born grandmother would make. Notice that the only chiles in this dish, adapted from my friend Iliana de la Vega, are the pickled jalapeños that garnish it. The chile-less sauce is a vestige of an older generation determined to distance itself from the chile-loving indigenous peoples.

SERVES 6 ACTIVE TIME: 40 MINUTES START TO FINISH: 1¼ HOURS TO 2¼ HOURS (DEPENDING ON THE MEAT USED)

2 pounds tomatoes (about 6 medium)

1 medium white onion, cut into ½-inch-thick rounds

6 garlic cloves, peeled

3 pounds skinless chicken pieces, or 2 pounds pork stewing meat, such as pork butt, cut into 1½-inch cubes

1 teaspoon fine salt, or 2 teaspoons kosher salt, divided

¼ cup mild olive oil or vegetable oil

4 ounces blanched almonds (¾ cup)

2 (1-inch-thick) slices baguette

8 whole black peppercorns

2 whole cloves

1 (scant 1-inch) piece canela (Mexican cinnamon)

1 teaspoon dried oregano, preferably Mexican

1 teaspoon sugar

1 to 2 cups chicken stock, divided

¼ cup raisins

¼ cup pitted green olives, halved

¼ cup sliced pickled jalapeño chiles (from a 7-ounce can)

SET the oven to broil and preheat. Alternatively, you can preheat the oven to 500°F. If you're using the oven broiler, position the rack 8 inches from the heat source. Core the tomatoes and cut a small "X" through the skin on the opposite ends. Roast the tomatoes, cored sides up, on a foil-lined baking pan, without turning them, until their tops are blackened and the tomatoes are cooked to the core, 20 to 30 minutes. Slip the skins from the tomatoes.

MEANWHILE, heat a comal, griddle, or heavy skillet over medium-low heat, and roast the onion slices and garlic, turning the garlic over once or twice, until it is just tender and golden brown with some blackened spots, 8 to 10 minutes; and turning the onions over once, until they're softened and charred on both sides, 15 to 20 minutes.

PAT the chicken or pork dry and season with ½ teaspoon of the salt. Heat the oil in a wide 5- to 6-quart pot over medium-high heat. Cook the chicken or pork, working in batches, if necessary, to prevent crowding, until it is golden brown on all sides, 8 to 10 minutes per batch. Transfer the meat to a large plate as it is browned.

FRY the almonds in the oil remaining in the pot over medium heat until golden brown, about 2 minutes. Using a slotted spoon, transfer the nuts to a large bowl. Fry the bread in the oil until golden on both sides, about 2 minutes. Transfer it to the large bowl. Remove the pot from the heat.

ADD the roasted tomatoes, onions, and garlic to the nuts and bread, then add the peppercorns, cloves, canela, oregano, sugar, the remaining ½ teaspoon of salt. Toss to combine, then blend the mixture in 2 batches, with ½ cup chicken stock per batch, at least 2 minutes per batch. Be careful when you're blending hot ingredients: Cover the top with a kitchen towel, and hold the top firmly in place with your hand.

REHEAT the oil in the pot over medium heat until it shimmers, then carefully pour in the sauce and simmer, stirring frequently, until it has thickened slightly, about 10 minutes.

As it's simmering, swish a little liquid around in the blender and add it to the pot. Stir in the raisins and olives and return the chicken or pork to the pot. Cover, turn the heat to low, and braise, stirring occasionally, until the chicken is cooked through, about 30 minutes, or until the pork is tender, about 1½ hours. Season to taste with additional salt.

GARNISH the dish with the pickled jalapeño chiles before serving.

Serve it with Corn Tortillas (page 39), rice, beans, or any other side you like (pages 246–256).

This almendrado keeps in the refrigerator for up to three days.

WHITE ALMOND SAUCE

PIPIÁN DE ALMENDRA

You'll come across this snowy white sauce in Mexico City, and it's so easy to make at home. The rich, savory pipián is surprisingly complex tasting, despite its short ingredient list. And each bite brings the unexpected saltiness and acidity of green olives, capers, and pickled jalapeños.

MAKES 6 CUPS SAUCE (ENOUGH FOR 6 TO 8 SERVINGS) **ACTIVE TIME: 1 HOUR** **START TO FINISH: 1 TO 2 HOURS**

½ cup unhulled sesame seeds (2½ ounces)

1 recipe Poached Chicken (page 242), including 4 to 5 cups of stock, divided

1½ cups blanched almonds (8 ounces)

2 fresh jalapeño or serrano chiles, coarsely chopped, including seeds

2 garlic cloves, peeled

4 fresh mint leaves

2 large whole allspice berries

1 whole clove

¼ teaspoon fine salt, or ½ teaspoon kosher salt

2 tablespoons mild olive oil or vegetable oil

1 cup pitted green olives (5 ounces)

½ cup sliced pickled jalapeño chiles (from a 7-ounce can)

¼ cup drained rinsed capers (1½ ounces)

———————————

HEAT a small skillet over medium heat and toast the sesame seeds, stirring and tossing constantly, until they're fragrant and a shade darker, about 4 minutes.

PUT the sesame seeds in the blender jar along with 2 cups of the stock and the almonds, fresh chiles, garlic, mint, allspice, clove, and salt. Blend until the mixture is smooth, about 3 minutes.

HEAT the oil in a 5- to 6-quart heavy pot (this will give you enough room to add the chicken later; if you're making just the sauce, a 3- to 4-quart pot is fine) over medium heat until

it shimmers. Then carefully pour the sauce into the pot (it may splatter). Simmer, uncovered (use a splatter screen so the sauce doesn't make a mess of the stove), stirring frequently, until it has thickened slightly, about 10 minutes. As it's simmering, swish a little liquid around in the blender and add it to the pot. Add about 2 more cups of stock to the sauce, or enough to thin it to a velvety consistency that thickly coats a wooden spoon, but isn't gloppy. Add the olives, pickled jalapeños, and capers, and simmer for 5 minutes. Season to taste with additional salt.

ADD the chicken to the sauce, reduce the heat to low, and cook until it's just heated through, 15 to 20 minutes.

Serve it with Corn Tortillas (page 39), rice, beans, or any other side you like (pages 246–256).

This almendrado keeps in the refrigerator for up to two days.

PIPIANES MADE WITH OTHER SEEDS AND NUTS The huge range of seeds and nuts employed by ingenious Mexican cooks demonstrates the cuisine's striking diversity. In some indigenous communities in the mountains, cooks go to great effort to make the seeds of the mamey fruit edible by boiling them for three days, peeling them, and then smoking them. Other cooks save chile seeds and turn those into tasty, fortifying sauces. But despite the different ingredients, these seemingly disparate sauces share common techniques and results.

PISTACHIO SAUCE PIPIÁN DE PISTACHE

Years ago, when I was the chef at the restaurant Fonda San Miguel in Austin, Texas, I was making a modern pipián from pistachios, excited to channel their fantastic flavor into a sauce for chicken, when one of my cooks smiled and exclaimed, "A pipián with pistachios! *Dios mio,* look what the world's coming to." In Mexico, pistachios are very expensive. Using the nut to make a pipián seemed as excessive as using a 1945 Bordeaux to make bordelaise sauce. He told me that when he was young, his family was too poor to afford even pumpkin seeds. His mother would toast and grind dried corn kernels with chiles and call it pipián. Some families are so poor that they save every seed from their chiles, toasting them and grinding them with garlic to make something delicious out of barely anything. Of course, pistachios are not particularly expensive in the United States, so my pipián was not so fancy. It just goes to show that not only aren't there set-in-stone rules about what nuts or seeds you can use to make pipianes, but as these resourceful cooks have shown us, there also aren't any rules to what makes something taste great. Try this sauce with chicken or fish—or even better, rack of lamb.

MAKES 5 CUPS SAUCE (ENOUGH FOR 5 TO 6 SERVINGS)   **ACTIVE TIME: 40 TO 55 MINUTES**   **START TO FINISH: 1¾ TO 2¾ HOURS**

2 poblano chiles (½ pound)

6 tablespoons unhulled sesame seeds

3 tablespoons chile seeds (from any non-smoked dried chile, like ancho or pasilla)

1 cup shelled unsalted roasted pistachios (4½ ounces), loose skins removed

2 small fresh serrano chiles, coarsely chopped, including seeds

2 small garlic cloves, peeled

¾ teaspoon fine salt, or 1½ teaspoons kosher salt

½ teaspoon aniseed

2 tablespoons mild olive oil or vegetable oil

½ recipe Poached Chicken (page 242), including 4 to 5 cups of chicken stock, divided

1 small avocado leaf

TURN 1 or 2 burners on the stove to high and roast the poblano chiles on the racks of the burners (or directly on the element of an electric stove), turning frequently with tongs, until they are blistered and charred all over, 4 to 6 minutes. Put the poblanos in a bowl and cover with a plate to sweat, 15 to 20 minutes.

RUB off the skin from the poblano chiles with a paper towel or your fingers, then cut them open lengthwise. Cut out the seed pods, veins, and stems, and lay the chiles flat. Wipe the chiles clean of seeds, discard the seeds, and tear the chiles into large pieces.

Rack of Lamb is the ultimate partner for Pistachio Sauce.

HEAT a small heavy skillet over medium heat and toast the sesame seeds and chile seeds, stirring and tossing constantly, until they're fragrant and a shade darker, about 4 minutes.

TRANSFER the poblanos and toasted seeds to the blender jar. Add the pistachios, serrano chiles, garlic, salt, aniseed, and 2 cups of the chicken stock, and blend until very smooth, about 3 minutes.

HEAT the oil in a 4- to 5-quart heavy pot (this will give you enough room to add the chicken later; if you're making just the sauce, a 3- to 4-quart pot is fine) over medium heat, then add the blended mixture and simmer, stirring frequently, until it has thickened slightly, about 5 minutes. As it's simmering, swish a little liquid around in the blender and add it to the pot. Reduce the heat to low and simmer the sauce, uncovered (use a splatter screen so the sauce doesn't make a mess of the stove), stirring frequently, until small pools of oil appear on the surface of the sauce, about 45 minutes. As the sauce simmers, add more stock, as necessary, to maintain a velvety consistency that thickly coats a wooden spoon, but isn't gloppy.

HEAT a comal, griddle, or heavy skillet over medium-low heat, and toast the avocado leaf, turning it frequently with tongs, until fragrant and lightly browned, 1 to 2 minutes. Crumble the leaf into the blender, add 1 cup of the sauce, and blend until smooth. Return the mixture to the remaining sauce in the pot and cook for 5 minutes more. Season to taste with additional salt.

ADD the chicken to the sauce, reduce the heat to low, and cook until it's just heated through, 15 to 20 minutes.

Serve it with Corn Tortillas (page 39), rice, beans, or any other side you like (pages 246–256).

This pipián keeps in the refrigerator for up to two days.

RED SESAME SEED SAUCE PIPIÁN ROJO

Sesame seeds make their way into so many moles and pipianes, but in this recipe, they take center stage. Their toasty fragrance, along with that of warm spices, roasting tomatoes, and garlic, fills your kitchen. Your guests may get to eat the sauce, but you'll have the pleasure of watching and smelling it take shape.

MAKES 4 CUPS SAUCE (ENOUGH FOR 4 TO 6 SERVINGS) ACTIVE TIME: **30 TO 45 MINUTES** START TO FINISH: **1½ TO 2½ HOURS**

⅔ pound tomatoes (about 2 medium)

1 (½-inch-thick) round slice white onion

1 large garlic clove, peeled

3 ounces ancho chiles (6), wiped clean, stemmed, slit open, seeded, and deveined

2 chipotle mora chiles (purplish-red color), wiped clean and stemmed

2½ ounces unhulled sesame seeds (½ cup)

1 (½-inch) piece canela (Mexican cinnamon), or ⅛ teaspoon ground cinnamon

1 whole clove

1 teaspoon fine salt, or 2 teaspoons kosher salt

½ teaspoon fresh thyme leaves

½ recipe Poached Chicken (page 242), including 3 to 4 cups of chicken stock, divided

3 tablespoons pork lard, mild olive oil, or vegetable oil

SET the oven or toaster oven to broil and preheat. Alternatively, you can preheat the oven to 500°F. If you're using the oven broiler, position the rack 8 inches from the heat source. Core the tomatoes and cut a small "X" through the skin on the opposite ends. Put the tomatoes, cored side up, on a foil-lined baking pan, and roast until their tops have blackened and the tomatoes are cooked to the core, 20 to 30 minutes. Slip the skins from the tomatoes.

MEANWHILE, heat a comal, griddle, or heavy skillet over medium-low heat, and toast the onion and garlic on one half of the comal, turning the garlic frequently until it's just tender and golden brown with some blackened spots, 8 to 10 minutes, and turning the onion once, until it's softened and charred on both sides, 15 to 20 minutes. At the same time, toast the chiles on the other half of the comal, a few at a time, turning them over and pressing them down with tongs frequently, until the anchos are fragrant and they've developed light-colored brown blisters, 1 to 1½ minutes per batch, and the chipotles are blistered in spots, 3 to 5 minutes, per batch. Soak the chiles in enough cold water to cover until they're soft, about 30 minutes. Drain and discard the soaking water.

HEAT a small heavy skillet over medium heat and toast the sesame seeds, canela, and clove, stirring constantly, until the sesame seeds are fragrant and a shade darker, about 4 minutes.

TRANSFER the sesame seed mixture to the blender jar along with the roasted tomatoes, onion, garlic, chiles, salt, thyme, and 2 cups of the chicken stock. Blend until the mixture is smooth, about 3 minutes. Be careful when you're blending hot ingredients: Cover the top with a kitchen towel, and hold the top firmly in place with your hand. Work in batches to avoid blending with a full jar.

HEAT the lard or oil in a 4- to 5-quart pot (this will give you enough room to add the chicken later; if you're making just the sauce, a 3- to 4-quart pot is fine) over medium heat until it shimmers. Carefully pour in the puree and simmer (use a splatter screen so the sauce doesn't make a mess of the stove), stirring frequently, until it has thickened slightly, about 10 minutes. As it's simmering, swish a little liquid around in the blender and add it to the pot. Add enough of the remaining chicken stock (1 to 1½ cups) to the sauce to thin it to a velvety consistency that thickly coats a wooden spoon, but isn't gloppy. Continue to simmer, partially covered, until pools of oil appear on the surface, about 20 minutes. Season to taste with additional salt.

ADD the chicken to the sauce, reduce the heat to low, and cook until it's just heated through, 15 to 20 minutes.

Serve it with Corn Tortillas (page 39), rice, beans, or any other side you like (pages 246–256).

This pipián keeps in the refrigerator for up to three days or in the freezer for up to a month.

NOW THAT YOU CAN MAKE SALSAS, GUACAMOLES, ADOBOS, MOLES, AND PIPIANES, YOU'LL FIND YOURSELF COMING UP WITH ALL SORTS OF SIMPLE BUT CREATIVE WAYS TO USE THEM. THERE YOU ARE SPREADING CHINTEXTLE ON YOUR TURKEY SANDWICH, TOSSING ROASTED TOMATO SALSA WITH CHIPOTLE AND HABANERO CHILES WITH PASTA, AND SPOONING SIMPLE PUMPKIN SEED SAUCE OR ROASTED TOMATILLO SALSAS OVER GRILLED CHICKEN BREASTS. THE POSSIBILITIES ARE ENDLESS.

Yet in this chapter, I've provided some common (but uncommonly delicious) ways to use these sauces as Mexicans do. Quesadillas and tacos are the perfect vehicles for salsas. Leftovers of your favorite saucy moles or adobos make great tacos. Homemade tortilla chips are great for scooping salsas and guacamoles, and for turning into sloppy, crunchy-soggy chilaquiles—which, along with eggs, is perhaps the world's best breakfast. Tamales and enchiladas are fantastic ways to use moles, pipianes, and adobos, whether you whip up a pot for the occasion or make use of leftovers.

TACOS

You're strolling down the streets or through the markets in Mexico, and the aroma hits you. Immediately, hunger strikes. A minute later, you're eating a little pile of tasty meat cushioned by a warm tortilla and electrified by a little salsa. Life is good.

Indeed, to Mexicans, anything can become a taco. Sure, luscious, crispy carnitas, grilled marinated steak or shrimp, or stewed chicken gets tucked into warm tortillas, but so does saucy meat from the mole pot, scoops of guacamole or beans, and scrambled eggs. You'll surely discover your favorites, and I've given you a few of mine—simple combinations of proteins and salsas from this book that are astoundingly good.

My favorite way to serve tacos at home is to set out a pile of sliced steak or shredded roasted chicken, a basket of warm tortillas, and a few bowls with salsas (if you're ambitious, try spooning two contrasting salsas on one taco!), chopped white onions and cilantro, and lime wedges. Letting your guests make tacos themselves, rather than assembling them beforehand, ensures the tortillas will stay warm and won't get soggy. Also, what could be more fun!

STEAK TACOS
TACOS DE CARNE ASADA

MAKES 12 TO 16 TACOS

1 recipe Grilled Adobo-Marinated Skirt Steak (page 135), cut into small pieces

12 to 16 warm Corn Tortillas, homemade (page 39) or store bought

1 cup salsa, such as Pico de Gallo (page 46), Roasted Pineapple Salsa (page 79), Chintextle (page 197), Drunken Salsa (page 81), or Spicy Cooked Tomatillo Table Salsa (page 74)

Finely chopped white onion

Chopped cilantro

Avocado slices

Lime wedges

CHICKEN TACOS
TACOS DE POLLO ASADO

MAKES 12 TO 16 TACOS

1 recipe Adobo-Marinated Chicken (page 133), cut into small pieces

12 to 16 warm corn tortillas, homemade (page 39) or store bought

1 cup salsa, such as Simple Roasted Tomato Salsa with Onion and Cilantro (page 62), Fresh Tomatillo Salsa with Avocado (page 51), Burnt Chipotle Chile Salsa (page 82), or Peanut and Árbol Chile Salsa (page 87)

Finely chopped white onion

Chopped cilantro

Lime wedges

How a Mexican holds a taco

MORE IDEAS FOR USING MEXICAN SAUCES

CARNITAS TACOS
TACOS DE CARNITAS

MAKES **24 TO 32 TACOS**

1 recipe Carnitas (page 240)

24 to 32 warm corn tortillas, homemade (page 39) or store bought

2 cups salsa, such as Fresh Tomatillo Salsa (page 50), Roasted Tomatillo Salsa with Toasted Chile Powder (page 67), Pico de Gallo (page 46), or Taco-Shop Guacamole (page 116)

Finely chopped white onion

Chopped cilantro

Lime wedges

SHRIMP TACOS
TACOS DE CAMARONES

MAKES **12 TACOS**

1 recipe Adobo-Marinated Shrimp (page 132), shelled

12 warm corn tortillas, homemade (page 39) or store bought

1 cup salsa, such as Fresh Mango and Pineapple Salsa (page 55), Fresh Peach Salsa (page 56), or Fried Serrano Chile Salsa (page 75)

Finely chopped white onion

Chopped cilantro

Avocado slices

Lime wedges

WARM TORTILLAS, GREAT TACOS

If your tortillas aren't warm and pliable, your tacos will suffer dearly. For a refresher on making tortillas, warming up tortillas (homemade or store-bought), and keeping them warm, see pages 36–39.

A carnitas taco with Taco-Shop Guacamole

ENCHILADAS

The word *enchilada* can refer to almost anything made with chile. Go to your favorite taqueria and, along with carnitas and carne asada, there's probably an option for *carne enchilada*, pounded pork marinated in a chile mixture. In the state of San Luis Potosi, cooks make *enchiladas potosinas*, which are fried cheese-filled tortillas made from masa that has been mixed with guajillo chiles. But my focus in this book is the enchilada in its most familiar form—filled tortillas doused in some lovely sauce. Enchiladas make a fabulous dinner and are a great way to use my cooking salsas, adobo sauces, thick moles, and pipianes. And you don't have to make your own tortillas—store-bought tortillas work fine. The following pages include a few ideas, but I'm sure you'll come up with many more yourself.

The process for making the enchiladas includes cooking tortillas in a little oil to soften them and then filling them. Once you fill the softened tortillas, all you do is warm them in the oven, then douse them with your favorite sauce.

TO SOFTEN TORTILLAS FOR ENCHILADAS

Have ready two layers of paper towels for blotting and a plate where you'll stack the finished tortillas. Heat 2 tablespoons of mild olive oil or vegetable oil in a small skillet (just large enough to fit a tortilla) over medium heat until it shimmers. Put a tortilla in the oil (the oil should be hot enough so that it sizzles around the edges of the tortilla) for 8 to 12 seconds, then carefully turn the tortilla over with tongs and cook until the other side bubbles but the tortilla is still soft, 8 to 12 seconds more. Transfer the tortilla with the tongs to the paper towels, and blot on both sides. Repeat the procedure with the remaining tortillas, adding more oil and using more towels as necessary and stacking the tortillas on the plate once they're blotted.

TO FILL TORTILLAS FOR ENCHILADAS

Put about ¼ cup of the filling on one half of a tortilla. Roll it up, and transfer it, seam-side down, to a baking pan or a heatproof serving dish, and repeat with the remaining tortillas.

A tortilla sizzling (left), bubbling (right), and waiting (right) to be made into enchiladas

217

SUPER-SIMPLE ENCHILADAS

For the most basic, but still wildly delicious, enchiladas, all you have to do is take the softened tortillas and submerge them with tongs in a tasty cooking salsa, adobo sauce (particularly one made from Adobo D.F. or Basic Ancho Adobo), thick mole, or pipián. Working with one tortilla at a time, you fold the tortilla in half while it's still submerged in the sauce, then you fold it in half again. Put the soaked tortillas on a plate (you can keep the plate in a low oven as you dunk the other tortillas), top them with chopped white onion and cilantro, a drizzle of crema, crumbled queso fresco and perhaps some eggs or chicken. No rolling or baking required!

ENCHILADAS WITH CHICKEN
ENCHILADAS DE POLLO

MAKES 8 ENCHILADAS **ACTIVE TIME: 35 MINUTES (NOT INCLUDING MAKING THE SAUCE OR COOKING THE CHICKEN)**
START TO FINISH: 35 MINUTES (NOT INCLUDING MAKING THE SAUCE OR COOKING THE CHICKEN)

4 to 6 tablespoons mild olive oil
or vegetable oil, divided

1 cup finely chopped white onion

2 cups shredded cooked chicken or turkey

2½ cups Ranchera Sauce (page 96), Cooked Green
Salsa (page 99), Adobo D.F. Sauce
(page 127), or Mole from Puebla (page 172)

Chicken stock or water, if necessary

8 corn tortillas, homemade (page 39) or store-bought

GARNISH
¼ cup Mexican crema, crème fraîche, or sour cream,
thinned slightly with water, if necessary, for drizzling

¼ cup grated queso fresco or ricotta salata

¼ cup finely chopped white onion

¼ cup chopped cilantro

2 teaspoons toasted unhulled sesame seeds, or
2 tablespoons finely chopped nuts (if used in the sauce)

———————————

PREHEAT the oven to 300°F.

HEAT 2 tablespoons of the oil in a medium heavy skillet over
medium-low heat and cook the onion, stirring, until softened,
about 5 minutes. Stir in the chicken or turkey and ½ cup
of the sauce and cook, stirring occasionally, until heated
through, about 5 minutes. Season to taste with salt.

MEANWHILE, heat the remaining 2 cups of sauce in a
saucepan over medium-low heat until heated through, adding
some chicken stock or water, if necessary, to maintain a
velvety consistency that is thick enough to coat a wooden
spoon, but not gloppy.

SOFTEN the tortillas in oil then fill them (see page 216)
with the chicken mixture. Arrange the rolled tortillas next to
each other in a baking pan or a heatproof serving dish, and
reheat them in the oven for 10 minutes. Transfer 2 rolled,
filled
tortillas to each of 4 plates (or keep them in the serving dish)
and spoon the warm sauce generously over them. Drizzle
with the crema, and top with the cheese, onion, cilantro, and
if appropriate, the sesame seeds or nuts.

Serve them with rice, beans, or any other side you like (pages
246–256).

These enchiladas can be assembled in a baking dish (before
you top them with the sauce) up to four hours ahead and kept
covered with plastic wrap in the refrigerator once they're cool.
Cover the enchiladas with foil and reheat them in a 350°F oven
for about 20 minutes, and then spoon the warm sauce over
them before garnishing and serving.

SPINACH AND MUSHROOM ENCHILADAS

ENCHILADAS DE ESPINACAS Y HONGOS

MAKES 8 ENCHILADAS   ACTIVE TIME: **30 MINUTES (NOT INCLUDING MAKING THE SAUCE)**
START TO FINISH: **40 MINUTES (NOT INCLUDING MAKING THE SAUCE)**

2 cups Sautéed Spinach and Mushrooms (page 255)

2 cups Roasted Tomato Salsa with
Chipotle and Habanero Chiles (page 97)
or Cooked Green Salsa (page 99)

Chicken stock or water, if necessary

2 to 4 tablespoons mild olive oil or vegetable oil

8 corn tortillas, homemade (page 39) or store-bought

GARNISH
¼ cup Mexican crema, crème fraîche, or sour cream,
thinned slightly with water, if necessary, for drizzling

¼ cup grated queso fresco or ricotta salata

¼ cup finely chopped white onion

¼ cup chopped cilantro

PREHEAT the oven to 300°F.

WARM the sautéed spinach and mushrooms, if necessary, in a small baking dish, covered with foil, 15 to 20 minutes.

MEANWHILE, heat the salsa in a saucepan over medium-low heat until heated through, adding some chicken stock or water, if necessary, to maintain a velvety consistency that is thick enough to coat a wooden spoon, but not gloppy.

SOFTEN the tortillas in oil, then fill them (see page 216) with the spinach and mushrooms. Arrange them next to each other in a baking pan or a heatproof serving dish, and reheat them in the oven for 10 minutes. Transfer 2 rolled, filled tortillas to each of 4 plates (or keep them in the serving dish) and spoon the salsa generously over them. Drizzle with the crema, and top with the cheese, onion, and cilantro.

Serve them with rice, beans, or any other side you like (pages 246–256).

These enchiladas can be assembled in a baking dish (before you top them with the sauce) up to four hours ahead and kept covered with plastic wrap in the refrigerator once they're cool. Cover the enchiladas with foil and reheat them in a 350°F oven for about 20 minutes, and then spoon the warm sauce over them before garnishing and serving.

LAMB ADOBO ENCHILADAS WITH COOKED GREEN SALSA

ENCHILADAS DE BORREGO ADOBADO CON SALSA VERDE COCIDA

MAKES 8 ENCHILADAS   ACTIVE TIME: 20 MINUTES (NOT INCLUDING MAKING LAMB OR GREEN SALSA)
START TO FINISH: 40 MINUTES (NOT INCLUDING MAKING LAMB OR GREEN SALSA)

2 cups shredded leftover Lamb Shanks Braised in Parchment (page 142), including ½ cup adobo sauce, or any other meat cooked in adobo

1½ cups Cooked Green Salsa (page 99)

2 to 4 tablespoons mild olive oil or vegetable oil

Chicken stock or water, if necessary

8 corn tortillas, homemade (page 39) or store-bought

GARNISH
¼ cup Mexican crema, crème fraîche, or sour cream, thinned slightly with water, if necessary, for drizzling

¼ cup grated queso fresco or ricotta salata

¼ cup finely chopped white onion

¼ cup chopped cilantro

PREHEAT the oven to 300°F.

WARM the shredded lamb in the adobo sauce in a small heavy saucepan over medium-low heat, about 15 minutes, or in a small baking dish covered with foil in the oven for 20 to 30 minutes.

MEANWHILE, heat the salsa in another saucepan over medium-low heat until heated through, adding some chicken stock or water, if necessary, to maintain a velvety consistency that is thick enough to coat a wooden spoon, but not gloppy.

SOFTEN the tortillas in oil, then fill them (see page 216) with the lamb mixture. Arrange them next to each other in a baking pan or a heatproof serving dish and reheat them in the oven for 10 minutes. Transfer 2 rolled, filled tortillas to each of 4 plates (or keep them in the serving dish) and spoon the salsa generously over them. Drizzle with the crema, and top with the cheese, onion, and cilantro.

Serve them with rice, beans, or any other side you like (pages 246–256).

These enchiladas can be assembled in a baking dish (before you top them with the salsa) up to four hours ahead and kept covered with plastic wrap in the refrigerator once they're cool. Cover the enchiladas with foil and reheat them in a 350°F oven for about 20 minutes, and then spoon the warm salsa over them before garnishing and serving.

Rustically rolled lamb enchiladas waiting for a little more green salsa

GUACAMOLE ENCHILADAS WITH GUAJILLO-TOMATILLO BEEF SAUCE

ENCHILADAS DE GUACAMOLE CON SALSA DE GUAJILLO

I have a very good friend who ran a hotel with a restaurant in Coatzacoalcos, Veracruz, and the cooks there made this incredibly delicious dish they called *tacos norteños*, or tacos from the North. I've never seen it in the North, or anywhere else for that matter, so I don't know about that title. Their invention seems more like enchiladas filled with guacamole to me—you roll my lively guacamole in tortillas and top it with a tangy sauce of tomatillos, guajillos, and beef—but either way, it's a fantastic alternative to serving guacamole in a bowl.

MAKES 12 ENCHILADAS　　**ACTIVE TIME: 1¼ HOURS**　　**START TO FINISH: 1½ HOURS**

1 pound tomatillos (10 to 12), husked and rinsed

3 ounces guajillo chiles (12), wiped clean, stemmed, slit open, seeded, and deveined

4 cups water, or more if necessary

2 large garlic cloves, peeled

¼ teaspoon aniseed

¼ teaspoon dried oregano, preferably Mexican

1 teaspoon fine salt, or 2 teaspoons kosher salt

2 tablespoons mild olive oil

1¼ pounds beef sirloin or chuck, excess fat removed and meat finely chopped, or 1 pound ground beef

12 corn tortillas, homemade (page 39) or store-bought

1 recipe Classic Guacamole (page 104), made at the last minute and with the avocado especially chunky

¼ cup vegetable oil

PUT the tomatillos and chiles in a 3- to 4-quart heavy saucepan or pot, add the 4 cups of water (or more to cover the tomatillos), and bring the water to a simmer over medium-high heat. Lower the heat and simmer gently, turning the tomatillos and chiles occasionally, until the tomatillos have turned a khaki-green color and are tender, but still intact, about 15 minutes. If necessary, let the tomatillos stand in the pan off the heat for up to 15 minutes longer or until the tomatillos are fully cooked through. Gently drain the tomatillos and chiles in a sieve set over a large bowl, being careful to keep the tomatillos intact and reserving the cooking liquid.

TRANSFER the tomatillos and chiles to the blender jar. Add the garlic, aniseed, oregano, and salt and blend until smooth, adding a little of the reserved cooking liquid if necessary to help blend. Be careful when you're blending hot ingredients: Cover the top with a kitchen towel, and hold the top firmly in place with your hand. Work in batches to avoid blending with a full jar. Strain the sauce through a medium-mesh sieve and into a bowl.

WIPE the saucepan clean, and heat the olive oil in the saucepan over medium-high heat until it shimmers. Carefully pour the sauce into the oil (it may splatter), and let the sauce simmer, stirring often, until it has thickened slightly, 5 to 7 minutes. To avoid making a mess of your stove, use a splatter screen or partially cover the pot.

ADD the rest of the reserved cooking liquid and return the sauce to a boil. Add the beef, stirring to break up the meat (a sturdy whisk is great for this), and simmer vigorously, stirring occasionally, until the sauce is just thick enough to coat the meat (like a thin Bolognese sauce or Sloppy Joe mixture), about 15 minutes. Season to taste with additional salt, and keep the sauce warm.

SOFTEN the tortillas in oil, then fill them (see page 216), using 2 tablespoons of guacamole for each tortilla. Transfer 3 rolled, filled tortillas to each of 4 plates, and spoon the meat sauce generously over them. Serve immediately.

Serve them with rice, beans, or any other side you like (pages 246–256).

The meat sauce keeps in the refrigerator for up to one day.

SHRIMP AND SCALLOP ENCHILADAS WITH HAZELNUT MOLE

ENCHILADAS DE MARISCOS CON MOLE DE AVELLANA

MAKES 8 ENCHILADAS   ACTIVE TIME: **35 MINUTES (NOT INCLUDING MAKING SALSA OR MOLE)**
START TO FINISH: **35 MINUTES (NOT INCLUDING MAKING SALSA OR MOLE)**

4 to 6 tablespoons mild olive oil
or vegetable oil, divided

½ pound small shrimp (about 20), peeled and deveined

½ pound sea scallops, tough ligament removed,
if necessary, and cut into ½-inch dice

½ teaspoon fine salt, or 1 teaspoon kosher salt

1 cup Simple Cooked Tomato Salsa (page 92)

2 cups Hazelnut Mole (page 180)

Chicken stock or water, if necessary

8 corn tortillas

GARNISH
¼ cup finely chopped, skinned roasted hazelnuts

2 tablespoons chopped chives, or
¼ cup finely chopped scallions

HEAT 2 tablespoons of the oil in a medium heavy skillet over medium-high heat until it just begins to smoke, and sauté the shrimp and scallops, stirring occasionally, until they're barely cooked through, 2 to 3 minutes. Sprinkle with salt, stirring to season the seafood evenly, then stir in the salsa and cook over medium heat, stirring occasionally, until the salsa is heated and the seafood is just cooked through, 2 to 3 minutes more. Using a slotted spoon, transfer the seafood to a bowl and boil the salsa left in the pan until it's thickened slightly, 3 to 5 minutes. Stir the salsa into the seafood.

HEAT the mole in another saucepan over medium-low heat until it's heated through, adding some chicken stock or water to maintain a velvety consistency that is thick enough to coat a wooden spoon, but not gloppy.

PREHEAT the oven to 300°F.

SOFTEN the tortillas in oil, then fill them (see page 216) with the seafood mixture. Arrange them next to each other in a baking pan or a heatproof serving dish, and reheat them in the oven for 10 minutes. Transfer 2 rolled, filled tortillas to each of 4 plates (or keep them in the serving dish) and spoon the warm mole generously over them, then sprinkle with the hazelnuts and chives and serve.

Serve them with rice, beans, or any other side you like (pages 246–256).

These enchiladas can be assembled in a baking dish (without the mole) up to four hours ahead and kept in the refrigerator, covered with plastic wrap once they're cold. Cover the enchiladas with foil and reheat them in a 350°F oven for about 20 minutes, and then spoon the warm mole over them before garnishing and serving.

QUESADILLAS QUESADILLAS

The grilled cheese sandwich of Mexico, this simple snack is gobbled in the country's markets and almost daily in the home kitchens of Mexicans around the world. It takes almost no time to make, though even I'll occasionally get impatient and make mine on the open flames of my stovetop burner—aka the Mexican microwave. Monterey Jack serves as an excellent and faithful stand-in for Chihuahua cheese, which is harder to find in the United States, but you can use anything from Manchego to cheddar to fresh goat cheese. The gooey, slightly crispy result calls out for Pico de Gallo (page 46), Classic Guacamole (page 104), D.F.-Style Roasted Serrano Salsa (page 88), and so many others!

SERVES 4 (12 QUESADILLAS)   **ACTIVE TIME: 20 MINUTES**   START TO FINISH: **20 MINUTES**

12 corn tortillas, homemade (page 39) or store bought, or 8 flour tortillas (see note)

2 cups grated Monterey Jack cheese, Manchego, or mozzarella

6 pickled jalapeño chiles (from a 7-ounce can), thinly sliced

HEAT a comal, griddle, or heavy skillet over medium heat. Put the tortillas, one or two at a time, on the comal and sprinkle each with about 3 tablespoons of cheese and a few slices of the pickled chiles. When the tortillas have softened, fold them over the cheese and press down slightly. Cook for an additional 45 seconds on each side or until the tortilla is lightly browned in spots and the cheese has melted. Serve immediately, and make more quesadillas in the same manner.

Make the quesadillas a meal by serving them with Chipotle-Avocado Leaf Black Beans (page 249) and Sautéed Spinach and Mushrooms (page 255).

MORE QUESADILLA FILLINGS

So long as there's a little cheese to hold them together, quesadillas can have almost any filling you can think of. Try substituting the pickled chiles in the recipe above with Sautéed Spinach and Mushrooms (page 255), Fast Mashed Pinto Beans (page 250), or Adobo-Marinated Chicken (page 133).

NOTE: Since the flour tortillas you find in stores are typically a little larger than corn tortillas, use about 8 flour tortillas for the same amount of cheese and chiles.

TAMALES TAMALES

These packets of masa dough, which can be wrapped in corn husks, banana leaves, and many other things, deserve an entire book of their own. But for now, you'll have to settle for this great recipe, which you can use to make a variety of tamales by filling them with the delicious leftovers from your adobo- and mole-making adventures and topping them with whatever salsa you'd like. Tamales also make a great stand-in for rice, potatoes, or other starchy sides when you're serving a saucy dish. Be sure to get dried masa that's specifically called tamal flour because it's a bit coarser than the kind you'd use to make tortillas.

MAKES 30 TAMALES　　**ACTIVE TIME: 35 MINUTES (USING A STANDING MIXER)**　　**START TO FINISH: 1¾ HOURS**

30 dried corn husks, preferably with rounded bases

1 cup (8 ounces) pork lard (see note)

3 cups tamal flour

2 cups barely hot water (about 110°F) (see note)

1 teaspoon fine salt, or 2 teaspoons kosher salt

⅔ cup vegetable oil

5 cups filling, such as pork or shredded chicken in any of the mole or adobo sauces, or Sautéed Spinach and Mushrooms (page 255)

SOAK the corn husks in cold water for 30 minutes.

MEANWHILE, using a standing mixer with the whisk attachment, beat the lard on medium-high speed in the mixer bowl until it's very fluffy, 3 to 5 minutes (if you are using a handheld electric mixer, double the beating times). Meanwhile, mix together the tamale flour, water, and salt with your hands in another large bowl until you have a uniform dough. Add half of the dough to the lard and beat to combine. Add the oil and the remaining dough to the lard mixture and beat on medium-high speed until it has the texture of a fluffy frosting and a tablespoonful of it floats in a glass of water, 10 to 15 minutes. Season the batter to taste with additional salt (the batter should taste salty, as some of the salt will leach out during steaming).

DRAIN the corn husks. Put a heaping serving spoon of the batter (about ⅓ cup) on the concave side of a husk. Spread the batter to flatten it slightly and evenly, so it roughly forms a rectangle. Put a couple of tablespoons of the filling in the middle of the batter. Enclose the filling in the batter as you fold over the husk, doubling the pointed end over the

bottom half. The rounded end will remain open. (See page 228.) Repeat with the remaining batter, filling, and husks.

FIT the tamales into the deep steamer basket of a pasta pot, standing them with the open ends up. Fill the pot with about 1 inch of water, and place a coin in the pot so you can tell if the water has evaporated (you'll know you need to add more water when the jiggling noise from the coin stops). Insert the tamale-filled steamer basket and cover the tamales with additional corn husks, a plastic shopping bag (as many Mexicans do), then a damp cloth and the lid. These coverings will ensure that no moisture escapes and the tamales steam properly.

BRING the water to a boil (you will hear the coin start to jiggle) and steam the tamales, adding more boiling water if you no longer hear the coin jiggling, until the tamale separates from the husk easily when you unwrap it, 45 to 50 minutes.

Traditionally served by themselves for breakfast, a light dinner, or a midday snack, tamales also make a great stand-in for rice and beans. Try serving them alongside Adobo-Marinated Chicken (page 133) or Thick Moles (beginning on page 164).

Tamales keep stored in a plastic bag in the refrigerator for up to three days or in freezer bags in the freezer for up to one month. You can also store the tamale batter in a sealable bag in the refrigerator for up to 3 days. If you freeze the tamales, defrost them overnight in the refrigerator before warming them. To reheat, either re-steam the tamales in their husks as before until they are heated through, about 30 minutes, or place a few at a time in a deep plate with a little water to cover the bottom of the plate. Cover the plate with another, inverted plate, and microwave 1 minute for every 1 or 2 tamales.

MORE IDEAS FOR USING MEXICAN SAUCES

NOTE ON OMITTING THE LARD: You can substitute an additional 1 cup of vegetable oil for the pork lard to make vegetarian tamales. If you do, just add all the oil at once to the masa dough and beat on medium-high speed, increasing the beating time, as necessary, to achieve a very fluffy batter.

NOTE ON WATER: To infuse more flavor into the masa, I love to start with 3 cups of boiling water in a small pot, add 4 or 5 tomatillo husks, ⅛ teaspoon aniseed, and ⅛ teaspoon cumin seeds, and cook for about 10 minutes. Then I strain the water, which has reduced to about 2 cups (add a little more water or pour a little out, if necessary), let it cool until it's barely hot, then use this water in the tamale recipe.

Forming tamales

TORTILLA CHIPS TOTOPOS

Bagged chips are no match for these crunchy, delicate fried tortilla wedges that you can use to scoop up my guacamoles and salsas or turn into Chilaquiles (page 231). They're so easy to make yourself that you'll never go back to the kind you can buy at the supermarket. In Mexico, cooks use stale but still pliable tortillas for chips to avoid waste and because they fry especially well.

MAKES 64 CHIPS   **ACTIVE TIME: 12 MINUTES**   **START TO FINISH: 12 MINUTES**

8 corn tortillas, homemade (page 39) or store bought

About ½ cup mild olive oil or vegetable oil

Fine salt to taste

STACK the tortillas, 4 at a time, and prick through the stack with a fork in several places (pricking is optional; it will prevent the tortillas from puffing up as they fry). Cut the tortillas, starting with a cut through the middle, into 8 equal-size wedges. You'll have 64 wedges total.

HEAT ½ inch of oil in a medium heavy skillet over medium-high heat until it shimmers. Add a handful of tortilla wedges in one layer to the oil and cook, stirring occasionally and turning them over with a slotted spoon, until they're golden on both sides and the oil stops sizzling, 1 to 2 minutes. Transfer the chips to paper towels to drain, then sprinkle them with salt while they're still hot and transfer them to a bowl. Repeat the procedure with the remaining tortilla wedges, adding more oil if necessary and letting it get hot before adding more wedges.

Serve them with Salsas (pages 46–89) or Guacamoles (pages 102–119), or turn them into Chilaquiles (page 231).

Tortilla chips are best served the day they're made.

TORTILLA STRIPS

Cut the tortillas in half, then cut each half crosswise into thin strips, and fry them as you would the wedges. These are great for garnishing soups and adding crunch to salads.

TOSTADAS

Fry whole tortillas, one by one, in a small skillet (just large enough to fit the tortilla), turning once, until golden brown on both sides, 1 to 2 minutes. These crunchy tortillas are a real treat topped with Fast Mashed Pinto Beans (page 250) or Chipotle–Avocado Leaf Black Beans (page 249), the meat from adobos (page 130–146) or moles (page 150–187), and fixings like shredded lettuce, salsa, finely chopped raw onion, avocado slices, crema or sour cream, and crumbled queso fresco.

CHILAQUILES

TORTILLA CHIPS SIMMERED WITH SAUCE

Only Mexico's culinary magicians could turn slightly stale tortilla chips into such a delicious meal: The chips are simmered briefly in sauce, so they soak up its flavor but still retain some of their lovely crunch. This textural quality is beloved in Mexico. It's fleeting, so eat up! Served with eggs, it's one of my favorite breakfasts in the world. If I'm craving chilaquiles later on, I'll top them with slices of Adobo-Marinated Chicken (page 133) or Grilled Adobo-Marinated Skirt Steak (page 135). Classic chilaquiles feature the herbal punch of epazote, but there's no need to add any if you're making this with the Chilaquiles variation of Cooked Green Salsa. Whatever sauce you use, just make sure that, as this recipe instructs, you add water to make it nice and loose.

SERVES 2 AS A MAIN COURSE AND 4 AS A SIDE   ACTIVE TIME: 10 MINUTES (NOT INCLUDING MAKING THE CHIPS OR SALSA)
START TO FINISH: 15 MINUTES (NOT INCLUDING MAKING THE CHIPS OR SALSA)

2 cups Ranchera Sauce (page 96) or Cooked Green Salsa (page 99), preferably Chilaquiles variation

1 cup water

2 or 3 sprigs epazote (if the salsa you use doesn't contain any already), optional

1 recipe Tortilla Chips (page 229), or the same amount good-quality store-bought corn tortilla chips

⅓ cup finely chopped white onion

¼ cup chopped cilantro

⅓ cup crumbled queso fresco or ricotta salata

2 tablespoons Mexican crema, crème fraîche, or sour cream, thinned slightly with water, if necessary, for drizzling

BRING the sauce, water, and epazote (if you're using it) to a boil in a 2-quart heavy pot, stirring occasionally. Reduce the heat and let the mixture simmer gently for 5 minutes. Discard the epazote sprig. Season to taste with salt.

ADD the chips to the pot and cook, shaking the pan or stirring gently to coat the chips, until the chips have absorbed some of the sauce but are still crunchy, about 2 minutes. Garnish with onion, cilantro, queso fresco, and crema in the skillet or divided among plates, and serve immediately.

NOTE: If you are using store-bought chips, don't salt your sauce as aggressively as you otherwise would.

MORE OPTIONS FOR CHILAQUILES

Chilaquiles can be made with many different sauces, as long as you thin the sauce with water, as I recommend in the recipe above. The sauce should be soupy, so that the tortillas are still saucy even after they absorb liquid. Try making chilaquiles with Adobo Sauce (page 147), moles like Mole from Puebla (page 172), and salsas like Roasted Tomatillo Salsa with Chipotle and Roasted Garlic (page 70).

BEANS WITH PORK FRIJOLES CON PUERCO

Pork and beans form a talented team that you'll see not just all over Mexico but all over South America. This one-bowl meal is one of my favorite ways to eat pinto beans, especially if I have some leftover carnitas lurking in the fridge. It's all flavored with a puree of chile, garlic, and spices (by now you should recognize this combination—it's an adobo!). Serve it over rice or with warm tortillas, a little avocado, and some pico de gallo.

SERVES 4 TO 6   **ACTIVE TIME: 35 MINUTES (NOT INCLUDING MAKING THE BEANS OR PORK)**
START TO FINISH: 1¼ HOURS (NOT INCLUDING MAKING THE BEANS OR PORK)

1¼ ounces guajillo chiles (8), wiped clean, stemmed, slit open, seeded, and deveined

⅓ ounce dried árbol chiles (10), wiped clean and stemmed

4 garlic cloves, peeled

¾ teaspoon cumin seeds

¼ teaspoon whole black peppercorns

5 whole cloves

1 cup water

1 recipe Basic Beans (made with pinto beans; page 246), including its liquid, or four 15-ounce cans, including liquid, plus 1 cup water

½ recipe Carnitas (about 4 cups; page 240)

2 ounces sliced bacon, diced (about 2 slices)

½ cup finely chopped white onion

ACCOMPANIMENTS
1½ cups Pico de Gallo (page 46) or Fresh Tomatillo Salsa (page 50)

2 avocados, pitted, peeled, and sliced

Warm corn tortillas, homemade (page 39) or store bought

HEAT a comal, griddle, or heavy skillet over medium-low heat, and toast the guajillos, a few at a time, turning them over and pressing them down frequently with tongs, until they're fragrant and their insides have changed color slightly, about 1 minute per batch. Toast the árbol chiles, turning them over and pressing them down frequently with tongs, until they are brown all over and blackened in spots, 3 to 4 minutes.

SOAK the chiles in enough cold water to cover until they're softened, about 30 minutes. Drain and discard the soaking water.

BLEND the chiles with the garlic, cumin, peppercorns, cloves, and the 1 cup of fresh water to form a smooth puree, at least 3 minutes.

COMBINE the chile puree, pinto beans (including the bean liquid), and the pork in a 4- to 5-quart heavy pot and bring to a simmer.

MEANWHILE, cook the bacon in a small heavy skillet over medium heat, stirring, until browned, 5 to 8 minutes. Add the onion to the skillet, and cook, stirring frequently, until the onion is softened, 3 to 5 minutes. Transfer the bacon mixture (including the fat) to the pot with the beans and pork, cover the pot, and simmer everything together for 20 minutes. Season to taste with salt.

Spoon the beans with pork into bowls and top with salsa and avocado. Serve with the warm tortillas.

The beans with pork keep in the refrigerator for up to five days or in the freezer for up to one month.

MEXICAN-STYLE NOODLES FIDEOS SECOS

It's almost an everyday thing for Mexicans to eat soups swimming with fideos, the thin little noodles that you also see in Spain. But this preparation is more like a pasta dish, or what Mexicans often call sopa seca, or "dry soup." The fabulous sauce made with anchos and guajillos is absorbed by the slippery little noodles, and the whole thing is crowned with toppings like salsa, avocado, cheese, and crema. Make it into a meal by serving Chipotle–Avocado Leaf Black Beans (page 249) alongside. You *have* to try this.

SERVES 4 TO 6 AS A MAIN COURSE, OR 8 TO 12 AS A FIRST COURSE   **ACTIVE TIME: 1 HOUR**   **START TO FINISH: 1½ HOUR**

FOR THE SAUCE

½ pound tomatoes (about 2 small)

2 dried árbol chiles, wiped clean and stemmed

¼ pound tomatillos (2 to 3), husked and rinsed

4 guajillo chiles, wiped clean, stemmed, slit open, seeded, and deveined

2 ancho chiles, wiped clean, stemmed, slit open, seeded, and deveined

½ cup finely chopped white onion

5 garlic cloves, peeled

1 (1-inch) piece canela (Mexican cinnamon)

1½ teaspoons cumin seeds

1 teaspoon dried oregano, preferably Mexican

1 teaspoon fine salt, or 2 teaspoons kosher salt

½ teaspoon sugar

5 to 6 cups chicken stock

FOR THE NOODLES

1 pound fideo noodles or thin spaghetti, such as capellini or spaghettini

½ cup mild olive oil or vegetable oil

2 pasilla chiles, wiped clean and stemmed

10 large sprigs cilantro

6 large sprigs flat-leaf parsley

6 large sprigs mint

1 (3-inch) piece canela (Mexican cinnamon)

FOR THE GARNISH

4 ounces queso fresco or ricotta salata, crumbled (1 cup)

½ cup chopped cilantro

½ cup Fresh Tomatillo Salsa (page 50)

¼ cup Mexican crema, crème fraîche, or sour cream, thinned slightly with water, if necessary, for drizzling

1 avocado, pitted, peeled, and thinly sliced

1 cup pork chicharrones, crumbled

MAKE THE SAUCE

SET the oven or toaster oven to broil and preheat. Alternatively, you can preheat the oven to 500°F. If you're using the oven broiler, position the rack 8 inches from the heat source. Core the tomato and cut a small "X" through the skin on the opposite end. Put the tomato, cored side up, árbol chiles, and tomatillos on a foil-lined baking pan, and roast, turning over the chiles frequently until they're brown with some blackened spots, about 8 minutes. Continue to roast the tomato and tomatillos until the tomatoes are blackened and cooked to the core, and the tomatillos turn a khaki-green color, turning the tomatillos over once halfway through, 20 to 30 minutes. Slip the skin from the tomatoes.

SOAK the guajillo and ancho chiles along with the toasted árbol chiles in enough cold water to cover until they're softened, about 30 minutes. Drain and discard the soaking water.

BLEND the chiles, tomato, tomatillos, onion, garlic, canela, cumin, oregano, salt, and sugar in the blender jar with 1½ cups of the chicken stock until the mixture is smooth, about 3 minutes. Strain through a medium-mesh sieve into a bowl, discarding any solids. Set the sauce aside.

MORE IDEAS FOR USING MEXICAN SAUCES

PREPARE THE NOODLES

BREAK the noodles (wrapped in a cloth so they don't scatter all over) into 2- to 3-inch pieces. If you have a very wide pot, break the noodles in half.

HEAT the oil in a wide 6- to 7-quart heavy pot set over medium-high heat until it shimmers. Fry the whole pasilla chiles in the oil, turning once or twice until puffed and crisp, about 1 minute total. Transfer to paper towels to drain. When cool, thinly slice the chiles crosswise and reserve them for garnish.

WORKING in about 4 batches, fry the noodles in the same oil, stirring and turning constantly with 2 flat-bottomed wooden spoons (or tongs) so they fry evenly, until they are a reddish-golden brown, about 2 minutes. Transfer the browned noodles to a large bowl lined with paper towels to drain.

REMOVE all but 2 tablespoons of the oil from the pot, if necessary, then carefully pour the sauce into the pot (it may splatter). Fry the sauce over medium heat, stirring frequently, until it thickens slightly, about 5 minutes. Stir in 4 cups of the chicken stock, then add the fried noodles, stirring briefly to coat them with sauce, and bring the liquid to a boil.

TIE the cilantro, parsley, mint, and canela into a bouquet with kitchen string and drop it into the pot. Reduce the heat to medium-low, cover the pot, and simmer the noodles until they are tender and have absorbed the sauce, about 10 minutes. Discard the bouquet of herbs and canela.

Serve the noodles in soup bowls topped with all the garnishes, including the fried pasilla chiles.

The cooked noodles keep for up to three days in the refrigerator. Put them in a baking dish with a little chicken stock to moisten them, then cover with foil and rewarm them in a 350°F oven for 20 to 30 minutes.

Fried noodles waiting to be finished in sauce.

CHICKEN IN TOMATO SAUCE
POLLO EN SALSA DE JITOMATE

This is the kind of magic a cooking salsa can bring to your weeknight dinners. Just pull the salsa out of the fridge or freezer, and you'll have a one-pot meal, enlivened by chipotle and habanero chiles, before you know it.

SERVES 6   ACTIVE TIME: 35 MINUTES (NOT INCLUDING MAKING THE SALSA)   START TO FINISH: 1 HOUR (NOT INCLUDING MAKING THE SALSA)

3 pounds chicken pieces

½ teaspoon fine salt, or 1 teaspoon kosher salt

1 tablespoon mild olive oil or vegetable oil

1 recipe Tomato and Habanero Salsa (page 94) or Ranchera Sauce (page 96)

¾ pound boiling potatoes (2 medium), peeled and diced

1 medium carrot, peeled and cut into thin slices

1 cup fresh or frozen peas

½ cup chopped cilantro

1½ tablespoons coarsely chopped fresh mint leaves

PAT the chicken pieces dry and season them with the salt. Heat the oil in a 5- to 6-quart wide heavy pot over medium-high heat until it shimmers. Brown the chicken pieces in batches without crowding the pot, turning occasionally, 8 to 10 minutes per batch.

RETURN all the chicken pieces to the pot, then add the salsa and bring it to a simmer. Stir in the potatoes and carrots, then cover and simmer over medium-low heat until the chicken, potatoes, and carrots are just cooked through, about 30 minutes. Stir in the peas and cook for 5 minutes. Stir in the cilantro and mint, season to taste with additional salt, and let stand covered and off the heat for 5 minutes.

Serve it with Corn Tortillas (page 39), rice, beans, or any other side you like (pages 246–256).

This dish keeps in the refrigerator for up to three days or in the freezer for up to one month.

CHICKEN IN CHUNKY TOMATILLO SAUCE POLLO ENTOMATADO

This easy, delicious braise makes a phenomenal dinner, whether you serve the tender, tangy, saucy chicken (duck or pork would be lovely, too) with tortillas and rice or crusty bread and potatoes. I strongly suggest you find epazote and use it here, but if you can't, just omit it.

SERVES 6   **ACTIVE TIME: 30 MINUTES (NOT INCLUDING MAKING THE SALSA)**   **START TO FINISH: 3 HOURS (NOT INCLUDING MAKING THE SALSA)**

3 pounds chicken pieces

½ teaspoon fine salt, or 1 teaspoon kosher salt

1 teaspoon freshly ground black pepper

2 teaspoons dried oregano, preferably Mexican

1 tablespoon mild olive oil or vegetable oil

1 recipe Chunky Tomatillo Sauce (page 93)

1 cup water

Distilled white vinegar to taste

½ cup chopped scallions

2 tablespoons chopped fresh epazote leaves (about 8)

PAT the chicken pieces dry them rub them with the salt, pepper, and oregano. Marinate, covered and chilled, for at least 2 or up to 6 hours.

HEAT the oil in a 5- to 6-quart wide heavy pot over medium-high heat until it shimmers. Brown the chicken pieces in batches without crowding the pot, turning occasionally, 8 to 10 minutes per batch.

RETURN all the chicken pieces to the pot, add the chunky tomatillo sauce and the water, and bring the liquid to a simmer. Cook, covered, over medium-low heat until the chicken is cooked through, about 30 minutes. Season to taste with vinegar and additional salt, and serve sprinkled with the scallions and epazote.

Serve it with Corn Tortillas (page 39) and Mexican White Rice (page 251).

This dish keeps in the refrigerator for up to three days or in the freezer for up to one month.

PORK BRAISED IN TOMATILLO SALSA
CERDO EN SALSA VERDE

I adore the way this tart, silky sauce tames the richness of tender pieces of pork shoulder floating next to gently crunchy green beans. But that's just one idea—once you've made the salsa, your options are endless. As you shop, maybe you'll decide to substitute chunks of zucchini or white beans or guajes (the green, purple-tinged pods you see in Mexican grocery stores). Maybe you'll use cubed potatoes and skip the pork altogether, swapping in about three pounds of chicken pieces and following the cooking instructions for Chicken in Tomato Sauce (page 237). Whatever you do, the technique for cooking this dish will be the same, so go wild!

SERVES 6   ACTIVE TIME: 30 MINUTES (NOT INCLUDING MAKING THE SALSA)   START TO FINISH: 2½ HOURS (NOT INCLUDING MAKING THE SALSA)

3 pounds boneless pork shoulder,
cut into 1½-inch pieces

½ teaspoon fine salt, or 1 teaspoon kosher salt

1 tablespoon mild olive oil or vegetable oil

1 recipe Cooked Green Salsa (page 99)

1½ cups water

½ pound green beans, trimmed and
cut into 1½-inch pieces

———————————

PAT the pork dry and season it with the salt. Heat the oil in a 5- to 6-quart wide heavy pot over medium-high heat until it shimmers. Brown the pork in batches (you want to avoid crowding the pot, though a little crowding is OK in this case), turning occasionally and adding more oil as necessary, 8 to 10 minutes per batch.

RETURN all the pork pieces to the pot, then add the salsa and water and bring to a simmer. Cover and cook over medium-low heat until the pork is tender, about 1½ hours. If you prefer, you can cook the pork, covered, in an ovenproof pot in a 350°F oven to braise for the same amount of time. Season to taste with additional salt, and stir in the green beans. Cover the pot and cook until the beans are cooked and the pork is very tender, 20 to 30 minutes more.

Serve it with Corn Tortillas (page 39), rice, beans, or any other side you like (pages 246–256).

This dish keeps in the refrigerator for up to three days or in the freezer for up to one month.

CARNITAS BRAISED AND FRIED PORK

Picture this: Mounds of juicy, tender, crispy-edged pieces of pork just waiting to be tucked into freshly made tortillas or piled on a plate along with rice and beans. This recipe is the classic way to make them—well, almost. Many restaurants and stalls put a whole butchered pig in a huge copper pot and let it simmer away until any liquid has evaporated. That's when the pork goes from being braised to being fried, browning in its own luscious fat. I do the same thing here, except I suggest using pork shoulder instead of the whole animal. And while the pork is traditionally browned on the stovetop, doing it in the oven is even easier and more effective. Pile the result on tortillas with salsa, chopped onions, and cilantro, or if you can bear it, reserve half the recipe to make Beans with Pork (page 232).

MAKES **ENOUGH FOR 8 MAIN COURSE SERVINGS, OR ENOUGH FOR 24 TO 32 TACOS**   ACTIVE TIME: **20 MINUTES**   START TO FINISH: **2 HOURS**

4 pounds fatty pork shoulder, cut into 2-inch pieces

3 cups water

1 medium white onion, thinly sliced

½ orange, cut into 2 pieces

¼ cup pork lard or vegetable oil

8 garlic cloves, peeled

3 bay leaves

1 tablespoon sweetened condensed milk

2 teaspoons dried oregano, preferably Mexican, crumbled

2 teaspoons fine salt, or 4 teaspoons kosher salt

PUT all the ingredients in a wide 6- to 7-quart heavy pot (don't worry if the pork is not completely covered) and bring the water to a boil, skimming the surface as necessary. Lower the heat and simmer vigorously, stirring occasionally, until the pork is fork-tender and the liquid has completely evaporated, 1½ to 2 hours. Discard the orange pieces and bay leaves. If the liquid hasn't evaporated after 2 hours, transfer the pork pieces to a bowl and let the liquid continue to bubble away, stirring often, until it has.

PREHEAT the oven to 450°F. Transfer the pork and fat to an ovenproof dish, if necessary, and brown the pork, uncovered, in the oven for 20 to 30 minutes. There's no need to stir.

Serve it with Chipotle-Avocado Leaf Black Beans (page 249), Mexican White Rice (page 251), and salsa, such as Pico de Gallo (page 46), Fresh Tomatillo Salsa (page 50), or Taco-Shop Guacamole (page 116). Or make it into Tacos (page 212–214).

Carnitas keeps in the refrigerator for up to three days.

NOTE: If you want to make half a batch, cut the amount of pork, salt, and oregano in half, but use the same amount of the remaining ingredients and water. You will need to use a slightly smaller pot.

POACHED CHICKEN AND CHICKEN STOCK POLLO COCIDO

This poached meat would be delicious in chicken salad, but I've included it because it's a very typical accompaniment to moles and pipianes. The mild-mannered meat is a great vehicle for all that flavor and spice, and it leaves you with a terrific stock that you can use in any recipe.

MAKES 8 TO 10 SERVINGS OF MEAT AND 2 QUARTS OF CHICKEN STOCK   ACTIVE TIME: 15 MINUTES   START TO FINISH: 1 HOUR

2 (3½-pound) whole chickens, cut into serving pieces, or 7 pounds chicken parts

12 cups water

2 carrots, peeled and cut into large pieces

1 celery stalk, cut into large pieces

1 small white onion, quartered

2 large parsley or cilantro sprigs

1 bay leaf

1 teaspoon fine salt, or 2 teaspoons kosher salt

PUT the chicken pieces in an 8-quart pot with the remaining ingredients and bring the water to a simmer over high heat, skimming any foam from the surface as necessary. Reduce the heat and simmer until the chicken is just cooked through, about 30 minutes.

REMOVE the chicken pieces from the stock. When they're cool enough to handle, remove the skin from the chicken, if desired.

STRAIN the stock into a wide bowl, discarding the vegetables and herbs.

Use the stock to make Moles (page 150–187) and Pipianes (pages 188–209), and serve them with the chicken.

You can keep the chicken in the stock and refrigerate it for up to two days. Or you can separate the two and keep the stock in the refrigerator for up to five days or in the freezer for three months. Be sure to let the meat and stock cool uncovered first.

POACHED TURKEY AND TURKEY STOCK

In Mexico, some moles, like Mole from Puebla (page 172), are traditionally served with turkey. You can substitute 7 pounds of turkey for the chicken in this recipe, but because they're slightly larger, cook the turkey parts for 45 minutes to 1 hour.

COOKED PORK AND STOCK CERDO COCIDO

Another fantastic accompaniment for moles and pipianes, these tender chunks of pork work best in especially bold sauces. Like the recipe for poached chicken, this one also gives you a flavorful stock.

MAKES 8 TO 10 SERVINGS OF MEAT AND 6 CUPS OF PORK STOCK   ACTIVE TIME: **15 MINUTES**   START TO FINISH: **1½ HOURS**

4 pounds pork shoulder, cut into 1½-inch pieces

8 cups water

1 medium white onion, finely chopped

8 garlic cloves, peeled

1 bay leaf

2 teaspoons dried oregano, preferably Mexican

1 teaspoon fine salt, or 2 teaspoons kosher salt

PUT all the ingredients in a 6- to 7-quart heavy pot and bring the water to a simmer over high heat, skimming any foam from the surface as necessary. Reduce the heat and simmer the pork, partially covered, until it is fork-tender, 1½ to 2 hours. Remove the pork from the pot and set aside.

STRAIN the stock into a wide bowl, pressing on and then discarding the solids.

Use the stock to make Moles (page 150–187) and Pipianes (pages 188–209), and serve them with the pork.

You can keep the pork in the stock and refrigerate it for up to two days. Or you can separate the two and keep the stock in the refrigerator for up to five days or in the freezer for up to three months. Be sure to let the meat and stock cool uncovered first.

SIDES

FOR ROUNDING OUT YOUR MEAL

THIS BOOK IS FOCUSED ON SAUCES, SO I'VE LIMITED THIS CHAPTER, WHICH COULD RUN ONE HUNDRED PAGES OR MORE, TO JUST A SMALL BUNCH OF ESSENTIAL DISHES THAT YOU CAN USE TO TURN A SALSA-TOPPED STEAK, BOWL OF ADOBO, OR MOLE-COATED ENCHILADAS INTO A FILLING MEAL. HERE YOU'LL FIND A FEW DELICIOUS PREPARATIONS OF BEANS, THREE OF MY FAVORITE MEXICAN RICES, AND A COUPLE OF SIMPLE VEGETABLE DISHES.

BASIC BEANS FRIJOLES SIMPLES

These simple cooked dried beans are as easy as can be and filled with enough flavor to serve on their own. Of course, there's no shame at all in using canned beans instead for my Chipotle–Avocado Leaf Black Beans (page 249) or Fast Mashed Pinto or Black Beans (page 250 and opposite page, respectively).

MAKES ABOUT 8 CUPS (6 CUPS BEANS AND ABOUT 2 CUPS BROTH)   **ACTIVE TIME: 10 MINUTES**   **START TO FINISH: 2 HOURS**

1 pound dried black or pinto beans, rinsed and picked over

9 cups water

½ cup chopped white onion

3 garlic cloves, peeled

1 teaspoon fine salt, or 2 teaspoons kosher salt

PUT the beans, water, onion, and garlic in a 3- to 4-quart heavy pot, and bring the water to a boil. Lower the heat and simmer gently until the beans are tender (add more hot water if necessary to keep the beans just covered), about 1½ hours. (If the dried beans have been sitting on a supermarket shelf for a while, they might take up to 3 hours.) Stir in the salt.

Serve them with Mexican White Rice (page 251), Mexican Red Rice (page 252), or Green Rice with Poblano Chiles (page 254) to accompany Adobos (pages 130–146), Moles (pages 150–187), and Pipianes (pages 188–209). Or make a meal of beans, rice, and any Salsas (pages 46–89) or Guacamoles (pages 102–119).

The beans keep in the refrigerator for up to five days.

FAST MASHED CANNED BLACK BEANS FRIJOLES NEGROS MACHACADOS

Sometimes, instead of a giant pot of beans for a family meal or dinner party, you just want a tasty dinner for one or side dish for two. So here's a way to quickly turn a simple can of beans into something special. If you make your own chipotle powder, all the better, but feel free to buy a jar at the store. After you make it once, I'm sure you'll start doubling, tripling, or quadrupling the recipe, just so you always have some tasty leftover beans in the refrigerator.

MAKES ABOUT 1½ CUPS   **ACTIVE TIME: 8 MINUTES**   **START TO FINISH: 8 MINUTES**

1 (15-ounce) can black beans, including liquid, plus ¼ cup water

1 tablespoon mild olive oil

½ teaspoon onion powder

¼ teaspoon garlic powder

¼ teaspoon Chipotle Chile Powder (page 21)

¼ teaspoon dried oregano, preferably Mexican, crumbled

PUT all the ingredients in a small saucepan and bring the mixture to a simmer over medium heat. Simmer the beans vigorously, mashing them slightly with a bean or potato masher (or a fork), for 2 to 3 minutes. Season to taste with salt.

Serve them with Mexican White Rice (page 251), Mexican Red Rice (page 252), or Green Rice with Poblano Chiles (page 254) to accompany Adobos (pages 130–146), Moles (pages 150–187), and Pipianes (pages 188–209). Or make a meal of beans, rice, and any Salsas (pages 46–89) or Guacamoles (pages 102–119).

CHIPOTLE-AVOCADO LEAF BLACK BEANS

FRIJOLES NEGROS CON CHIPOTLE Y HOJA DE AGUACATE

I can't say for sure, but I think I've eaten beans every single day of my life. And this is my favorite way to make black beans, mellow but seriously flavorful and with a texture that reminds me of mashed potatoes. Inspired by the beans you'll find in Oaxaca, I add chiles and avocado leaves, which add a real depth of flavor. In Oaxaca, cooks typically use chiles de árbol, but here I use chipotle moras (I prefer pasillas de Oaxaca, but they can be tough to find) because I love the smoky flavor they bring to the beans. For a delicious snack, try spreading these on crusty bread and melting cheese on top—the resulting treat, called a *mollete,* is perfect by itself or with a salsa like Pico de Gallo (page 46).

MAKES ABOUT 8 CUPS   **ACTIVE TIME: 30 MINUTES**   **START TO FINISH: 30 MINUTES (NOT INCLUDING COOKING THE BEANS)**

1 recipe Basic Beans (made with black beans; page 246), with its liquid, or 4 (15-ounce) cans black beans, including liquid, plus 1 cup water

½ cup mild olive oil or vegetable oil

½ medium white onion, finely chopped

2 chipotle mora chiles (purplish-red color) wiped clean and stemmed, or 1 pasilla de Oaxaca chile, wiped clean, stemmed, slit open, seeded, and deveined

2 large fresh or dried avocado leaves, or 4 smaller leaves

WARM the beans (either the cooked dried beans or canned beans with the fresh cup of water added) in a large pot over medium-low heat.

HEAT the oil in a small skillet over medium-high heat and cook the onion until it's browned on the edges, 10 to 15 minutes. Tear the chiles into a few pieces and coarsely crumble or tear the avocado leaves into the onions, and cook until

they're fragrant and the chiles turn a lighter color, 1 to 2 minutes. Add 1 cup of the beans to the blender jar, then transfer the contents of the skillet, oil and all, to the jar. Blend until smooth. Be careful when you're blending hot ingredients: Cover the top with a kitchen towel and hold the top firmly in place with your hand.

RETURN the blended bean mixture to the pot, then swish a little water (about ¼ cup, or more if the beans are very thick) around in the blender jar and add it to the beans. Let them cook for a few minutes or until thickened, stirring occasionally, then season to taste with salt.

Serve them with Mexican White Rice (page 251), Mexican Red Rice (page 252), or Green Rice with Poblano Chiles (page 254) to accompany Adobos (pages 130–146), Moles (pages 150–187), and Pipianes (pages 188–209). Or make a meal of beans, rice, and any Salsas (pages 46–89) or Guacamoles (pages 102–119).

The beans keep in the refrigerator for up to five days.

The fried avocado leaf, chile, and onion before they're blended for the beans

FAST MASHED PINTO BEANS
FRIJOLES PINTOS MACHACADOS

This is a quick way to turn pinto beans into an exciting side dish. You can buy chipotle chile powder at the grocery store nowadays, but making your own (see page 21), which keeps for months in the cupboard, will give you a particularly smoky, spicy result.

MAKES ABOUT 7 CUPS   ACTIVE TIME: **8 MINUTES (NOT INCLUDING COOKING THE BEANS)**
START TO FINISH: **8 MINUTES (NOT INCLUDING COOKING THE BEANS)**

1 recipe Basic Beans (made with pinto beans; page 246) with its liquid, or 4 (15-ounce) cans of pinto beans, including liquid, plus 1 cup water

2 tablespoons mild olive oil or vegetable oil

1 teaspoon dried oregano, preferably Mexican, crumbled

1 teaspoon ground cumin

½ teaspoon Chipotle Chile Powder (page 21)

HEAT all the ingredients together in a medium heavy pot over medium heat. Simmer, mashing the beans with a bean or potato masher (or a fork), until they are thickened to the consistency of mashed potatoes, about 5 minutes. Season to taste with salt.

Serve them with Mexican White Rice (page 251), Mexican Red Rice (page 252), or Green Rice with Poblano Chiles (page 254) to accompany Adobos (pages 130–146), Moles (pages 150–187), and Pipianes (pages 188–209). Or make a meal of beans, rice, and any Salsas (pages 46–89) or Guacamoles (pages 102–119).

The beans keep in the refrigerator for up to five days.

MEXICAN WHITE RICE ARROZ BLANCO

A truly great pot of rice only seems simple. In this version of the classic Mexican white rice, each grain retains its integrity—the result won't be lumpy or one big mush—and is imbued with the subtle flavor of the chiles and garlic in the cooking liquid. You'll never go back to the plain boiled kind.

SERVES 6 TO 8   **ACTIVE TIME: 10 MINUTES**   **START TO FINISH: 50 MINUTES**

2 cups long-grain white rice, such as Texmati, basmati, or jasmine

¼ cup roughly chopped white onion

1 small garlic clove, peeled

½ teaspoon fine salt, or 1 teaspoon kosher salt

4 cups water

¼ cup mild olive oil or vegetable oil

1 large parsley sprig

1 fresh serrano or jalapeño chile, stemmed

RINSE the rice thoroughly in a large strainer until the water runs clear. Drain well, at least 15 minutes.

PUT the onion, garlic, salt, and water in the blender jar and blend until smooth, at least 1 minute.

HEAT the oil in a wide 3- to 4-quart heavy pot over medium heat until it shimmers, then add the rice and cook, stirring frequently (the rice will clump at first), until the grains of rice separate and turn a brighter white, 3 to 5 minutes. Stir in the blended mixture, then add the parsley sprig and the whole chile. Bring to a boil over high heat. Boil the rice, uncovered, just until the surface of the rice is visible, about 5 minutes. Cover the pot and turn the heat to very low. Cook the rice gently for 10 minutes more. Turn the heat off. Drape a clean dry cloth over the pot, then recover with the lid and let the rice stand to finish cooking, 10 to 15 minutes. Discard the chile and parsley, or reserve the chile and make salsa.

Serve it with Chipotle–Avocado Leaf Black Beans (page 249) or Fast Mashed Pinto Beans (page 250) to accompany Adobos (pages 130–146), Moles (pages 150–187), and Pipianes (pages 188–209). Or make a meal of rice, beans, and any Salsas (pages 46–89) or Guacamoles (pages 102–119).

The rice keeps in the refrigerator for up to three days. Reheat it in a 350°F oven with a sprinkle of additional water, covered, until heated through, about 30 minutes.

MEXICAN RED RICE ARROZ A LA MEXICANA

A different take on rice for a different mood. A few spices and tomatoes conspire to bump up the flavor and color of this side dish.

SERVES 6 TO 8   ACTIVE TIME: **15 MINUTES**   START TO FINISH: **1 HOUR**

2 cups long-grain white rice, such as Texmati, basmati, or jasmine

1 pound tomatoes (about 3 medium), cored, halved, and coarsely chopped

¼ cup chopped white onion

2 small garlic cloves, peeled

1 whole clove

1 whole allspice berry

½ bay leaf

¾ teaspoon fine salt, or 1½ teaspoons kosher salt

About 1½ cups water

¼ cup mild olive oil or vegetable oil

RINSE the rice thoroughly in a large strainer until the water runs clear. Drain well, at least 15 minutes.

PUT the tomatoes, onion, garlic, clove, allspice, bay leaf, and salt in the blender jar along with 1 cup of water and blend to a smooth puree, at least 2 minutes. Add enough water (about ½ cup more) to the blender jar so the mixture measures 4½ cups. Strain the tomato mixture through a medium-mesh sieve into a large bowl.

HEAT the oil in a wide 3- to 4-quart heavy pot over medium heat until it shimmers, then add the rice and cook, stirring frequently (the rice will clump at first), until the grains of rice separate and begin to turn pale golden, 8 to 10 minutes. Stir in the tomato mixture and bring to a boil over high heat. Boil the rice, uncovered, until the surface of the rice is visible, about 5 minutes. Cover the pot and turn the heat to very low. Cook the rice gently for 10 minutes more. Turn the heat off. Drape a clean dry cloth over the pot, then cover with the lid and let the rice stand to finish cooking, 10 to 15 minutes.

Serve it with Chipotle–Avocado Leaf Black Beans (page 249) or Fast Mashed Pinto Beans (page 250) to accompany Adobos (pages 130–146), Moles (pages 150–187), and Pipianes (pages 188–209). Or make a meal of rice, beans, and any Salsas (pages 46–89) or Guacamoles (pages 102–119).

The rice keeps in the refrigerator for up to three days. Reheat it in a 350°F oven with a sprinkle of additional water, covered, until heated through, about 30 minutes.

GREEN RICE WITH POBLANO CHILES
ARROZ VERDE CON CHILE POBLANO

Another classic Mexican rice. This green version, along with the white and red kinds in the previous two recipes, completes the trio that matches the colors of the Mexican flag. Whereas the white rice is cooked with onion and garlic and the red rice is cooked with tomatoes, this rice gets its color from a cooking liquid made from pureed poblano chile, zucchini, and cilantro—a pretty typical trick employed by cooks south of the border. This particular version comes from Rebecca Rosas, who comes from Puebla and a family of great cooks.

SERVES 6 TO 8   ACTIVE TIME: 25 MINUTES   START TO FINISH: 1 HOUR

2 cups long-grain white rice, such as Texmati, basmati or jasmine

½ pound poblano chiles (about 2 large)

½ pound green zucchini (about 1 large), coarsely chopped

½ packed cup fresh epazote leaves or chopped cilantro

¼ cup chopped white onion

2 garlic cloves, peeled

1 whole clove

¾ teaspoon fine salt, or 1½ teaspoons kosher salt

About 1½ cups water

¼ cup mild olive oil or vegetable oil

½ cup shredded queso fresco or ricotta salata

RINSE the rice thoroughly in a large strainer until the water runs clear. Drain well, at least 15 minutes.

REMOVE the stem from 1 of the poblano chiles, then halve, seed, and devein it. Chop it coarsely and put it in the blender jar along with the zucchini, epazote or cilantro, onion, garlic, clove, salt, and 1 cup of the water, and blend to a smooth puree, at least 2 minutes. Add enough water to the blender jar (about ½ cup) so the mixture measures 4½ cups.

HEAT the oil in a wide 3- to 4-quart heavy pot over medium heat until it shimmers, then add the rice and cook, stirring frequently (the rice will clump at first), until the grains of rice separate and turn pale golden, 8 to 10 minutes. Stir in the blended mixture and bring to a boil over high heat. Boil the rice, uncovered, until the surface of the rice is visible, about 5 minutes. Cover the pot and turn the heat to very low. Cook the rice for 10 minutes more. Turn the heat off. Drape a clean dry cloth over the pot, then cover with the lid and let the rice stand to finish cooking, 10 to 15 minutes.

WHILE the rice is cooking, turn another burner to high and roast the remaining poblano chile on the rack of the burner (or directly on the element of an electric stove), turning frequently with tongs until it is blistered and charred all over, 4 to 6 minutes. Put the roasted poblano in a bowl and cover with a plate to sweat for 15 to 20 minutes. Rub off the skin from the poblano chile with a paper towel. Then cut it open lengthwise, cut out the seed pod, veins, and stem with scissors, and lay the chile flat. Wipe the chile clean of seeds with another paper towel and cut it into thin strips.

TRANSFER the cooked rice to a wide serving dish and top with the roasted poblano strips and the shredded queso fresco.

Serve it with Chipotle–Avocado Leaf Black Beans (page 249) or Fast Mashed Pinto Beans (page 250) to accompany Adobos (pages 130–146), Moles (pages 150–187), and Pipianes (pages 188–209). Or make a meal of rice, beans, and any Salsas (pages 46–89) or Guacamoles (pages 102–119).

The rice keeps in the refrigerator for up to three days. Reheat it in a 350°F oven with a sprinkle of additional water, covered, until heated through, about 30 minutes.

SAUTÉED SPINACH AND MUSHROOMS ESPINACAS Y HONGOS SALTEADAS

Whether you make this for a fresh, delicious side dish or use it as a filling in a vegetarian version of enchiladas (page 219), you'll love the way the hint of lime and slight kick from jalapeños make each bite exciting.

SERVES 4 TO 6   **ACTIVE TIME: 25 MINUTES**   **START TO FINISH: 25 MINUTES**

¼ cup mild olive oil or vegetable oil

1 medium white onion, halved and thinly sliced lengthwise

¾ pound mixed or button mushrooms, trimmed and sliced

1 to 2 fresh jalapeño chiles, thinly sliced, including seeds

¼ teaspoon fine salt, or ½ teaspoon kosher salt

1½ pounds spinach (2 large bunches), stems discarded, and leaves well rinsed and spun dry

Freshly squeezed lime juice to taste

HEAT the oil in a large heavy skillet over high heat until it is almost smoking. Add the onion, mushrooms, and chiles, and cook, stirring frequently, until the mushrooms and onion are softened and any liquid the mushrooms have given off has evaporated, 5 to 8 minutes.

ADD the salt, and add the spinach by the handful, stirring or tossing to wilt it until it all fits in the skillet. Then cover and cook until all the spinach is just wilted, about 1 minute. Season to taste with lime juice and additional salt.

Serve it with Chipotle–Avocado Leaf Black Beans (page 249) or Fast Mashed Pinto Beans (page 250) and Mexican White Rice (page 251), Mexican Red Rice (page 252), or Green Rice with Poblano Chiles (page 254). You can also serve it alongside Adobos (pages 130–146), Moles (pages 150–187), and Pipianes (pages 188–209), or turn it into Enchiladas (pages 216–224) and Tacos (pages 212–214).

This dish keeps in the refrigerator for up to two days.

ZUCCHINI AND CORN WITH CREAM

CALABACITAS CON CREMA

This thrilling side dish is one of my favorite ways to eat the little summer squashes called *calabacitas* that you find in markets in Mexico and that are very similar to zucchini. An aromatic sauté of onion, garlic, and chile is enough to make the squash and corn special, but roasted tomatoes, cream (just a bit), and cheese push the dish into unforgettable territory.

SERVES 10   **ACTIVE TIME: 50 MINUTES**   **START TO FINISH: 50 MINUTES**

1 pound tomatoes (about 3 medium)

¼ cup mild olive oil or vegetable oil

1 cup finely chopped white onion

2 large garlic cloves, minced

1 fresh serrano or jalapeño chile, minced, including seeds

2 cups fresh corn kernels (from 2 to 3 ears), or 10 ounces frozen corn kernels, thawed

1½ teaspoons dried oregano, preferably Mexican, crumbled

½ teaspoon freshly ground nutmeg

¼ teaspoon freshly ground black pepper

2 pounds calabacitas or zucchini, cut into ½-inch dice

½ cup Mexican crema or heavy cream

4 ounces cheddar cheese, coarsely grated (1 cup)

¾ teaspoon fine salt, or 1½ teaspoons kosher salt

1 cup chopped cilantro

SET the oven or toaster oven to broil and preheat. Alternatively, you can preheat the oven to 500°F. If you're using the oven broiler, position the rack 8 inches from the heat source.

CORE the tomatoes and cut a small "X" through the skin on the opposite ends. Put the tomatoes, cored sides up, on a foil-lined baking pan and roast until their tops have blackened and the tomatoes are cooked to the core, 20 to 30 minutes. Slip the skins from the tomatoes, discard the skins, and coarsely chop the tomatoes.

MEANWHILE, heat the oil in a 6- to 7-quart heavy pot over medium-high heat until it shimmers. Add the onions, garlic, and chile and cook, stirring, until softened, 3 to 5 minutes.

ADD the corn, oregano, nutmeg, and pepper and cook, stirring, until the corn is lightly browned, about 7 minutes. Add the zucchini and cook, stirring, until it is just tender, 3 to 5 minutes. Add the tomatoes, crema, cheese, and salt and cook, stirring, 5 minutes more. Season to taste with additional salt, and stir in the cilantro just before serving.

Serve it with Adobo-Marinated Chicken (page 133) or Grilled Adobo-Marinated Skirt Steak (page 135).

This dish keeps in the refrigerator for up to two days.

SOURCES

Finding Mexican ingredients has never been easier. Chain supermarkets often stock tomatillos, serranos, and habaneros. Online retailers will ship molcajetes and tortilla presses, chiles pasillas and chiles de árbol, to your door. And while vibrant Mexican communities were once located mainly in big cities, such as Los Angeles, Houston, Chicago, and New York, the American landscape is changing. Today, they've sprouted in places that you might not expect, like Durham, North Carolina, and Portland, Oregon. Even small towns have a block or neighborhood nearby where you'll find stores and markets catering to customers looking for epazote and chiles mulatos, cotija cheese, and Mexican cinnamon. If you're not sure where that is, ask a Mexican friend or colleague where he would get these ingredients. Almost nothing will make someone from Puebla light up like hearing you ask where to find *papalo*. "You know *achiote*?" someone from the Yucatán might exclaim before eagerly guiding you to a store that sells it. Note that the best produce is local and seasonal, but I've included sources for certain fruits and vegetables that may be hard to find in your local market.

MELISSA'S

www.melissas.com • 800-588-0151

Melissa's game is produce, and you'll find a ton of Mexican ingredients that many people will have a hard time finding at the supermarket: fresh chiles, including habaneros and manazanos, ataulfo mangoes, chayote, tomatillos, and banana leaves, to name just a few.

MELISSA GUERRA: TIENDA DE COCINA

www.melissaguerra.com • 877-875-2665

Melissa has rounded up a variety of excellent Mexican cooking equipment, including cast-iron comales, molcajetes made from real volcanic stone, and my preferred brand of cast-aluminum tortilla presses (plus woven tortilla baskets). There's also some great pantry staples (corn husks for tamales, canela, high-quality Mexican chocolate, and the unrefined Mexican sugar called piloncillo), and for the ambitious among you, there's dried corn, metates, and crank-operated corn grinders, in case you feel like making fresh masa.

PENZEYS SPICES

www.penzeys.com • 800-741-7787

Just about any spice or dried herb you can think of is sold here. Think harder-to-find items, like Mexican oregano and canela, as well as very fine examples of the usual suspects, like clove, allspice, and aniseed.

MEXGROCER.COM

www.mexgrocer.com • 877-463-9476

A reliable place for pantry ingredients, like canned chipotles in adobo, dried masa, corn husks, and pickled jalapeños.

DONALDO'S CHILES & SPICES

www.donaldoschilesandspices.com • 773-277-8313

Donaldo's has one of the largest online retail selections of chiles I've found: It has almost as many varieties—cascabeles and mulatos, pasillas and puyas!—as the chile guy who supplies my restaurant. There are avocado leaves, too.

GOURMETSTORE.COM

www.gourmetstore.com • 847-625-8600

Yet another fine place to buy dried chiles, like chiles de árbol, guajillos, and mulatos. You can even buy in bulk— 30 pounds of ancho chiles anyone? Plus, they sell raw, hulled pumpkin seeds.

FRIEDA'S

www.friedas.com • 714-826-6100

Besides being a great source for dried chiles, this company specializing in produce will ship you fabulous fresh chiles, like poblanos, serranos, and habaneros, along with other beloved Mexican ingredients, like nopales (cactus pads) and plantains.

PENDERY'S

www.penderys.com • 800-533-1870

Yet another source for dried chiles, but unlike many of the others, Pendery's sells the hard-to-find and incomparably delicious pasillas de Oaxaca.

INDEX

Page numbers in *italics* indicate illustrations

A

Adobo(s), 122–123
  adobo-meat ratio, 123
  Ancho, Basic, 126
  Beef in, *125*, 140
  Chicken in, 137
  as cooking sauce, 136–146
  D.F., 127
  Guajillo, Basic, 124
  Lamb, -Braised, 146
  Lamb, Enchiladas with Cooked Green
      Salsa, 220, *221*
  Lamb Shanks Braised in Parchment, 142
  as marinade, 130
  -Marinated
      Chicken, 133
      Chicken Paillards, (variation), 135
      Fish, 130, *131*
      Shrimp, 132
      Skirt Steak, Grilled, *134, 135*, 135
  Pasilla-Guajillo, 128
  paste, making, 123
  Pork in, 138, *139*
  Ribs from La Huasteca Veracruzana,
      143–144
  Sauce, 147
  Short Ribs in, Braised, 145
  storing, 140
Almond(s)
  Mole, Blackberry, 176–177
  Mole, Black, from Oaxaca, 185–187
  Mole from Puebla, 172–174, *173, 175*
  Mole, Xico-Style, *182*, 183–184
  Sauce, Red, Braised Chicken in, 203–204
  Sauce, White, 204–205, *205*
Ancho Chile(s), 18–19, *126*
  Adobo, Basic, 126
  Adobo D.F., 127
  Adobo, Short Ribs Braised in, 145
  Mole, Blackberry, 176–177
  Mole from Puebla, 172–174, *173, 175*
  Mole, Red, "Little," Mexico City–Style,
      165–166
  Mole, Red, Oaxacan, 168–169
  Mole, Red, Soupy, "In a Pot" with Beef,
      153–154, *155*
  Mole, Yellow, Oaxacan, 159–160
  Noodles, Mexican-Style, *234*, 235–236
  Ribs from La Huasteca Veracruzana,
      143–144
      Sesame and Pumpkin Seed Sauce,
          Veracruz-Style, 194
      Sesame Seed Sauce, Red, 209
Apple
  and Pasilla Mole, 178–179
  in Red Peanut Mole, 167–168
  -Tequila Guacamole, 109
Arbol Chile(s), 18–19, *92*
  Beans with Pork, 232, *233*
  in Chile Powder, *21*, 21
  Guajillo Salsa, Jalisco-Style, 77
  Lamb, Adobo-Braised, 146
  Noodles, Mexican-Style, *234*, 235–236
  and Peanut Salsa, *86*, 87
  Peanut Sauce, Red, 200, *201*
  with Strawberry Salsa, Sweet, 90
  Tomatillo Salsa, Roasted, with Chipotle
      and, 72
  Tomatillo Salsa, Roasted, with Roasted
      Garlic and (variation), 70
  Tomato and Pineapple Salsa, Roasted,
      64–65
  Yellow Mole, Modern, Lamb in, 161–162,
      162
Arbol chile powder, 21, 48
Avocado(s). *See also* Guacamole(s)
  pitting/cutting, *23*, 24
  ripeness, 23, 102–103
  Sauce, *119*, 119
  selecting, 102
  storing, 23
  with Tomatillo Salsa, Fresh, 51
Avocado Leaf–Chipotle Black Beans, *248, 249*
Avocado leaves, 4, *5*

B

Beans
  Basic, 246
  Chipotle–Avocado Leaf Black, *248, 249*
  Fast Mashed Black, Canned, 247
  Fast Mashed Pinto, 250
  with Pork, 232, *233*
Beef
  in Adobo, *125*, 140
  Guajillo-Tomatillo, Tangy Guacamole
      Enchiladas with, *222*, 223
  Red Mole, Soupy, "In a Pot" with, 153–154,
      155
  Shank in Mulato Adobo, 141
  Shank, in Yellow Mole, Modern
      (variation), 162
      Short Ribs, Braised, in Adobo, 145
      Skirt Steak, Grilled, Adobo-Marinated,
          134, 135, 135
      Steak Tacos, 213
      in Yellow Mole, Oaxacan, 159–160
Beer
  Drunken Salsa, 81
  Pasilla-Guajillo Adobo, 128
Beet Salsa with Habanero, 85
Black Beans
  Basic, 246
  Chipotle–Avocado Leaf, *248, 249*
  Fast Mashed, Canned, 247
Blackberry Mole, 176–177
Black Mole from Oaxaca, 185–187
Blender, 40, *76*
Blue Cheese Guacamole, *112*, 113
Boiling method
  tomatillos, *30*, 31
  tomatoes, 29
Burnt Chipotle Chile Salsa, 82, *83*

C

Carnitas, 240, *241*
  Tacos, 214, *215*
Cascabel Chile(s), *16*, 18–19
  Adobo, Three-Chile, 129
  in Chile Powder, *21*, 21
  and Pumpkin Seed Dip, 195
  with Tomatillo Salsa, Roasted, 69
Cast-iron pans, 40
Cazuela, 40
Chayote, *24*, 24–25
Cheese
  Blue Cheese Guacamole, *112*, 113
  Chilaquiles, *230*, 231
  Quesadillas, 225
  Zucchini and Corn with Cream, 256, *257*
Cherry Tomato Salsa, Roasted, 63
Chicharrón (pork skin), Guacamole with,
      114, *115*
Chicken
  in Adobo, 137
  Adobo-Marinated, 133
  Adobo-Marinated Chicken Paillards
      (variation), 135
  in Almond Sauce, Red, Braised, 203–204
  in Almond Sauce, White, 204–205, *205*
  Enchiladas with, 218

Chicken, continued
    in Mole
        Black, from Oaxaca, 185–187
        Blackberry, 176–177
        Green, Guanajuato-Style, 170
        Hazelnut, 180–181
        Pasilla and Apple, 178–179
        from Puebla, 172–174, *173*
        Red, "Little," Mexico City–Style,
            165–166
        Red, Oaxacan, 168–169
        Red Peanut, 167–168
        Xico-Style, *182*, 183–184, *184*
        Yellow, from Querétaro, 163–164
    in Peanut Sauce, Classic, 199
    in Peanut Sauce, Green, 202
    in Peanut Sauce, Red, 200
    in Pistachio Sauce, 206, 208
    Poached, 242
    in Pumpkin Seed Sauce, Puebla-Style,
        192
    in Pumpkin Seed Sauce, Simple, 189–190
    in Sesame and Pumpkin Seed Sauce,
        Veracruz-Style, 194
    in Sesame Seed Sauce, Red, 209
    Stock, 242
    Tacos, 213
    in Tomatillo Sauce, Chunky, 238
    in Tomato Sauce, *94*, 237
    in Totonac-Style Sauce, 193
Chilaquiles, *230*, 231
Chile Paste
    adobo, making, 123
    Green, 89
    in Guacamole, Classic, 104, *105*
    Pumpkin Seed and Pasilla de Oaxaca,
        196, 197
Chile Powder
    making, 20, *21*, 21
    Toasted, Roasted Tomatillo Salsa with,
        67–68, *68*
Chile Salsa(s)
    Chipotle, Burnt, 82, *83*
    Chipotle, and Roasted Garlic, 84
    Drunken, 81
    Guajillo, Jalisco-Style, 77, *78*
    Habanero-Orange, 80
    Serrano, Fried, 75
    Serrano, Roasted, D.F.-Style, 88
Chiles, dried. *See also specific chiles*
    deseeding, 20
    size of, 15
    toasting, 17, 19, 20
    varieties of, 15–19, *16–17*
Chiles, fresh. *See also specific chiles*
    heat of, 11
    roasted, peeling, 14
    roasting, 12, *13*, 13, 14, 15

        seeding/deveining, 123
        varieties of, 12
Chilhuacle Chile(s)
    Black Mole from Oaxaca, 185–187
    Yellow Mole, Oaxacan, 159–160
Chipotle Chile(s), 18–19
    Adobo, Short Ribs Braised in, 145
    Black Beans, –Avocado Leaf, *248*, 249
    in Chile Powder, 21
    Guacamole, Seafood, 110, *111*
    Mole, Hazelnut, 180–181, *182*
    Mole from Puebla, 172–174, *173*, *175*
    Salsa, Burnt, 82, *83*
    Salsa, and Roasted Garlic, 84
    Sesame Seed Sauce, Red, 209
    toasting, *16*, *17*, 19
    Tomatillo Salsa, Roasted, with Arbol
        Chiles and, 72
    Tomatillo Salsa, Roasted, with Garlic,
        Roasted, and, 70, *71*
    Tomatillo Salsa, Roasted, with Jalapeño
        and, 73
    Tomatillo Sauce, Chunky, 93
    Tomato Salsa, Roasted, with Habanero
        Chiles and, 97
Chochoyotes (Masa Dumplings), 160
Chocolate, Mexican, 35
    Adobo D.F., 127
    Mole from Puebla, 172–174, *173*
    Mole, Xico-Style, *182*, 183–184, *184*
Cilantro, 4, 6, *9*
    chopping, 6–7, 7, *8*
Cinnamon, Mexican, *33*, 35, *179*
Comal, *17*, 40–41
Comapeño Chile(s), in Sesame and Pumpkin
        Seed Sauce, Veracruz-Style, 194
Cooking pans, 40–41
Corn
    in masa, 35
    Red Mole "In a Pot" with Beef, 153–154,
        155
    and Zucchini with Cream, 256, *257*
Corn Tortillas, 37, *38*, 39
Crabmeat, in Seafood Guacamole, 110, *111*
Cucumber
    and Pineapple Guacamole, 106, *107*
    Salsa, 59

D
D.F. Adobo, 127
D.F.-Style Roasted Serrano Salsa, 88
Dip(s)
    Guacamole-Tomatillo, Creamy, 118
    Pumpkin Seed and Cascabel Chile, 195
    Pumpkin Seed and Jalapeño, 198
Drunken Salsa, 81
Dumplings, Masa, 160

E
Enchiladas, *175*, *217*
    with Chicken, 218
    Guacamole, Tangy, with Guajillo-
        Tomatillo Beef, *222*, 223
    sauce-soaked, *217*, 217
    Shrimp and Scallop, with Hazelnut Mole,
        224
    softening/filling tortillas, *216*, 216
    Spinach and Mushroom, 219
Epazote, 7, *7*
    Salsa Verde con (variation), 99
Equipment and tools, 40–41

F
Fish
    Adobo-Marinated, 130, *131*
    in Pumpkin Seed Sauce, Simple, 189–190
    Red Snapper Papillotes in Green Mole,
        158
    in Totonac-Style Sauce, 193
Freezer, 41
Fruit Guacamole, 108

G
Garlic
    Chile Paste, Green, 89
    Roasted, and Chipotle Chile Salsa, 84
    Roasted, Tomatillo Salsa, Roasted, with
        Chipotle and, 70, *71*
    roasting, 25
Ginger, 78
    Guajillo Salsa, Jalisco-Style, 77
Green Chile Paste, 89
Green Mole
    Guanajuato-Style, 170–171
    from Oaxaca, 156–157, *157*
    Red Snapper Papillotes in, 158
Green Peanut Sauce, 202
Green Rice with Poblano Chiles, 254
Green Salsa, Cooked, 99
Guacamole(s), 3, 102–103
    Apple-Tequila, 109
    Avocado Sauce, *119*, 119
    avocados for, 102–103
    Blue Cheese, *112*, 113
    with Chicharrón, 114, *115*
    chunky, 102, 104–115
    Classic, 104
    Enchiladas, Tangy, with Guajillo-
        Tomatillo Beef, *222*, 223
    Fruit, 108
    Pineapple and Cucumber, 106, *107*
    Seafood, 110, *111*
    smooth, 103, 116–119

Taco-Shop, 116, *117*, *215*
-Tomatillo Dip, Creamy, 118
Guajillo Chile(s), 18–19, *144*
    Adobo, Basic, 124
    Adobo, Lamb, -Braised, 146
    Adobo, -Pasilla, 128
    adobo paste, preparing, 123
    Adobo, Three-Chile, 129
    Beans with Pork, 232, *233*
    Mole, Black, from Oaxaca, 185–187
    Mole, Hazelnut, 180–181, *182*
    Mole, Red, "Little," Mexico City–Style,
        165–166
    Mole, Red, Oaxacan, 168–169
    Mole, Red Peanut, 167–168
    Mole, Yellow, Modern, Lamb in, 161–162,
        162
    Mole, Yellow, Oaxacan, 159–160
    Noodles, Mexican-Style, *234*, 235–236
    Peanut Sauce, Red, 200, *201*
    Ribs from La Huasteca Veracruzana,
        143–144
    Salsa, Jalisco-Style, 77, *78*
    toasting, *17*, 19
    -Tomatillo Beef, Tangy Guacamole
        Enchiladas with, *222*, 223
Guanajuato-Style Green Mole, 170–171

H

Habanero Chile(s), *10*, 12
    Beet Salsa with, 85
    Cucumber Salsa, 59
    freezing, 11
    Mango and Pineapple Salsa, Fresh, 55
    -Orange Salsa, 80
    Papaya Salsa, 58
    Peach Salsa, Fresh, 56, *57*
    Pineapple Salsa, Roasted, 79
    Tomatillo and Manzano Chile Salsa,
        Fresh, 52
    Tomato and Mango Cocktail Salsa, 66
    and Tomato Salsa, 94, *95*
    Tomato Salsa, Roasted, with Chipotle
        Chiles and, 97
    Tomato Salsa, Yellow, Fresh, 49
Hazelnut(s)
    Mole, 180–181, *181*
    Mole, Shrimp and Scallop Enchiladas
        with, 224
    in Xico-Style Mole, 182, 183–184, *184*
Herbs, 4–9
Hoja santa (holy leaves), 8

I

Ingredients
    chiles, dried, 15–20, *16–17*
    chiles, fresh, *10*, 11–15
    fruits and vegetables, 22–32
    herbs, 4–9
    pantry staples, 34–36
    peanuts, 32, 179
    seeds, 32–33, 166
    sources, 258
    spices, 78
    substitutions, 3
    vinegars, 127

J

Jalapeño Chile(s), 12
    Almond Sauce, White, 204–205, *205*
    Cherry Tomato Salsa, Roasted, 63
    Chile Paste, Green, 89
    in Guacamole. *See* Guacamole(s)
    Mole, Green, from Oaxaca, 156–157, *157*
    Mole, Green, Red Snapper Papillotes in,
        158
    Mole, Yellow, from Querétaro, 163–164
    Pico de Gallo, 46, *47*
    Pineapple Salsa, Spicy Fresh, 54
    and Pumpkin Seed Dip, 198
    Pumpkin Seed Sauce, Puebla-Style, 192
    Pumpkin Seed Sauce, Simple, 189–190,
        191
    Ranchera Sauce, 96
    Tomatillo Salsa, Fresh, 50
    Tomatillo Salsa, Fresh, with Avocado, 51
    Tomatillo Salsa, Roasted, with Chipotle
        and, 73
    Tomatillo Table Salsa, Spicy Cooked, 74
    Tomato and Pineapple Salsa, Roasted,
        64–65
    Tomato Salsa, Simple Cooked, 91
    Tomato Salsa, Simple Roasted, 60–61, *61*
    Totonac-Style Sauce, 193
Jalisco-Style Guajillo Salsa, 77, *78*

L

Lamb
    Adobo-Braised, 146
    Adobo Enchiladas with Cooked Green
        Salsa, 220, *221*
    in Pistachio Sauce, 206, *207*, 208
    Shanks Braised in Parchment, 142
    in Yellow Mole, Modern, 161–162, *162*
Lard, 34
    melted (manteca), 34
    in Tamales, *226*, 227–228, *228*
Lime, *24*, 25–26
Lobster, in Seafood Guacamole, 110, *111*

M

Mango, 26
    cutting, 26
    in Fruit Guacamole, 108
    and Pineapple Salsa, Fresh, 55
    and Tomato Cocktail Salsa, 66
Manzano Chile(s), 12
    and Tomatilla Salsa, Fresh, 52
Marinade, adobo as, 130–135
Masa, 35
Masa Dough, in Tamales, *226*, 227–228, *228*
Masa Dumplings (Chochoyotes), 160
Mexican cooking. *See also* Ingredients
    equipment and tools, 40–41
    five commandments of, 3
    techniques. *See* Boiling method;
        Roasting method; Toasting
        method
Mint, 8
    Tomato Salsa, Fresh, with Parsley, Olive
        Oil and, 48
Mixtamal, 35
Molcajete, 41
Mole(s), 150–151
    Black, from Oaxaca, 185–187
    Blackberry, 176–177
    dark thick, 172–187
    Green
        Guanajuato-Style, 170–171
        from Oaxaca, 156–157, *157*
        Red Snapper Papillotes in, 158
    Hazelnut, 180–181, *181*
    Hazelnut, Shrimp and Scallop
        Enchiladas with, 224
    Pasilla and Apple, 178–179
    from Puebla, 172–174, *173*, *175*
    Red
        "Little," Mexico City–Style, 165–166
        Peanut, 167–168
        Soupy, "In a Pot" with Beef, 153–154,
            155
    serving, 152
    thick, 164–187
    thin, 152–164
    tips for, 151–152
    Xico-Style, *182*, 183–184, *184*
    Yellow
        Modern, Beef Shank in (variation),
            162
        Modern, Lamb in, 161–162, *162*
        Modern, Oxtail in (variation), 162
        Oaxacan, 159–160
        from Querétaro, 163–164
Mulato Chile(s), 18–19
    Adobo, Beef Shank in, 141
    Mole, Black, from Oaxaca, 185–187
    Mole, Blackberry, 176–177

Mulato Chile(s), continued
        Mole from Puebla, 172–174, *173*, *175*
        Mole, Xico-Style, *182*, 183–184, *184*
Mushroom(s)
        Beef in Adobo, *125*, 140
        and Spinach, Sautéed, 255
        and Spinach Enchiladas, 219

N

Noodles, Mexican-Style, *234*, 235–236

O

Oaxaca
        Black Mole from, 185–187
        Green Mole from, 156–157, *157*
        Yellow Mole, Oaxacan, 159–160
Oil, cooking, 36
Olive Oil, Tomato Salsa, Fresh, with Mint,
        Parsley and, 48
Onions, roasting, 27, *28*
Orange-Habanero Salsa, 80
Oregano, Mexican, 8, *9*
Oxtail, in Yellow Mole, Modern (variation),
        162

P

Pantry staples, 34–36
Papalo, *9*
Papaya Salsa, 58
Pasilla Chile(s), 18–19, *177*
        Adobo, -Guajillo, 128
        Adobo, Three-Chile, 129
        Drunken Salsa, 81
        Mole, and Apple, 178–179
        Mole, Black, from Oaxaca, 185–187
        Mole, Blackberry, 176–177
        Mole from Puebla, 172–174, *173*, *175*
        Mole, Red, "Little," Mexico City–Style,
                165–166
        Mole, Red, Soupy, "In a Pot" with Beef,
                153–154, *155*
        Mole, Xico-Style, *182*, 183–184
        Noodles, Mexican-Style, *234*, 235–236
Pasilla de Oaxaca Chile(s), *16*, 18–19
        and Pumpkin Seed Paste, *196*, 197
        Red Peanut Mole, 167–168
        Tomatillo Salsa, Roasted, with Roasted
                Garlic and (variation), 70
Peach
        in Fruit Guacamole, 108
        Salsa, Fresh, 56, *57*
Peanut(s), 32, 179
        and Arbol Chile Salsa, *86*, 87
        Mole, Black, from Oaxaca, 185–187

Mole, Pasilla and Apple, 178–179
Mole, Red, 167–168
Sauce, Classic, 199
Sauce, Green, 202
Sauce, Red, 200, *201*
sauces, about, 198
Pecans
        Guacamole, Apple-Tequila, 109
        Mole, Black, from Oaxaca, 185–187
        Mole, Xico-Style, *182*, 183–184
Pepicha, *9*
Pico de Gallo, 46, *47*
Piloncillo, 93, 157, 184
Pineapple
        and Cucumber Guacamole, 106, *107*
        in Fruit Guacamole, 108
        and Mango Salsa, Fresh, 55
        roasting, 27
        Salsa, Roasted, 79
        Salsa, Spicy Fresh, 54
        and Tomato Salsa, Roasted, 64–65
        in Yellow Mole from Querétaro, 163–164
Pine Nuts, in Mole, Xico-Style, *182*, 183–184
Pinto Beans
        Basic, 246
        Fast Mashed, 250
        with Pork, 232, *233*
Pipianes, 150–151
        Almond Sauce, Red, Braised Chicken in,
                203–204
        Almond Sauce, White, 204–205, *205*
        Peanut Sauce, Classic, 199
        Peanut Sauce, Green, 202
        Peanut Sauce, Red, 200, *201*
        Pistachio Sauce, 206, *207*, 208
        Pumpkin Seed and Cascabel Chile Dip,
                195
        Pumpkin Seed and Jalapeño Dip, 198
        Pumpkin Seed and Pasilla de Oaxaca
                Paste, *196*, 197
        Pumpkin Seed Sauce, Simple, 192
        serving, 152
        Sesame Seed Sauce, Red, 209
        tips for, 151–152
        Totonac-Style Sauce, 193
        varieties of, 188
Pistachio Sauce, 206, *207*, 208
Poblano Chile(s), 12
        Green Rice with, 254
        Pistachio Sauce, 206, *207*, 208
        roasting, *12*, 12
Pork
        in Adobo, 138, *139*
        Beans with, 232, *233*
        Carnitas, 240, *241*
        Carnitas Tacos, 214, *215*
        Chicharrón (pork skin), Guacamole with,
                114, *115*

Cooked, 243
in Mole
        Blackberry, 176–177
        Green, Guanajuato-Style, 170
        Green, from Oaxaca, 156–157, *157*
        Pasilla and Apple, 178–179
        Red, "Little," Mexico City–Style,
                165–166
        Red, Oaxacan, 168–169
        Red Peanut, 167–168
in Peanut Sauce, Red, 200, *201*
in Pumpkin Seed Sauce, Puebla-Style,
        192
in Pumpkin Seed Sauce, Simple, 189–190
Ribs from La Huasteca Veracruzana,
        143–144
Stock, 243
in Tomatillo Salsa, Braised, *98*, 239
in Totonac-Style Sauce, 193
Prickly pear (xoconostle), 31–32
Puebla, Mole from, 172–174, *173*, *175*
Puebla-Style Pumpkin Seed Sauce, 192
Pumpkin Seed(s)
        and Cascabel Chile Dip, 195
        green moles with, 170
        hulled raw, *188*, 189
        and Jalapeño Dip, 198
        Mole, Blackberry, 176–177
        Mole, Green, Guanajuato-Style, 170–171
        Mole from Puebla, 172–174, *173*, *175*
        Mole, Red, "Little," Mexico City–Style,
                165–166
        and Pasilla de Oaxaca Paste, *196*, 197
        pipianes with, 189
        Sauce, Puebla-Style, 192
        Sauce, Simple, 189–190, *191*
        Sauce, Totonac-Style, 193
        and Sesame Seed Sauce, Veracruz-Style,
                195
        toasted, 32, *188*
Puya (pulla), 18–19

Q

Querétaro, Yellow Mole from, 163–164
Quesadillas, 225

R

Ranchera Sauce, 96
Red Almond Sauce, Braised Chicken in,
        203–204
Red Mole
        "Little," Mexico City–Style, 165–166
        Peanut, 167–168
        Soupy, "In a Pot" with Beef, 153–154, *155*
Red Peanut Sauce, 200, *201*
Red Rice, Mexican, 252, *253*

Red Sesame Seed Sauce, 209
Red Snapper Papillotes in Green Mole, 158
Refrigerator, 41
Ribs from La Huasteca Veracruzana,
    143–144
Rice
    Green, with Poblano Chiles, 254
    Red, Mexican, 252, *253*
    White, Mexican, 251
Roasting method, 3, 14
    chiles, fresh, 12, *13*, 13, 14, 15
    garlic, 25
    onions, 27, *28*
    pans for, 40
    pineapple, 27
    tomatillos, *30*, 31, 67
    tomatoes, *28*, 29

S

Salsa(s), *42–43*
    cooked, 60–90
        Beet, with Habanero, 85
        Cherry Tomato, Roasted, 63
        Chipotle Chile, Burnt, 82, *83*
        Chipotle Chile and Roasted Garlic, 84
        Drunken, 81
        Guajillo, Jalisco-Style, 77, *78*
        Habanero-Orange, 80
        Peanut and Arbol Chile, *86*, 87
        Pineapple, Roasted, 79
        Serrano Chile, Fried, 75
        Serrano, Roasted, D.F.-Style, 88
        Strawberry, Sweet, with Arbol Chiles,
            90
        Tomatillo, Roasted, 69
        Tomatillo, Roasted, with Chiles
            Cascabel, 69
        Tomatillo, Roasted, with Chipotle and
            Arbol Chiles, 72
        Tomatillo, Roasted, with Chipotle and
            Roasted Garlic, 70, *71*
        Tomatillo, Roasted, with Jalapeño
            and Chipotle, 73
        Tomatillo, Roasted, with Toasted
            Chile Powder, 67
        Tomatillo, Spicy Cooked Table Salsa,
            74
        Tomato and Mango Cocktail, 66
        Tomato and Pineapple, Roasted,
            64–65
        Tomato, Roasted, Simple, 60–61, *61*
        Tomato, Roasted, Simple, with Onion
            and Cilantro, 62
    for cooking, 91–99
        Green, Cooked, *98*, 99
        Green, Cooked, Lamb Adobo
            Enchiladas with, 220, *221*

Ranchera Sauce, 96
Salsa Verde con Epazote (variation), 99
Tomatillo, Pork Braised in, *98*, 239
Tomatillo Sauce, Chunky, 93
Tomato, Chicken in, 237
Tomato and Habanero, 94, *95*
Tomato, Roasted, with Chipotle and
    Habanero Chiles, 97
Tomato, Simple Cooked, 91
    keys to, 45
    raw, 45–59
        Cucumber, 59
        Mango and Pineapple, Fresh, 55
        Papaya, 58
        Peach, Fresh, 56, *57*
        Pico de Gallo, 46, *47*
        Pineapple, Spicy Fresh, 54
        Tomatillo, Fresh, 50
        Tomatillo, with Avocado, Fresh, 51
        Tomatillo and Manzano Chile, Fresh, 52
        Tomato, with Parsley, Mint, and Olive
            Oil, Fresh, 48
        Tomato, Yellow, Fresh, 49
    tastes and textures, 3, 44–45
Salt, 36, 45
Sauce(s). *See also* Mole(s); Pipianes
    Adobo, 147
        Beef in, 140
        Chicken in, 137
        as cooking sauce, 136
        Lamb, -Braised, 146
        Lamb Shanks Braised in Parchment,
            142
        Mulato, Beef Shank in, 141
        Pork in, 138, *139*
        Ribs from La Huasteca Veracruzana,
            143–144
        Short Ribs in, Braised, 145
    Avocado, *119*, 119
    for Chilaquiles, *230*, 231
    for Noodles, Mexican-Style, *234*, 235–236
    Salsa
        Green, Cooked, *98*, 99
        Green, Cooked, Lamb Adobo
            Enchiladas with, 220, *221*
        Ranchera, 96
        Tomatillo, Chunky, 93
        Tomatillo, Chunky, Chicken in, 238
        Tomatillo, Pork Braised in, *98*, 239
        Tomato, Chicken in, 237
        Tomato and Habanero, 94, *95*
        Tomato, Roasted, with Chipotle and
            Habanero Chiles, 97
        Tomato, Simple Cooked, 91
Scallop(s)
    in Hazelnut Mole, 180–181, *181*
    and Shrimp Enchiladas with Hazelnut
        Mole, 224

Seafood. *See also specific seafoods*
    Guacamole, 110, *111*
Serrano Chile(s), 12
    Almond Sauce, White, 204–205, *205*
    Cherry Tomato Salsa, Roasted, 63
    Chile Paste, Green, 89
    in Guacamole. *See* Guacamole(s)
    Mole, Green, Guanajuato-Style, 170–171
    Mole, Green, from Oaxaca, 156–157, *157*
    Mole, Green, Red Snapper Papillotes in,
        158
    Mole, Yellow, from Querétaro, 163–164
    Peanut Sauce, Classic, 199
    Peanut Sauce, Green, 202
    Pico de Gallo, 46, *47*
    Pistachio Sauce, 206, *207*, 208
    Pumpkin Seed and Cascabel Chile Dip,
        195
    Pumpkin Seed Sauce, Puebla-Style, 192
    Pumpkin Seed Sauce, Simple, 189–190,
        191
    Ranchera Sauce, 96
    roasting, 15
    Salsa, Fried, 75
    Salsa, Roasted, D.F.-Style, 88
    Tomatillo Salsa, Fresh, 50
    Tomatillo Salsa, Fresh, with Avocado, 51
    Tomatillo Table Salsa, Spicy Cooked, 74
    Tomato Salsa, Simple Roasted, 60–61, *61*
    Tomato Salsa, Simple Cooked, 91
    Totonac-Style Sauce, 193
Sesame Seed(s), *33*, 33
    Mole, Black, from Oaxaca, 185–187
    Mole, Blackberry, 176–177
    Mole from Puebla, 172–174, *173*, *175*
    Mole, Red, "Little," Mexico City–Style,
        165–166
    Mole, Red, Oaxacan, 168–169
    and Pumpkin Seed Sauce, Veracruz-
        Style, 195
    Sauce, Red, 209
    toasting, 33
    unhulled, 166
Shrimp
    Adobo-Marinated, 132
    Guacamole, Seafood, 110, *111*
    Papillotes in Green Mole (variation), 158
    in Pumpkin Seed Sauce, Simple, 189–
        190, *191*
    and Scallop Enchiladas with Hazelnut
        Mole, 224
    Tacos, 214
    in Totonac-Style Sauce, 193
Skirt Steak, Grilled, Adobo-Marinated, *134*,
    135, 135
Spearmint, 8
Spices, 78
Spicy Cooked Tomatillo Table Salsa, 74

Spicy Fresh Pineapple Salsa, 54
Spinach
    and Mushroom Enchiladas, 219
    and Mushrooms, Sautéed, 255
Steak(s)
    Skirt, Grilled, Adobo-Marinated, *134,*
        135, 135
    Tacos, 213
Stock
    Chicken, 242
    Pork, 243
    Turkey (variation), 242
Strawberry Salsa, Sweet, with Arbol Chiles,
    90

T

Tacos
    Carnitas, 214, *215*
    Chicken, 213
    holding, *213*
    serving, 212
    Shrimp, 214
    Steak, 213
Taco-Shop Guacamole, 116, *117, 215*
Tamales, *226,* 227–228, *228*
    lard in, 34
    Vegetarian (variation), 228
Tequila-Apple Guacamole, 109
Texture, in Mexican cooking, 3
Toasting method
    avocado leaves, 4
    chiles, dried, 17, 19, 20
    pumpkin seeds, 32
    sesame seeds, 33
Tomatillo(s), 29–30, 50, *53, 171*
    blending, 50
    boiling, *30,* 31
    -Guacamole Dip, Creamy, 118
    Guacamole, Taco-Shop, 116
    -Guajillo Beef, Tangy Guacamole
        Enchiladas with, *222,* 223
    Mole, Black, from Oaxaca, 185–187
    Mole, Green, Guanajuato-Style, 170–171
    Mole, Green, from Oaxaca, 156–157, *157*
    Mole, Green, Red Snapper Papillotes in,
        158
    Mole, Hazelnut, 180–181, *182*
    Mole from Puebla, 172–174, *173, 175*
    Mole, Yellow, Modern, Lamb in, 161–162,
        162
    Mole, Yellow, from Queretaro, 163-164
    Noodles, Mexican-Style, *234,* 235–236
    Peanut Sauce, Green, 202
    Pumpkin Seed and Cascabel Chile Dip,
        195
    Pumpkin Seed Sauce, Puebla-Style, 192
    rinsing, 30

roasting, *30,* 31, 67
Sauce, Chunky, 93
Sauce, Chunky, Chicken in, 238
Strawberry Salsa with Arbol Chiles, 90
Totonac-Style Sauce, 193
Tomatillo Salsa
    Fresh, 50
    Fresh, with Avocado, 51
    Fresh, and Manzano Chile, 52
    Green, Cooked, *98,* 99
    Pork Braised in, *98,* 239
    Roasted, with Chiles Cascabel, 69
    Roasted, with Chipotle and Arbol Chiles,
        72
    Roasted, with Chipotle and Roasted
        Garlic, 70, *71*
    Roasted, with Jalapeño and Chipotle, 73
    Roasted, with Toasted Chile Powder,
        67–68, *68*
    Table, Spicy Cooked, 74
Tomato(es)
    Almond Sauce, Red, Braised Chicken in,
        203–204
    boiling, 29
    canned, 28–29
    coring, 29
    Mole, Black, from Oaxaca, 185–187
    Mole, Red, Oaxacan, 168–169
    Mole, Red, Soupy, "In a Pot" with Beef,
        153–154, *155*
    Mole, Yellow, Oaxacan, 159–160
    Mole, Yellow, from Querétaro, 163–164
    Noodles, Mexican-Style, *234,* 235–236
    Peanut Sauce, Classic, 199
    Peanut Sauce, Red, 200, *201*
    Ranchera Sauce, 96
    Rice, Red, Mexican, 252, *253*
    roasted salsas, 60, *65*
    roasting, 3, *28,* 29
    Sauce, Chicken in, 237
    selecting, 28
    Sesame Seed Sauce, Red, 209
Tomato Salsa
    Cherry Tomato, Roasted, 63
    with Chipotle and Habanero Chiles,
        Roasted, 97
    Cooked, Simple, 91
    and Habanero, 94, *95*
    and Mango Cocktail, 66
    with Onion and Cilantro, Simple Roasted,
        62
    with Parsley, Mint, and Olive Oil, Fresh,
        48
    Pico de Gallo, 46, *47*
    and Pineapple, Roasted, 64–65
    raw, about, 46
    Roasted, Simple, 60–61, *61*
    Yellow, Fresh, 49

Tortilla(s). *See also* Enchiladas; Tacos
    Chilaquiles, *230,* 231
    Chips, *229,* 229
    Corn, 37, *38,* 39
    making, 36, 37
    Quesadillas, 225
    storing, 36–37
    Strips, 229
    Tostados, 229
    warming, 36, 37, 214
Tortilla press, 41
Tostados, 229
Totonac-Style Sauce, 193
Turkey
    in Mole, Black, from Oaxaca, 185–187
    in Mole from Puebla, 172–174, *173*
    in Mole, Xico-Style, *182,* 183–184, *184*
    Poached (variation), 242
    Stock (variation), 242

V

Veracruzana, La Huasteca, Ribs from,
    143–144
Veracruz-Style Sesame and Pumpkin Seed
    Sauce, 195
Vinegars, 127

W

White Almond Sauce, 204–205, *205*

X

Xico-Style Mole, *182,* 183–184, *184*
Xoconostle (prickly pear), 31–32
    peeling, 154
    in Red Mole, Soupy, "In a Pot" with Beef,
        153–154, *155*

Y

Yellow Mole
    Modern, Beef Shank in (variation), 162
    Modern, Lamb in, 161–162, *162*
    Modern, Oxtail in (variation), 162
    Oaxacan, 159–160
    from Querétaro, 163–164
Yellow Tomato Salsa, Fresh, 49

Z

Zucchini
    and Corn with Cream, 256, *257*
    Green Rice with Poblano Chiles, 252
    Red Mole "In a Pot" with Beef, 153–154,
        155